School Sense

How to Help Your Child Succeed in Elementary School

Tiffani Chin, Ph.D.

Executive Director, Ed*Boost*

SANTA
MONICA
PRESS

SANTA
MONICA
PRESS

Published by:
Santa Monica Press LLC
P.O. Box 1076
Santa Monica, CA 90406-1076
1-800-784-9553
www.santamonicapress.com
books@santamonicapress.com

Printed in the United States

Santa Monica Press books are available at special quantity discounts when purchased in bulk by corporations, organizations, or groups. Please call our Special Sales department at 1-800-784-9553.

This book is intended to provide general information. The publisher, author, distributor, and copyright owner are not engaged in rendering health, medical, legal, financial, or other professional advice or services, and are not liable or responsible to any person or group with respect to any loss, illness, or injury caused or alleged to be caused by the information found in this book.

Library of Congress Cataloging-in-Publication Data

Chin, Tiffani.
  School sense : how to help your child succeed in elementary school / by Tiffani Chin.
     p. cm.
Includes bibliographical references.
ISBN 1-891661-40-X
1. Education, Elementary--Parent participation. 2. Home and school. I. Title.

LB1048.5.C46 2004

2004008647

Cover and interior design by Future Studio

Contents

This book is dedicated to my mom—
who went to every Back to School Night, every Open House,
every parent-teacher conference and who was always there to help—
even when I was too stubborn to listen to her suggestions.

Preface

THIS BOOK HAS BEEN AN EXCITING, BUT UNEXPECTED, PRODUCT OF THE TUTOR-ing and education research I have done over the past 12 years. I began tutoring in high school (doing mostly SAT preparation through the now-defunct Ronkin Educational Group), continued with volunteer tutoring in the Crenshaw District of Los Angeles as an undergraduate at UCLA, took up private tutoring (mostly for private elementary and middle school students) again after I graduated from college to help pay my bills, and then began studying education in earnest when I started graduate school. For my master's thesis I observed and interviewed families as their children did test preparation and wrote applications to elite private high schools. For my dissertation, I spent a year doing fieldwork with a classroom of public-school fourth-graders. For my post-doctoral fellowship, I coordinated a research project tracking students as they transitioned from elementary school to middle school and once again found myself observing from the backs of classrooms, talking with teachers, and interviewing students and their families. As I went about writing my dissertation and various academic papers, I found that what I really love is not research but working with kids. Thus, with some colleagues, I founded EdBoost, a non-profit organization that provides tutoring and enrichment classes to students in Los Angeles.

In the process of research and writing, I also found that I had become the "go-to" person for school-related questions. Kids were constantly asking me to help them with their projects (especially projects they needed to have done the next day). Parents asked me for advice about how to request teachers or convince their children to read more. Colleagues stopped me in the halls to ask for the "inside track" on how to get their kids into "the best" magnet or private schools. Although I had always thought of my research as a way to get to know more about kids and how they learn, I found that along the way I had spent more time in schools than any parent I knew. And, I had observed in more classrooms than any teacher I knew. Through my research I had seen a much wider range of parent-teacher and parent-student problems than most families ever experience (thank goodness!). These observations gave me a broad perspective on the positive ways (and unfortunately also the not-so-positive ways) in which parents interact with teachers, work with schools, and try to help their kids with schoolwork.

I had also gained an insider's view of how schools work. Unlike most parents, I'd heard the hallway chatter as teachers gossiped (both positively and negatively) about parents and I'd seen kids misrepresent to their parents (sometimes carelessly, sometimes deliberately) what happened at school. I'd seen how thrilled teachers became over the smallest consideration (a kind word, a nice note) and how frustrated they became over parents' missteps (parents being late to a conference or doing their children's homework for them). And, the more I chatted with parents, the more I found that they asked me similar questions. Many did not have the information they needed to do everything they could to help their kids succeed in school. I just kept thinking that there had to be a way to share what I knew with more people. Short of talking to parents in my community, what could I do?

I sat down at my computer to see if I could sketch out a few paragraphs of advice, thinking that I might send them to a parenting magazine or the district newsletter. Several hours later, I was looking at over 25 single-spaced pages— and I knew that I had only just begun. Thus, this book was born. The pages of this book are full of ideas and practices that I have seen scores of teachers, parents, and students use effectively over the years (and which I hope they'll forgive me for "borrowing"). This book is also a compilation of mistakes I've observed— in the hope that I can allow other parents to learn from the mistakes of strangers.

So, this book represents the wisdom (sometimes that special kind of wisdom that only comes from learning from our mistakes) of every kid, parent, and teacher I've ever worked with. I wish I could name them all—but I can't, both because it would take pages and pages and because I've promised many of them that their contributions to my research would remain anonymous. But I hope they all know who they are and how much I appreciate being a part of their lives—and how much so many of them have touched my life by welcoming me into their families and their hearts.

By name I must thank three teachers who have been my friends and mentors over the years: Sue Shultz, Elaine Lessman, and Claudine Phillips. I could not ask for better models of good, caring teachers and I feel honored to have been able to watch them work, talk with them, and learn from them. This book would not exist without them. (Sue and Claudine both gave me invaluable comments on the manuscript.)

As a product of the California public school system myself, I look back and see a long line of teachers who contributed to making me the person that I am and, in their own ways, contributed to this book. I cannot possibly name all of them, but four stand out as unforgettable: Mrs. Darlette Dexter (who taught me to write), Mr. Jim Shields (who forced me to think), Professor Bob Emerson (who encouraged me to come to graduate school and introduced me to ethnography—the research method that put me in classrooms to begin with), and Professor Meredith Phillips (who shares my passion for education and has been my primary advisor and collaborator through my dissertation and postdoctoral work).

I also want to thank my family and friends. My mom, to whom this book is dedicated, deserves most of the credit for my academic accomplishments. She was always there to help me—even when I fought every one of her suggestions tooth and nail. I also thank my father (who started building my fourth-grade California Mission without me) and my younger brother, Justin (who has always believed in me—even as he put up with the baggage of being my little brother!). My friend Alisa Anderson read the book cover to cover in its early stages and has been unflaggingly confident in my ability to write something parents would find useful. Her sons, Kyle and Jason—who will be starting school soon—have frequently been my models as I tried to envision the kids who might benefit from this book. And, again, Meredith Phillips was the first to read the book, the first to believe in it, and always the first to volunteer to read it again. I can't thank you enough. I also want to thank the UCLA graduate division and the Spencer Foundation for Research in

Education for supporting me while I conducted the research that informed much of this book.

And last, but not least, I thank my publisher, Jeffrey Goldman, who was willing to give me and the book a chance.

—Tiffani Chin, Ph.D.
June 2004

Introduction

W E ALL ATTENDED ELEMENTARY SCHOOL, BUT BY NOW, MOST OF US HAVE
only vague and fuzzy memories about what it was like. And, let's be
honest. How much do we really remember—or did we ever really
know—about the struggles that our parents went through to make sure we did
our homework or got the best teachers? And yet, it's often precisely these hazy
memories that parents draw on while trying to help their children succeed in
school. As adults, we try to remember how we learned to add fractions, which
books we liked to read in the third grade, what we did our science projects on,
and how we ended up in "a good school." But, these memories often don't seem
sufficient to help today's twenty-first-century students succeed in school (especially if our science projects weren't that wonderful to begin with!). That's where
this book comes in.

Having spent over 3,000 hours observing in classrooms, tutoring students,
and interviewing parents and teachers, I've found that although most parents want
their children to get the best education possible, many don't quite know how to
make that happen. How do you know which school is the best? How do you get
your child to do homework without battling every night? How do you approach a
teacher if your child isn't being challenged? How do you request a teacher or some
kind of special service for your child?

Even when parents have a sense of how to "help," they often waste a lot of
time and effort—fighting with their kids over where to do their homework, buying workbooks that their children will never use, and struggling with teachers over
avoidable misunderstandings. The point of this book is to show you, as a parent,
how to make the most of the hard work you put into your children's education—
to show you how to get the greatest payoff, in terms of your child's grades, test
scores, and love of learning, from every single hour you spend helping your child

with homework, attending parent-teacher conferences, and even helping out at the school car wash.

I designed this book to do two things: to show you how schools "work" and to show you how to "work the school." By "work the school," I don't mean anything sneaky or unethical (or illegal), but simply how to be an effective part of the school system and how to make it work for you and in your child's best interests. This book recognizes that the vast majority of U.S. parents work as a "teaching tag-team" with their child's teacher. They hand their kids off to school at 8 o'clock in the morning and then are expected to expand on what their children have learned (in the form of homework, projects, and enrichment) after the three o'clock bell rings. And yet, most parents know very little about what actually goes on in the classroom. They have to rely on their kids (even their kindergartners!) to keep them informed. This book removes the guesswork. It tells you precisely what teachers expect from you, what you should expect from your child's teacher, what you should expect from your child, how to recognize when the whole tag-team system is breaking down, and what you can do to fix it.

This book begins with three assumptions. First, it assumes that you know your children (what they like, what they don't like, their strengths and weaknesses, their personalities, etc.). Second, it assumes that you know your own family's priorities and values. Third, it assumes that you, as a reader and a parent, want your children to do well in school.

The first assumption—that you know your own child—is important because no book can tell you which school is best for your child. No book can tell you what time your children should start their homework in order to be done before your family's dinner time. No book can tell you exactly which free reading books your child will love. Instead, this book gives you the information you need in order to answer these questions for your particular child yourself. As a competent adult, you make good decisions all of the time, using your own common sense. But schools often seem to defy common sense. Whether it's the "unspoken" process of requesting teachers or the "new" ways of teaching reading or adding fractions—schools and homework can seem daunting even to parents who were very successful students themselves. The goal of this book is to provide you with information that will help you to develop your own common sense—or "school sense," if you will—to help you navigate the elementary school years.

This book also assumes that you and your family have your own political, moral, and religious values. In the tips and advice given throughout this book, I don't try to shape or change those values. My sole goal is to help you achieve the best elementary school education that you can for your children. That means, for instance, that I tell you how to assess all kinds of schools, from neighborhood schools to charter schools to private schools. I leave it to you to decide how much you value having your child in an ethnically diverse school, a neighborhood school, or a religious school. I also assume that by the time your child has begun elementary school, your family has developed its own disciplinary style. Although I discuss instances in which your children should face the "consequences" of their behavior, I leave the particulars to you.

As you read through this book, some of the advice may seem selfish. I walk you through how to choose a school that is the very best match for your child. I discuss ways to make sure your children get every available school resource that they need. I explain strategies for working with teachers to create a maximally challenging curriculum for your child. I believe every parent should have this information, although how much you choose to use it is up to you. Of course, every time you succeed in getting "the best" teacher or extra services for your child, you may prevent another child from getting that teacher or those services. When you put your child in private school, you may be depriving your neighborhood school of the leader and role model that your child might become. But, I leave it to you to decide how to weigh benefits for your child against the costs and benefits for the school or the community as a whole. My aim, with this book at least, is to give you the insights you need to make good, informed decisions based on your own personal values.

This book's final assumption—that you want your child to do well in school —reflects my personal bias: that your child's education should be your first priority. You may not agree. For instance, if your child has the potential to play World Cup soccer or become a world-class pianist, you might want to take my advice that they put schoolwork before extracurricular activities with a grain of salt. But, even if you disagree with the notion that your child's education should be a major focus in your family, the advice in this book should help you to make the most of any effort that you do put into your child's education.

Before you dive into the chapters, you should bear one important caveat in mind. This book proposes hundreds of tactics and strategies that you can use to build good relationships with your children's school and teachers, help your children get organized and do homework efficiently, and help your children develop and use their natural curiosity . . . and much more. I subscribe to the theory that more is actually more—especially when parents are trying to find the style that works for them. But more (and more and more and more) can be overwhelming. Treat this book as you do the good advice you receive from family, friends, neighbors, and colleagues. You'll use a lot of it. You'll dismiss some of it as "not right for me." You'll store some of it in case you need it later. The book is designed to give you a range of tips, activities, and ideas—so you can choose the ones that best fit your lifestyle and will best benefit your child.

Because most parents have very hectic lives, I've tried to organize this book so that you can use it in several ways. Some of you may want to sit down with this book and read it from cover to cover. But, you should also feel free to skip around. If your child hasn't started school yet, you may want to start with the appendix on what you can do now to help your child get ready for school. If you are about to move to a new city, you may want to start with Chapter 1 and learn how to assess the schools in your future neighborhood. If your child is already in school, or you're already thrilled with the school that your child is going to attend, then skip ahead. Read Chapter 2 if you're coming up on your parent-teacher conference or are struggling to find out more about what your child is learning in school. Skip to Chapters 3 and 4 if homework and projects are causing you headaches. Skip to Chapter 5 if you want to find fun, stimulating activities you can do with your child at home. Read Chapter 6 if you think your child might be gifted or might have a learning disability. Or, use the index to find the information you need when you need it.

Once you start reading, you'll see that each chapter begins with several guiding principles and then presents specific information as answers to common parent questions. You can read the questions and answers straight through, like an advice column, or skip around to find the questions that you might someday need the answers to. My hope is that this book will become a reference for you and your children—a reference that will help you make the most of your children's elementary school years.

A Quick Note about Gender Pronouns

For simplicity's sake, I have tried to avoid using "he/she" and "his or her" throughout this book. When referring to children, I alternate between referring to boys and girls from question to question. When referring to teachers, I use the pronoun "she." I don't mean to, in any way, downplay the significance of dedicated male teachers—but as they remain a distinct minority in elementary schools, I hope they'll forgive me for referring to all teachers as "she" in the name of more streamlined prose.

Attention Teachers!

Although this book was designed for parents, several teachers who reviewed it remarked that they might like to photocopy some of the sidebars and "Tip Boxes" to send home to parents. If you think that your students' parents would find them useful, please feel free to copy any of the sidebars or "Tip Boxes" throughout the up-coming chapters to send home with your students.

Don't See Your Question in the Book?

Check out www.school-sense.com. I'll be posting more answers to parent questions on the Internet and taking questions from readers by e-mail.

CHAPTER 1

Choosing a School

M OST CHILDREN SPEND THE MAJORITY OF THEIR EDUCATIONAL CAREERS IN SCHOOLS. So, choosing a school is one of the biggest decisions that you will make for your child. The difficulty you will encounter in finding the right school will vary dramatically depending on where you live. In some suburban areas, *most* schools are high achieving, safe, and thought to be "good" schools. In many urban areas, *most* schools are under-achieving and thought to be "bad" schools. No matter what type of area you live in, however, it is worth taking some time to compare the various school options available to your child. Be vigilant, both when choosing a neighborhood (assuming you intend to send your child to the neighborhood school) and when investigating schools of choice. If you live in an area where all children attend the neighborhood school, this chapter will help you research local schools before you choose a new home. If you live in an area with many public and private school options, this chapter will help you to choose among your options. Try to remember the following three guidelines as you think about choosing an elementary school that will be right for your child:

Choose a school that is a good match for *your* child.

No matter where you live, you will find people who will swear that a certain school or set of schools are "the best" in the city. You may also find people who will claim that parents must be crazy not to enroll their child in a particular school if they can afford it and their child can gain admission. However, schools, like children, have various strengths and weaknesses and a school will be good for your child only if those strengths and weaknesses compliment one another. If your child needs structure and rigorous academics, don't choose the new "open" school that lets children work independently or specializes in arts and drama—even if that's the school that everyone is talking about. Conversely, if your child is sensitive and artistic or doesn't thrive under pressure, don't place her in a school that is known for giving hours and hours of homework and pitting children against each other in academic competition—even if that school is known for sending graduates to prestigious private high schools. No matter what social pressures you face or what your personal preferences are, try to put them aside and choose a school for your child that will optimally help her grow and learn. And when you talk to parents, teachers, and school administrators during the process of choosing schools, make sure to ask questions that will help you to determine how good a "match" a particular school will be for your child.

Think about the years ahead and the pathways that different elementary schools offer your child.

Although middle school and high school may seem very far off when you enroll your child in kindergarten, before you choose an elementary school, take the time to investigate how your choice of elementary schools may affect or limit your choice of middle schools or high schools. For instance, many private and religious elementary schools "feed" into particular high schools. Some private high schools have "lower schools" and essentially guarantee high school admission to students who attend for the elementary grades (which eliminates the stress of applying later). Similarly, some public magnet programs make it easier for students to attend magnet high schools if they attended magnet elementary schools. So, even if you love your local non-magnet public school, if you really want your child to attend a magnet high school, check out your school district's Web site, and call the district to find out if your child will have a harder time getting into a magnet high school if he doesn't attend a magnet elementary school. Finally, learn the basics of your local school systems (public and private). Sometimes simple differences between systems can become important considerations. In Los Angeles, for instance, public elementary schools end at fifth grade while many private middle schools do not begin until seventh grade. Thus, students who attend public elementary schools but want to attend private middle schools often have to scramble to find a school to attend for sixth grade. For this reason, many L.A. parents who want their children to attend private middle schools (and then private high schools) start their children in the private system from kindergarten (even if they think that their local public elementary school is "good enough"). Most students go through school knowing that they will attend the local elementary school, the local middle school, and the local high school—in which case the transitions are smooth and easy. But, it's better to take the time now to investigate all possible pathways so that you don't regret your choice when your child is ready to go to high school.

Try not to judge a school by its cover.

When you investigate schools, some might seem wonderful because they have beautiful buildings, others might be disappointing because they do not look well-maintained, and others may be a little intimidating because they have a lot of kids from a different ethnic group than your own. Take all of these factors into consideration. But make sure you also spend some time *inside* the school, looking around, talking to teachers and administrators and, ideally, talking with parents and students. Sometimes schools spend less on buildings and maintenance but more on teachers and academic enrichment. Sometimes schools attract ethnically diverse students from all over the city precisely because they have a wonderful academic program. Definitely consider how proud your child can be of her school and how safe she will feel while she is there, but make sure that you examine schools closely enough to get past purely cosmetic considerations.

The remainder of this chapter discusses how to gather information about all types of schools. It will walk you through the process of assessing the different types of demographic, staffing, and performance statistics you can learn about schools and what to look for when you make school visits. The chapter will then answer the questions specific to public schools of choice and private schools. Although this chapter should give you a good basis for understanding your local schools, systems can vary dramatically by state and region, even by city. So, make sure to learn the specifics that apply to your area before you make any major decisions.

Getting Information about School Systems

"I've never enrolled a child in the school district I live in now. How can I get information?"

There are many ways to get information about a school system. Each source has its advantages and disadvantages, so try a few different routes.

♦ *Use the Internet.* If you don't have Internet access at home, most public libraries do. Most large school districts have Web sites that contain "official" district information. Ideally your local district Web site will tell you information about the individual schools in your district as well as different programs (such as magnet programs or schools for children with special needs). Your state's department of education Web site might also have comprehensive statistical information about the schools in your area.

♦ *Go to the district office.* This is particularly important if your school district does not have a Web site. Although you may be able to get information and brochures from your local school, there's no guarantee that each school has all of the relevant information about the entire district. (In fact, some schools may be reluctant to provide you with information about school choice or magnet programs because they don't want local students to leave the school.) When you get to the district office, explain that you are about to enroll your child and would like all of the information that they give to new parents (brochures, handouts, etc.). The district should also have a map that shows each school's attendance areas. If you are thinking of buying a new house or renting a new apartment, the district office is the best source of up-to-date information about school attendance areas.

♦ *Visit local schools.* The schools probably have district information and handouts. Schools can also show you their own attendance areas.

♦ *Talk to other parents.* This is crucial. Although the district's Web site and district office can give you official information, only other parents can give you the inside track. Only parents can tell you about an incredibly caring set of teachers at your neighborhood school or about how the new principal is making impressive improvements at a school that had been under-performing. Other times parents can tell you how to strategize. For instance, some magnet schools admit students on a first-come, first-served basis. If you want to get your child into a magnet school like that, local parents may be able to tell you the time by which you need to line up in order to have a good chance of admission (some parents even camp out overnight to get their children into good magnet programs).

"I've heard that my district does not require students to attend their neighborhood school. How do I find out if this is true? How do I find out if there are any restrictions or limitations on the enrollment process?"

Many districts have open-enrollment programs and allow parents to enroll their children in public schools that are not in their neighborhoods. These programs vary dramatically from district to district and almost all of these programs have significant restrictions and limitations (e.g., schools usually only have to accept students from outside their local neighborhood if they are under-enrolled, and the best school in the district is often over-enrolled). There are many different types of open enrollment (see the term box on school choice terminology for more details).

To learn about your local open enrollment system, check your district's Web site if you have one. Many districts provide information about open enrollment as well as applications on the Internet. When you visit the district office, ask specifically if the district allows inter- or intra-district transfers or has a magnet program or charter schools. You can also ask at your local school, but neighborhood schools often want to keep good students, so they may be reluctant to tell you how you can enroll your child in a different school. No matter what you hear from the school, check with

the district as well.

You can also contact the school you want to enroll your child in and see if there are any circumstances in which they will accept a child from your neighborhood. They may not take intra-district transfers but they may accept students through a magnet program or on work permits or childcare permits.

"I would like to enroll my child in a private school. Is there a central place where I can learn about the local private schools?"

Because private schools are independent, no central "district office" collects information about them. The U.S. Department of Education does, however, survey all private schools every two years. You can look up private schools by name, zip code, religious affiliation, and a few other school characteristics on the National Center for Education Statistics Web site (http://nces.ed.gov/surveys/pss/private schoolsearch/). This Web site will give you basic information about most private schools, including enrollment by grade, enrollment by ethnicity, student:teacher ratio, religious affiliation, and whether the school is coed. This Web site also lists the private school associations that the school belongs to. Most associations accredit schools or require their members to be accredited by particular accrediting agencies

School Choice Terminology

School districts offer many different types of school choice. These are terms you might hear as you investigate school choice in your district:

- *Attendance area*—Most regular public schools draw their students from a particular group of neighborhoods called the "attendance area." Although attendance areas are sometimes obvious, *always* check with the school before you buy a home. You might have found a good deal on a house exactly because it lies just outside the attendance area of a good school. Don't trust the real estate agent—check it out for yourself.
- *Assigned school*—The school assigned to the attendance area you live in.
- *Catchment area*—Same as attendance area.
- *Child care permits*—Some districts allow students to opt out of their assigned school into a choice school if their primary day care provider is in the choice school's attendance area.
- *Choice school*—Any school that is not your assigned school.
- *Charter schools*—While some charter schools are neighborhood schools, others accept applications from all over the district. If you want your child to attend a charter school, call the school directly to learn its policies. Charter schools are somewhat independent of the district, so the district office is not the best source of information about them.
- *Inter-district transfers*—Transfers into another school district. Almost 40 percent of school districts in the U.S. allow inter-district transfers.
- *Intra-district transfers*—Transfers to different schools within your school district. About half of all U.S. districts allow intra-district transfers.
- *Magnet schools*—Most major urban districts have magnet schools. Students are not usually assigned to magnet schools based on where they live; instead students apply to attend magnet schools.
- *Open enrollment*—This is a catch-all term that means that the district does not require students to attend their neighborhood schools. Although it implies that students can attend any school within their district, the policy usually includes a caveat giving first dibs to students who live within a school's attendance area. Then, if the school has extra space, students from other attendance areas can enroll (usually by lottery).
- *Work permits*—Some districts allow students to opt out of their assigned schools if their parents work closer to another school.

(look up the associations on the Internet to see what their specific requirements are). Although schools do not have to belong to private school associations, if the school you are looking into does not belong to any associations, make sure that it is accredited. Many associations (e.g., the National Association of Independent Schools) provide an online look-up service where you can learn about member schools (although usually not much more information than you can get from the NCES Web site).

Some large communities have private school guidebooks that can give you basic descriptions of private schools (e.g., *The Manhattan Family Guide to Private Schools* by Victoria Goldman and Katherine Hausman or *The Los Angeles Guide to Private Schools* by Victoria Goldman). But, for the most part, you will have to call each private school you are considering. Fortunately, most private schools want your business, so they will be happy to provide you with information. When you talk to an admissions officer or even a receptionist at a private school, be assertive. Ask the questions you really want to know (e.g., How successful are they at getting students into the top private high schools? How good is their arts program?). Be concerned if you do not receive answers that seem forthcoming and honest. Other parents will also be an essential source of information about private schools.

If you have your heart set on a particular private high school, it's a good idea to call that school and see if they can recommend any elementary schools. Of course, no high school can promise you admission to an elementary school (nor will they recommend a school for your particular child without knowing the child) but they will be able to tell you the elementary schools from which many of their current students graduated.

Finally, some communities (especially urban areas with very competitive private school systems) have private school counselors. These counselors work in much the same way that college counselors do, helping you find a "good match" for your child and helping you through the private school application process. Most people learn of these counselors through word of mouth. But, a good way to start to look for one is to call a local college counselor. He or she may also offer private school counseling or may be able to recommend someone who does.

General Considerations When Choosing Schools

"I always just assumed that my child would go to our neighborhood schools. What is all the hubbub about choosing schools?"

Any time you buy a house or a condo or move into a new apartment, you choose an elementary school. In many areas, choosing a home in a neighborhood that you like is enough to assure you that your children will attend "good" schools. But, before you move, always take the time to check out the local schools (if you plan to stay in the neighborhood for a while, visit the local elementary, middle school, and high school). Not all schools are of the same quality and just because a school is located in a "good neighborhood" doesn't mean that the local school is "good." Be especially vigilant if you live in an urban area, an area where many children attend private schools (including religious schools), or in a district that allows open enrollment. You might be surprised to find that many of the neighborhood kids do not actually attend the neighborhood school!

Moreover, when you visit your local school, tell the receptionist your address (or your potential address) to make sure that you are checking out the right school. Sometimes school boundaries are unclear and they sometimes change from year to year. You could end up buying a home just outside the boundary of the school you want your child to attend. In fact, in some urban areas, children get bussed to their "neighborhood" school because the school that is actually closest to their houses has turned into a magnet school and no longer accepts neighborhood children (except through the magnet process). Although these situations are rare, you definitely want to find out where your child is supposed to go to school before you sign a lease or put money down on a house.

"My real estate agent says that only certain schools are 'good ones.' When I visited some of the schools, that didn't seem to be true, but should I just trust the agent?"

Listen to your real estate agent—but don't trust his or her judgment entirely. Real estate agents are experts on *real estate*. When they tell you that the local schools in a particular area are not good, they likely know what they are talking about—from a real estate perspective. In areas where school quality varies a lot, houses in neighborhoods with schools that everyone considers to be good often appreciate faster than houses in areas with less obviously good schools. So, your real estate agent likely knows what schools are usually "considered to be good" and which neighborhoods have higher housing prices *because* of a school's reputation. However, public opinion and housing values do not always accurately reflect a school's *academic* quality. For instance, schools that people consider good are usually schools that serve larger percentages of white and middle class children. Schools that serve many children of color are often looked upon as "bad" schools even if they have strong academic programs. If you value diversity, you may want to consider a school that real estate agents would hesitate to call "good" simply because many potential home buyers would not consider it "white enough."

But, regardless of how much you trust your agent's opinions, real estate agents are sometimes a good source of statistics on schools. Visit local agents' Web sites or offices if you are having trouble finding statistics from other sources.

"I can afford a home in a neighborhood with low-performing schools. I can only afford an apartment in a neighborhood with higher performing schools. I think that it's important for my kids to have a good education, but I also think that it's important for my kids to have a yard. What should I do?"

Seriously consider the apartment—especially if you do not have many opportunities to transfer your child out of the neighborhood school (e.g., through magnet schools or open enrollment). The trade-off between a nicer home and a better school is one that middle-income parents debate all of the time. And it's not an easy question to answer. But, in addition to deciding what you value more (your

child's education or the comforts of a home), you also want to consider the peer group your child will find in each neighborhood. Children learn best when the other students at their school value education (in other words, where students work hard, pay attention when the teacher is talking, and encourage each other to do homework and study for tests). When you choose a nicer home over a better school, you may be putting your child in a school where other parents made a similar choice. When you choose to sacrifice comfort for better schools, you may be putting your child in a school where other parents are doing the same—and these children may be a more motivated peer group and one that makes less trouble for teachers. So, before you buy the house, investigate the local school carefully. What do the teachers at the school have to say about their students and their parents? A school's test scores should not determine your decision about where to live, but surrounding your child with motivated, academically interested students should be a priority.

Of course, as you will read later on, many areas have "choice" programs in which children can apply to schools outside of their neighborhood. So, many parents do manage to have a home in an area that they can afford and put their kids in good schools. But parents who choose to live in neighborhoods with low-performing schools have to work much harder to ensure that their children receive a high-quality education.

"The other parents in our neighborhood all send their kids to private schools. They say that they _have_ to because our local school is not very good. Does this mean that in order to be a good parent, I have to send my kids to private school, too?"

OR

"The other parents in our neighborhood all send their kids to the local public school—they say it's a really good school. I'm not so sure. But could they all be wrong?"

You can learn information from other parents that you would never learn from a school administrator or the Internet. Only parents can tell you about phenomenal teachers in a particular school. Only parents can tell you if the principal in your neighborhood school is insane. Keep your ears open!

But, remember that everyone has an agenda. Any parent who is paying a lot of money (sometimes over $10,000 a year!) for a private school has to firmly believe (and continue to convince himself or herself) that the public schools simply are not good enough. Similarly, parents who put their kids in "questionable" public

schools need to justify to themselves why they don't pay whatever it takes to put their kids in a private school. So, listen to other parents but take whatever they have to say with a grain of salt. Sometimes, when the debate between public and private gets particularly heated, parents even get accusatory. I have heard university professors complain that their colleagues were shocked that they had their kids in public schools—implying that any parents who did not put their children in private school were somehow short-changing them. Bottom line: listen to what your neighbors have to say, but don't forget to do your own research.

"I can afford to send my kids to private schools. Are private schools always better?"

No. Some private schools are wonderful. Some public schools are wonderful. But, because each school has various strengths and weaknesses, there is no hard and fast rule about whether private or public schools are better. Some private schools have high standards, very well-qualified teachers, excellent facilities, and great success getting students into elite high schools and colleges. But others are less well-funded and have less-qualified teachers than their local public schools (remember, private schools are not even required to hire credentialed or certified teachers—and they often pay teachers considerably less than public schools do). In most states, *anyone* can open a private school, regardless of education background or criminal record.

Moreover, just because you can afford private school does not mean that your money would be best spent on private school. Suppose, for example, that private school tuition is $5,000 a year (this is just an estimate—tuition varies tremendously from school to school) and you have great local public schools. If you sent your child to public school, you could spend that extra $5,000 a year on tutoring, enrichment classes, lessons and other extras for your child instead of spending it on tuition.

Of course, you may have a local private school that is exemplary or local public schools that are poor or mediocre. Or, you may find a private school that would be a perfect match for your child's needs and interests. In those cases, you need to seriously consider private school (even if it means that your child may get fewer extras).

Assessing Individual Schools

"So, how in the world do I evaluate whether or not a school is good?"

There are some basic steps you should follow when evaluating a school:

1. Get the basic facts about the schools you are considering.

2. Get demographic and staffing statistics about the schools you are considering.

3. Do a "drive-by" past the schools you are considering to see what they look like.

4. Get inside the schools to see what the classrooms look like and to talk to administrators, teachers, and possibly some parents (most schools will not allow strangers to talk to students).

The following sections will tell you how to go through each step, gathering and assessing the information and impressions you receive. As you read the next few sections, however, try not to feel overwhelmed. I describe a lot of statistics (and hopefully make them easier to interpret), but most of them should influence your decisions only marginally. Don't feel obligated to ferret out every single statistic! Your goal should be to make an informed choice—use the following tips to make your information gathering process easier.

"What are the basic facts I should learn about the schools I am considering?"

You might be surprised at how much schools vary in terms of the basics.

Make sure to find out:

♦ **What grades do they serve?** While many parents assume that all schools follow the same grade system they went through, systems often change over time and different regions have different policies. Find out at which grades children transition to middle school and high school. If there are private schools in your area, do they transition at the same grades? (If they do, it will be much easier for you if you decide to switch from public to private, or vice versa, in the future.)

♦ **What school calendar do they follow?** Although most schools still follow a traditional calendar (September to June), many districts have year-round schools or schools with multiple tracks which have breaks at different times. If the school is "year-round" or "multi-track" find out when your child's vacations will be (some systems give students a month off three times a year rather than three months off in the summer). Also find out if all of your children can enroll in the same "track" (in other words, can you make it so that your children all have vacation at the same time?).

♦ **How big is the school?** Whether or not you want a big or small school should be determined by your child's personality, temperament, interests, and needs. Small schools offer more closeness and a greater likelihood that your child will get personal attention (I have actually walked through some

small high schools where the counselors could call out to every student by name!). Small schools can also be socially limiting, however, especially if they span many grades (i.e., serve students in grades K-12). At the high school level, small schools also have the drawback of not being able to offer as many sports, clubs, and programs (such as drama, a school newspaper, an orchestra) because they may not have enough students to participate. On the other hand, your child may have a better chance of participating in activities at a small school (e.g., getting on a sports team, getting on the yearbook staff) since they may be more eager for members. Small schools also make it more likely that teachers and counselors will know your child well enough to write good recommendations for middle/high school or college.

♦ **What programs do the schools offer?** Does your child qualify for any special services? If your child qualifies for resource help, GATE (Gifted and Talented) programs, speech services, occupational therapy or other services, find out if and how these programs and services are administered in each school. (For more about programs and services, see Chapter 6.) Also, some schools may offer better before- or after-school care.

♦ **How does the school organize students?** Does it track high achievers into classrooms with other high achievers and low achievers into classrooms with other low achievers? Does it try to mix all students together? Do children who excel in particular subjects get enrichment in those subjects? (See the next question on grouping and tracking to learn more about these practices and whether they are likely to benefit your child.)

◗ Even if you are focusing on elementary schools, *pay attention to the middle schools and high schools that those elementary schools feed into.* Some wonderful elementary schools feed into much weaker middle schools, which might force you to go through this decision process all over again in five or six years.

School Calendar Terms

- *Traditional calendar*—Schools that follow a traditional calendar run from September until June. Students get "the summer" (usually July and August) off and a few weeks off in December (winter break) and March or April (spring break).
- *Year-round calendar*—Although many parents think that students in year-round schools attend more school than children in schools that have traditional calendars, they usually don't. In fact, many schools with year-round calendars have the same or fewer school days than nearby schools with traditional calendars. Schools with year-round calendars usually have several month-long breaks throughout the year (rather than two consecutive months off in summer).
- *Multi-track calendars*—Multi-tracking is a way for overcrowded schools to accommodate more students. Multi-track schools usually follow staggered year-round schedules. Tracks are staggered so that while some students (and teachers) are on vacation, others are in school. Multi-track calendars are arranged so that they best alleviate the overcrowding. While some schools have two tracks, others may have three or four. Some multi-track calendars give students two six-week breaks during the year; others give students four three-week breaks. Consult with the school for exact dates (also ask what kind of day-care activities the school provides for children when they are "off-track" since many traditional summer camps are not available to children who have a break in February!).

"How do I find out how a school organizes students? Do I just ask if they track students?"

Tracking, leveling, and ability-grouping all refer to the process of sorting children into different classes or groups based on their academic skills. These processes are very common (remember being in "reading groups" in elementary school?) and many teachers find them essential in order to provide students with skill-appropriate materials. Some students, parents, teachers, and policy-makers argue that the practice of sorting students gives "smart kids" a boost while holding back students who are slower. Others argue that tracking tends to unfairly put white, Asian, and middle class students in higher groups while putting African-American, Latino, and poor students in lower groups. Because of these arguments, "tracking" has become a dirty word in many public schools. You may have a hard time getting a direct answer if you ask, "Do you track students?" Instead ask teachers and principals how they group students and how they ensure that high-achieving students get enrichment and low-achieving students get extra help. Also, ask about your child specifically. If your child is designated as gifted or GATE, ask how they will accommodate her. If your child is still learning English, ask how they will place her. Also listen for other key words that sometimes indicate that a school uses tracking (or doesn't):

▶ *Balancing/balanced*—Balanced classes are mixed-achievement group classes (although teachers often group children within balanced classes).

▶ *Homogeneous groups*—these are groups where children have similar skill levels.

▶ *Heterogeneous groups*—these are mixed-ability groups.

▶ *Teaming/team teaching/rotating classes/switching classes*—Although many teachers team-teach without ability grouping, in some schools team-teaching indicates that "homeroom" classes are balanced but that students go to skill-segregated classes for core subjects. Likewise, if a school has students switch teachers for different subjects, ask how they determine which students go to which teachers. You may find that these groups are determined based on academic skill.

"Why do schools track or group students? Will tracking and grouping be good for my child?"

There are two main reasons that schools and teachers track and group students:

1. Many teachers and schools feel that they can serve all children best if they can work with them in similarly skilled groups. When teachers try to teach mixed-skill groups, they often struggle to pace lessons (i.e., moving fast enough so that quick children don't get bored but slowly enough so that slower children can fully comprehend) and find appropriate materials (i.e., books that are both challenging enough for good readers and easy enough for struggling readers). On the other hand, if they divide children into groups, they can work with each group at a pace that is perfect and with materials that are appropriate for that group of students.

2. Schools with diverse populations often struggle to keep high achieving students at their school. Many parents worry that their children are not being sufficiently challenged. Some pull their children out of schools that they perceive to be too easy. Thus, schools that serve both low- and high-achieving students might create special classes for high-achievers to show parents that the school is committed to providing a rigorous education to its highest-achieving students.

Your opinion about tracking and grouping will likely depend upon your personal opinions about how children should be educated, your child's achievement level, and how your school implements grouping. Here are some aspects of tracking and grouping that many parents like:

◆ Tracking and grouping often help high achieving students get extra enrichment and a more fast-paced, challenging curriculum.

◆ Tracking and grouping can help lower-achieving students get the extra help or slower pace that they need to understand and enjoy school.

◆ Tracking and grouping control children's peer groups. By putting children in classes with other children with comparable academic skills, children often tend to be in classes with children who have similar family backgrounds.

◆ Tracking and grouping can ensure those children with special educational needs (e.g., English Language Learners (ELL) or students with learning disabilities) the special attention they need without holding back students without special needs. (In other words, a school may have a large ELL population, but if your child will be in an English-only class, you probably do not have to worry about her receiving a slower-paced language arts curriculum.)

Of course, parents also dislike many aspects of grouping and tracking:

◆ Tracking and grouping can make high-achieving kids get "big heads" and feel superior to children in lower groups.

◆ Tracking and grouping can make lower-achieving students feel bad about themselves (and yes—even first-graders usually know who is in the "high group" and who is not).

◆ Tracking and grouping systems can make it hard for children to work their way up into higher groups and may punish "late-bloomers."

♦ Classes for lower-achieving students are often harder to control and waste more time on classroom management.

♦ Isolating children in a "high" or "GATE" class can rob them of the benefits of attending a diverse school and keep them from learning to get along with children who are "different."

♦ Isolating children in "low" classes or special ELL classes can prevent them from learning from higher-achieving peers and having good student role models.

Whether or not tracking and grouping are good for your child will depend a lot about your child's skill level, personality, and your own philosophies about teaching and learning. However, when thinking about tracking and grouping remember that *mobility* is the key to making any grouping system work to your child's advantage. If your child can move to higher groups as he improves his skills (or switch down if the work in his current class is too hard), he will receive the instruction that he needs in a grouping system. Make sure that teachers at the schools you are considering reassess children frequently to make sure that they are placed correctly. (And, once your child starts school, if you have questions about his placement, make an appointment to talk to the teacher.)

"What statistics can I learn about a school? Where do I get them?"

Statistics won't tell you everything about a school but they are a good starting point. Many schools and districts post test scores and other relevant information on the Internet. Many states have a unified system where you can look up the test scores, poverty level, racial composition, average teacher experience, and teacher qualifications on the states' department of education Web sites. (Read on for how to interpret and use these numbers.) Many local newspapers also publish annual test scores for local school districts. Schools generally report test score results in the form of percentiles. Percentiles either refer to the school's average national rank or the percentage of students who scored above a certain cutoff on the exam. (It's not easy to interpret what many of these statistics mean—so read the next section before you jump to any conclusions based on test score statistics.)

Perhaps even better, several Web sites are dedicated to making school statistics easy to find (although these statistics may not be as comprehensive as the ones made available by your own state, district, or school). For instance, www.greatschools.com allows you to look up schools (public and private) within a radius of your home (or potential home) and compare them in terms of test scores, teacher experience, percentage of teachers with full credentials, and student demographics (ethnicity, poverty, ELL population). If you are looking to relocate, a new Web site called www.schoolmatch.com will allow you to look up school districts in different areas by school and community characteristics to find a school that is a good match for your family.

"What should I learn from a school's demographics?"

Statistics about schools' student populations are usually the easiest to find (either on state, district, or school Web sites or at www.greatschools.com). Here's what you should expect to find:

▶ *Ethnic breakdown.* The ethnic composition of a school is one of the most frequently cited, and sometimes the most misleading indicator of school quality. Often schools that real estate agents consider "bad" schools are schools with large minority populations. Many parents (of all ethnic backgrounds) avoid schools that are "all black" or "mostly minority." Many parents feel that the education at minority-majority schools must be subpar or that their children might be in danger at those schools. But, despite these widely held notions, you should not dismiss integrated or ethnically diverse schools out of hand.

A school's ethnic statistics (or the color of the students on the play-ground) don't necessarily indicate a school's academic quality. Many schools with many minority students have a great deal to offer—and may be academically superior to other, whiter schools. Moreover, many students have a lot to gain socially by attending a diverse school and learning about different cultures, customs, and ways of interacting. In an increasingly multicultural society, students can learn very important interpersonal skills in diverse schools.

However, you should also consider how your child will fit in at the schools you are considering. Many children feel uncomfortable if they are one of the only members of a particular race or ethnic group at a school (and this goes for a white child attending an all-Latino school or a Black child attending an all-White school). And, if your child is part of a very small ethnic group at a school, you need to be particularly vigilant to make sure that he is being treated fairly and his teachers' expectations for him are appropriate.

▶ *Free/reduced lunch population.* The percentage of students in a school who qualify for free or reduced price lunch is a measure of school poverty. Children whose family incomes are less than 130 percent of the poverty line qualify for free lunch (for a family of four in 2004 the poverty line is about $18,850 a year—so students qualify for free lunch if their families earn less than $24,505). Children whose families earn less than 185 percent of the poverty line ($34,873 in 2004) qualify for reduced price lunch. Although some schools with large numbers of poor children are academically strong, on average, they tend to have lower academic achievement, less-qualified teachers, and less well-maintained facilities. If you are considering a school in which more than 60 percent of the children qualify for free or reduced lunch, make sure to closely examine the school's test scores and instructional quality (in other words, you should observe some classes).

▶ *English Language Learner (ELL) population.* Many schools report the percentage of students who are not native English speakers or who are in programs for students who speak English as a second language. Many schools that serve a lot of ELL students have special bilingual programs. Some people argue that these bilingual programs are very useful in helping to transition non-native English speaking students to fluency in English. Others argue that bilingual programs prevent children from learning English as fast as they would in regular classes. If your child is not yet fluent in English, talk with teachers and any ELL specialists at the schools you are considering to see what their approach is and how it meshes with your philosophy. If your child is a native English speaker, you probably do not want to place her in a school where very few other children are native speakers. Schools that serve all ELL students often spend a great deal of time on English—which would probably not be a good use of your child's time. However, many schools that serve ELL students have strategies for helping ELL students learn English while maintaining academic rigor for English-only (EO) students. If you are concerned about the number of ELL students in a school that you are considering, talk to the principal and teachers at the school. Do ELL students have separate classes? Do they have special pull-out classes? How fluent is the average ELL student? How quickly do they become fluent? ELL students at some schools are very fluent and transition out of ELL quickly.

"What can I learn from statistics about a school's teaching staff?"

Many schools report basic statistics about their teaching staff (and sometimes their administrative staff as well). Since the figures reported are averages, they can't tell you very much about the particular teachers that your child will get, but they can tell you some things about the schools you are considering. (Some districts are moving towards providing more comprehensive profiles of individual teachers online—ask your district (or check its Web site) if it has such a system.)

▶ *Teacher experience.* Average measures of teacher experience cannot tell

Common Statistics Used to Describe School Populations

Schools often report the proportion of students they serve in the following categories:

- *Free or reduced price lunch*—This is a measure of poverty. Students qualify for reduced price lunch of their family income is less than 185 percent of the poverty line. They qualify for free lunches if their families earn less than 130 percent of the poverty line.

- *GATE or Gifted and Talented*—Gifted and talented students are students who have surpassed a predefined score on an IQ test or other standardized test or have been recommended by a teacher and qualify for special enrichment programs.

- *LEP or ELL or ESL*—LEP stands for "Limited English Proficient." ELL stands for "English Language Learner." ESL stands for "English as a Second Language." All of these statistics show the proportion of students who are not fully fluent in English. To learn what the students' native language is or what their average level of fluency is, you need to contact the school.

- *Public subsidy, AFDC, or Calworks*—Public subsidy refers to welfare. These students used to be categorized as AFDC, which stands for "Aid for Families with Dependent Children." Since the federal AFDC program was dismantled, many states have instituted their own welfare programs. In California, for instance, this program is called Calworks. No matter what it's called, this statistic indicates the proportion of the students who qualify for welfare support and indicates a more severe level of poverty than the free/reduced price lunch statistic.

- *Migrant Students*—Migrant students are children of laborers who move seasonally to find work in agriculture or the fishing or timber industries. Migrant students usually live in extreme poverty, and—because they move so often—usually have spotty educational backgrounds. Schools with large migrant student populations receive supplemental government funds to provide for their education.

- *Minority*—"Minority" includes all non-white students (African-American, Asian-American/Pacific Islander, Latino, or Native-American).

- *Special education/students with disabilities:* These students have some kind of diagnosed disability that can be physical, mental, or emotional (including everything from blindness to dyslexia.)

you much but you probably want to try to avoid schools where all teachers are brand new (less than two years of experience). Not only may these teachers lack teaching and classroom management skills, but schools with a lot of new teachers often have problems with teacher turnover as well. High teacher turnover may indicate poor administration or generally disgruntled teachers. But, other than that, experience is a mixed bag. Many teachers get better as they gain experience. But some older teachers burn out and some young teachers are talented, energetic, and enthusiastic.

▶ *Percentage of credentialed teachers.* Since many teachers gain credentials simply by taking some courses at a mediocre college, it's not clear that most teachers learn a great deal through the credentialing process. And, I've found that some excellent teachers have never officially gotten a credential. However, knowing the percentage of uncredentialed teachers at a school does tell you some things about school quality. First, many districts will hire uncredentialed teachers (or teachers who have not yet finished all of the requirements to get a credential) but most require teachers to finish the credential in order to keep their positions. Thus, uncredentialed teachers are more likely to be brand new teachers, who tend to struggle the most with teaching and classroom management. Also, when schools have large numbers

of new teachers it usually means that other teachers have recently left the school. Although retirements and other moves are normal, a school with a lot of turnover is probably not a good choice for your child. Second, most schools would prefer to hire credentialed teachers over uncredentialed teachers (although some schools make exceptions for candidates they really love). So, a school with many uncredentialed teachers may be a school that has trouble attracting good teachers—especially if that school has far more uncredentialed teachers than other local schools. (As a general rule, schools in areas with a "teacher shortage" will have more uncredentialed teachers than schools in areas with a "teacher surplus.")

▶ *Class size.* The fewer students a teacher has to deal with, the more she can focus on your child. Everything else equal, you should probably choose schools with smaller class sizes. Given a choice between 35 students and 22 students, I would choose a school with classes of 22 students. But tiny differences in class size should not determine your choice of a school—especially if the school with the large classes seems to have better teachers or stronger academic programs.

"What can I learn from a school's test scores?"

At the most basic level, test scores tell

Staff Statistics

- *Teachers*—Pupil:teacher ratios (or dividing the number of students by the number of teachers) will give you some idea of class size, but remember that many schools employ teachers who do not work in regular classrooms (they may be special education teachers or "teacher coaches" who are responsible for helping other teachers). If you want to know how many students are in a typical classroom at a school, ask specifically about class size (and because some schools have different class sizes for different grades, ask about every grade you are interested in).
- *Administrators/Other Professionals*—Some schools report how many principals, counselors, nurses, librarians, etc. they have. Other schools and districts simply lump all "non-teaching professionals" into a general administrator category. If you are interested in a specific position, ask (e.g., if your child has a health condition and you want to make sure the school has a nurse on staff all the time).
- *Paraprofessionals*—These are more commonly known as "teacher's aides" or "T.A.s." Schools vary widely in the qualifications they require for teacher's aides as well as the tasks that they assign to their aides.

Schools often report the qualifications of their teaching staff using the following terms:
- *Credentialed/certified/with certificate*—Teachers who have received a teaching credential or certificate have gone through your state's mandated teacher training coursework (which usually includes student teaching). High school teachers are generally certified within academic subjects (e.g., history or math) but elementary school teachers usually receive a general elementary education credential.

Per-student staffing is usually reported as "student:staff ratios." Schools and districts usually report these ratios per one staff member (i.e., student:counselor ratio=200). This statistic means that, on average, each counselor serves 200 students.

you how well the students in a school do in the subjects for which test scores are reported—usually reading and math (see sidebar for information on different ways in which test score data may be presented). Obviously, you don't want to enroll your child in a school with rock-bottom test scores if you can help it. And, everything else being equal, schools with higher test scores are likely better than schools with lower test scores.

But, a school's test scores do *not* simply show you how well the school teaches. You want to bear in mind that schools do not *create* students' test scores—students have varying test scores before they even start school. As a general rule, children from more affluent backgrounds have higher test scores than students from poorer backgrounds. An incredible school may raise its students' scores significantly but still have lower test scores than another school whose students come from wealthier backgrounds and begin kindergarten with higher scores. However, regardless of why students' test scores are high, if you send your child to a school with higher average test scores, she will probably have classmates with better academic skills than if you choose a school with lower scores.

If you look at a school that has scores in the middle range, question someone at the school to learn more about how the students score. The way

averages work, middle scores (say 50th percentile) could mean that most students score at the 50th percentile, or that half of the students score at the 90th and half of the students score at the 10th. These are very different schools. A school that works to accommodate both its very high achievers and its struggling students could be an excellent school for a child in either group—even though the school's average scores are only mediocre.

"Are there any other school statistics I can look for?"

Beyond demographics, staffing, and test scores, there are a few other statistics that many schools and districts report.

◆ *Stability or transience measures*. Stability statistics show the percent of students who remain at the same school from one year to the next (conversely, transience measures how many students move into the school each year). As a general rule, you do not want to enroll your child in a high-transience school. Students who move around a lot tend to lack academic skills and have disruptive home lives. Schools that serve many new students every year also have a hard time building a sense of community and maintaining academic momentum from year to year.

◆ *Student:computer ratio*. Many schools report how many computers they have per student. This ratio gives you some sense of how technologically advanced a school is. At computer-rich schools your child will probably learn to do some research at school and gain familiarity with computers in school computer labs. Plus, kids usually love computers so their very presence seems to make school more fun. However, try not to place too much value on the number of computers at school. Often these computers are outdated or suffer from poor Internet connections. And, unless the student:computer ratio is 2-to-1 or less, too many students will have to share the computers for them to use them really effectively. Instead of worrying about the number of computers in your child's school, you would be better off investing in a computer for your home that your child can explore, learn from, and use for homework (if you have a computer that you don't want your young child touching—and possibly breaking—consider getting an additional, cheaper model for your child's use).

Some schools also report crime, suspension and expulsion statistics. For most elementary schools, these numbers are very low:

▶ **Crime incidents**. You obviously don't want to send your child to a school where a lot of crime occurs. Compare the crime statistics from a variety of schools in your area to see what looks like an "average" amount of crime in your local elementary schools. Or, look up a school that you know to be "very safe" and compare other schools to that benchmark.

▶ **Suspension and expulsion statistics**. These statistics tell you something about the behavior of students in a school and something about the school's willingness to punish students who behave badly. Like crime statistics, suspension and expulsion statistics are best understood when you compare different schools.

"I don't know anything at all about schools. None of these statistics mean anything to me. What can I compare them to? What's a good baseline?"

Comparisons will vary dramatically from community to community—it's impossible to give a baseline that will apply to everyone. However, one way to form a comparison group is to think of schools that you know are good (ideally, choose schools in the same state as the schools you are considering so that you are at least comparing test scores from the same test). You might think of the schools that some of your friend's children attend, or an exemplary school in the next neighborhood. Even if you can't afford to live in the neighborhood with the exemplary school, this will give you a "dream" baseline to which you can compare the schools in more affordable neighbor-

Understanding School-Level Test Results

School level test results are typically reported in several different ways (read the introduction to the table presenting the statistics to see which interpretation you should use).

- *Percentile Ranking*—This measure ranks all schools (or districts or states) on a scale from 1 to 100. The percentile ranking tells you where a school ranks relative to other schools. For instance, if, in a table presenting test scores for every school in the state, your child's school is ranked at the 75th percentile, it means that 25 percent of schools in your state scored above your school and 75 percent scored below your school. In other words, your school is better than the average school in your state, but is not one of the very top schools. Or, if you are looking at a ranking of all of the districts in the country and your school district scores at the 90th percentile, you will know that your district performs better (on average) than 90 percent of the school districts in the country.

- *Percentage of students who score above the 50th percentile on the administered standardized test*—This measure shows you what percentage of students in a school scored "above average" on the test. The tests are designed so that every student who takes the test is ranked on a scale from 1 to 100. The student who has the middle score (also known as the median score) in the entire country is assigned to the 50th percentile. These figures then show you the percentage of students at your school who scored better than that "middle" score. For example, if 90 percent of students in a school score above the 50th percentile, then most of the students are above the national median (you cannot tell from this statistic if they are barely above or way above). If only 10 percent of students score above the 50th percentile, then you know that most of the students are below the national median (but, again, you don't know if they are way below or just a little below).

- *Percentage of students scoring above "basic," "proficient," or "advanced"*—Most states have academic standards that they want all students to meet. They often use tests that correspond with these standards and report test scores by showing how many students could be considered "basic," "proficient," or "advanced" according to those state standards. If you see test results reported this way, you want to choose hoods. If you are moving from a neighborhood in which you know a lot about the schools, think of a school you really like in your old neighborhood and try to find a similar school in the new town you're moving to.

"What's a drive-by? How do I do one? What am I looking for?"

Statistics are a good start, but they don't really let you get a feel for a school. Once you choose a school, you will have to send your child there every day. You want to make sure you feel comfortable going there and leaving

him on the playground. So, get in your car and drive past the schools you are interested in. Bring a notebook or even a camera (especially if you want to discuss schools with your partner, child, or friends).

Simply looking at a school can tell you a great deal. Pay attention to:

▶ *Overall maintenance.* Is the school well cared for? Is the paint maintained? Is trash picked up? Is the landscaping kept up? Although none of these factors will play a huge role in your child's education, decent maintenance does make going to school more pleasant. Maintenance also shows how much

schools in which a greater percentage of students score above proficient or advanced and a smaller percentage of students score "below basic." (Sometimes schools use "poor," "proficient," and "advanced" or other, similar labels—again, choose schools where more children are scoring above advanced and fewer are scoring below poor.)

- *School Performance Score*—Some states have developed school performance scores (e.g., California uses the Academic Performance Index (API), Michigan uses report cards) that simplify test score data. Higher scores (or letter grades) are usually better.
- *Similar Schools Score*—Many states also report "similar schools" scores that compare schools to other schools that are similar in terms of student demographics (e.g., ethnicity and poverty). No matter what a school's overall score is, make sure that it ranks well compared to similar schools.
- *Adequate Yearly Progress (AYP)*—Federal law requires that all schools meet annual progress goals towards achieving 100% proficiency by 2014. Most states make AYP data available through their Web sites but because states are still developing standards (and challenging federal requirements) these measures are not entirely useful to parents. Suffice to say that schools that do not meet AYP targets probably deserve extra scrutiny.

pride the school administrators and the students (who are probably the ones leaving trash around or drawing graffiti on the walls) have in their school.

♦ *Overall environment.* Does the school look friendly? Are there murals, signs, or schoolwork posted in the windows? Does the school look as though it loves and values children? Do you think your child would be happy on that playground?

♦ *Buildings.* How crowded does the school look? Many schools nowadays have portable classrooms (like little mobile homes) to help accommodate growing populations of students— portables alone do not indicate that a school is bad or even overcrowded. But, if the portables take up most of the playground, you may be dealing with an overcrowded school.

♦ *How the children interact with each other.* If you go at recess or lunchtime, you have the perfect opportunity to peek through the fence and see how children interact with each other. Every school will have a certain amount of yelling and squabbling during games. But do the kids seem to cooperate with each other? When they have a problem, is an adult nearby and can the adult resolve the problem? Do the kids solve their problems verbally or physically? Do the kids seem active and happy? Also, look for aspects of the student body that might make good playmates for your child. If you want your child to have a diverse group of friends, see if children from different racial groups seem to play together or in segregated groups. If you have a girl who loves to play sports, look to see if girls are involved in the basketball and soccer games. If you have a child who adores jump rope or handball, look around to see if other children (who are about the same age as your child) are engaged in those games. Of course, jump rope availability should not make or break your decision about a school, but it's something to consider. (If sports could be a decision breaker for you, make sure you get all the information. Some schools only allow certain sports on certain days, so if you don't see anyone playing basketball the day you drive by, don't cross a school off your list until you talk to someone at the school and find out its playground schedule.)

♦ *How involved are the parents?* If you drive by right as school lets out you will get a glimpse of the parents. See how many come to pick their children up. See how many go into the school and talk with students and teachers. If you are bold, pick a friendly looking parent and strike up a conversation.

"I have driven by the schools I am interested in, but how do I find out if the teachers are nice and the academic programs are strong?"

You actually need to get inside the school, look at some classrooms, and talk to some administrators and teachers. There are several ways to "get inside" a school.

▶ *Call the school and see if there are parent orientations* (some schools hold them periodically). If so, sign up. This way you can go and see the school's official orientation, see the grounds, maybe hear from the principal, and probably talk with other parents. You might even hear some interesting facts and tidbits about other schools while you are there.

▶ *Attend Back to School Night or Open House.* These events are designed for current parents but most schools will allow prospective parents to attend. At Back to School Night (usually in September or October) teachers explain to parents their organization systems, their expectations for students, and their agenda for the year. You will probably be able to sit in on a presentation or two. Open Houses (usually in the spring) are less formal (and it would be easier for you to attend unnoticed). At Open House teachers display student work, students give their parents tours of the school, and parents talk more informally with teachers. Go and look around. Pop your head into different classrooms to see the type of work the students do. Talk to some teachers—most will be glad to answer any questions you have about the school. Call

schools you are interested in and ask about dates for these events (some schools also post calendars on the Internet).

▶ *Make an appointment to talk with the principal and a teacher who teaches the grade your child would be in.* As long as you are not calling at a particularly crazy time of the year (e.g., during standardized testing or right before a vacation), most principals will make appointments to talk with prospective parents. They may even set you up with a parent volunteer to give you a little tour. Teachers may be harder to get in contact with but when you talk to the principal ask if you can meet with a teacher or sit in on a few lessons. While you're there, don't only pay attention to what the principal and teacher tell you, but how the adults interact with each other and how they interact with the kids. Try to take in the overall atmosphere of the school.

"I have an appointment to meet with the principal at a school I'm considering. What kinds of questions should I ask?"

Many of the questions that you will want to ask a prospective principal or teacher will depend on your child's particular needs and interests. If your child is academically gifted, ask what sorts of enrichment programs the school offers. If your child has a learning disability, ask what kinds of special education resources are available. If your child loves sports, ask about the school's physical education program and if there is an after-school sports program. In addition, make sure to cover the following points:

♦ **What is the school's teaching philosophy?** This may sound like a corny question. But, you should know what a school—in its most idealistic moments—values. Does it value focusing entirely on academics, nurturing the "whole" student including his or her artistic and interpersonal skills, or emphasizing religion, character education, community involvement, or the arts. Ask yourself if the school's professed values match your own.

♦ **What types of teaching strategies does the school employ?** Does it focus on basic skills? Does it emphasize projects and other "hands-on" learning? Although a school may have a fabulous program in which students put on plays or create projects for every lesson, that school may not be a good fit for your child if he struggles to learn basic reading and math skills or needs a highly structured learning environment.

♦ **How does the school group or track students?** Some schools group students by academic ability. Some have all GATE classes, all ELL classes, or all remedial classes. (See earlier question for more information about grouping and tracking.)

♦ **What does the school expect from parents?** Are most parents involved in school government? Do they volunteer at the school? Although you don't want to put your child in a school that requires you to be there all the time, a school that expects a lot from students' parents probably has strong community support, may benefit from good fundraising, and probably has students who tend to come to school well-prepared for the school day. Schools with high standards for parental involvement usually have high standards for students as well. (Some charter schools require prospective parents to commit to a set amount of involvement.)

"The principal says that I can observe a class, but what should I look for when I go?"

Observing a class is a great way to get a feel for a school even though you probably won't see the exact same class that your child will be in (next year there will be different students and possibly a different teacher). But, the principal will probably steer you towards a teacher she thinks is one of her best. Observing a school's "best teacher" tells you a lot about the school's philosophy. If the teacher is great, you have found a school that has good ideals and at least some teachers who reach those ideals. If you are disappointed with the teacher you observe, you may well worry that she is the best the school has to offer. Pay attention to:

▶ *The classroom.* Examine students' work on the walls. Do the assignments look fun and interesting? Are they well done? Is the room decorated cheerfully? Does it demonstrate the teacher's pride in her students' work?

▶ *The teacher's teaching style.* Does she provide the children with a lot of information? Does she allow them to discuss new ideas? You want a teacher who can communicate information quickly and efficiently but in a way that lets children absorb and understand—not just memorize.

▶ *Classroom management.* The best teachers can keep their classes under control. A phenomenal amount of time is wasted in elementary school classes when teachers have to keep asking students to be quiet or pay attention. Good teachers (somehow) manage to keep 20-30 young children quiet and under control during lessons. (Remember, the children shouldn't look terrified or too bored to participate; they just need to be quiet and focused enough for their classmates to follow the lesson.) If you observe a class that is in the middle of a lively discussion or group project, don't interpret noise as poor class management. If the teacher can call the class to order quickly and reorients students to new tasks easily, she has the class under control.

▶ *The teacher's interaction style.* Does the teacher treat the children kindly? Does she treat them with respect or talk down to them? You want a teacher who commands respect but does not intimidate or put down students.

▶ *The content of the lesson.* Does the content of the lesson that you are observing seem to be at an appropriate level for your child? Does the vocabulary that the teacher is using seem appropriate for your child? Do the classwork and homework seem like work that your child could complete but that would also challenge him?

▶ *The children's interactions with the teacher.* Again, good teachers command respect and affection. Children should feel free to raise their hands and talk to the teacher (when appropriate) but should not take advantage of the teacher (e.g., continue to misbehave after being warned).

▶ *The children's interactions with each other.* Are the children kind and friendly to each other? How do they react when a classmate makes a mistake? (And, if they react badly, by booing or laughing, does the teacher chide them for it?) When you choose a school, you choose your child's peers and future friends. Ideally, they will be motivated, eager to learn, and respectful of one another.

While you are observing, remember that the teacher (and the children) may be on their best behavior while they are being observed, so don't expect every lesson to go as smoothly as the one that you saw. (It does not bode well if you observe a class that seems to be acting *particularly* bad because you are observing—most students like their teacher well enough not to want to embarrass her in front of observers.) And again, when you observe a classroom, try to think about how well *your child* will fit in (for instance you may love a loud, enthusiastic classroom full of students who are constantly participating in discussion, but this might be an intimidating environment if your child is shy).

Specific Questions about Public Schools of Choice

(i.e., charter schools and magnet schools)

When you choose a public school of choice, make sure you walk through all of the previous steps involved in choosing and assessing schools. However, many parents find that their search through the public school system turns up even more questions. This section should help you understand and negotiate the public school "choice" process.

"What is a charter school?"

Charter schools are usually located geographically within traditional public school districts, but are run at least somewhat independently of the district. Charter schools have been designed to create school choice for parents and to try innovative new ways to raise achievement without the restrictions and bureaucracy that govern regular public schools.

The driving idea behind charter schools is that they don't have to follow district rules or abide by district bureaucracy, but they are held accountable for fulfilling their charters. Charter schools submit their charter—which is essentially a contract or plan for how the school will be run—to their local district or state. Within the charter, charter schools set their own standards for hiring and paying teachers, choose their own curricula, explain how they will select students, and elucidate any other special rules or programs they intend to implement. For instance, most charter schools have a requirement that students' parents be involved—many require parents to sign a contract agreeing to volunteer a certain amount of time at the school. Charter schools are then allowed to essentially run themselves (again, free from district regulations) according to their plan. They are assessed at the end of their charter (usually 3-5 years) on how well they raised achievement and how well they executed their charter. Charter schools that do not raise achievement or abide by their plan risk losing their charter status.

Many politicians and policy-makers like charter schools because they think that they provide competition and push regular public schools to improve. Many parents like charter schools because their independence (and relative lack of bureaucratic red tape) makes them appealing to good teachers. Sometimes (but not always) charter schools have better programs and better teachers than other nearby schools.

"Who can go to a charter school?"

Different charter schools have different rules. One overarching rule is that charter schools are supposed to recruit students from their community (including conducting outreach to tell people in the community about the school). Some charter schools automatically admit all of the students in their catchment area. Many charter schools allow students from outside their usual attendance area to apply for admission. Charter schools often do not have enough capacity for all the children who would like to attend. When more children apply than can fit in a charter school, charter schools are required to admit students fairly, usually with some kind of lottery system. However, because one of the main characteristics of charter schools is that they have their own charters and set their own rules, you need to contact the charter school that you are interest-ed in to learn the exact details of its enrollment process.

"What is a magnet school?"

Magnet schools were developed 50 years ago in an attempt to facilitate voluntary desegregation. The Magnet School Assistance section of the "No Child Left Behind" legislation defines magnet schools as a school or learning center "that offers a special curriculum capable of attracting substantial numbers of students of different racial backgrounds."[1] So, although districts operate magnet schools in scores of different ways, they are all supposed to advance this goal (which explains why many magnet programs use race as a factor in their admission processes).

The idea was that magnet schools could develop special programs that would attract students from all over the city in which they were based. This would pull students out of typically segregated neighborhood schools into integrated magnet schools. Because of these special programs and specialized curricula, magnet schools are often considered some of the best forms of public education in urban areas. Some magnet schools specialize in science, others in arts. Still others

---

[1] U.S. Department of Education. *No Child Left Behind Act of 2001.* Washington, D.C.: U.S. Department of Education, 2004. World Wide Web. 16 April 2004 <http://www. ed.gov.legislation/ESEA02/pg65.html>

cater to gifted students or students who want to become doctors or engineers. When these specialized programs are executed well, children can get very strong, specialized educations.

Perhaps even more important than the curriculum, all magnet schools admit students through an application process. Although many magnet schools admit students in a lottery process without considering children's grades or achievement, the very fact that an application is required usually weeds out students whose parents don't care enough about their education to apply. Given how important parental involvement is in education, the mere fact that magnet schools require families to exert a little extra effort to get in often results in a higher achieving, more motivated student body (even if the school itself is not better than other local schools).

"I keep hearing about magnet schools in my district. How do I get my child into one?"

Districts have widely varying policies on how to admit students to magnet schools. Several rules are relatively consistent, however. First, unlike regular public schools, magnet schools do not limit themselves to children in their catchment area—by design, they admit students from all over the district. Districts do, however, differ as to whether they require magnet schools

to give priority enrollment to children who live in the local neighborhood or if they require all students, regardless of where they live, to participate in the full application process. So, before you assume that moving into a neighborhood will give you access to the local magnet school, talk to someone at the district office to learn what its policies are (district Web sites often have this information).

Because magnet school admission is usually in high demand, most magnet schools have a process by which they admit students when there are more applicants than spaces available. Most districts use lottery systems, through which they claim to "randomly" choose who gains admission. Although some randomness is involved in all of these processes, it would be more accurate to call them "stratified random lotteries" since, often, not every student has an equal chance of being drawn in the lottery (read on for the factors that influence students' odds of admission). Other districts still use the "first come, first served" admission method, which sometimes leads to parents camping out on the sidewalk outside of the school to make sure they can sign up their child for one of the limited number of slots. Be sure to check with your district and with the specific magnet schools to which you want to apply to find out exactly what system they use.

Almost all magnet schools

require parents to fill out an application. All of the following criteria might influence your child's chances of getting in to a magnet school:

▶ *Race/ethnicity.* Because magnet schools are supposed to foster integration, many magnet schools use students' race or ethnicity to determine their odds of admissions. Some districts require all magnet schools to serve a certain percentage of white students and a certain percentage of students of color. Thus, while they admit students randomly, they admit from different pools in order to achieve and maintain these percentages. For example, if a school is trying to maintain equal numbers of white and Latino students and 10 white applicants and 100 Latino applicants apply for 20 open slots, all of the white applicants would probably be admitted while only 10 (10%) of the Latino applicants would gain admission. Some districts also consider the racial composition of the school that a child would be leaving if he gained admission to a magnet school (in other words, a white child whose assigned school is predominately white will have a better chance of being admitted to an integrated magnet school than a white child who is leaving an integrated assigned school for a predominately white magnet school). Other districts have specific race quotas that they try to reach in particular schools. Still other districts do not ask about race in the application and do not seem to use race in their admissions policies.

▶ *Siblings.* For the most part, magnet schools offer priority enrollment to children who have siblings already attending the school. Some districts guarantee sibling enrollment, others simply give siblings greater weight in the lottery. Either way, most applications ask about siblings (even younger siblings) and many schools require parents to "put themselves in the sibling pool" when they first apply with their eldest child. (Putting yourself in the sibling pool lowers the odds that your first child will get in, but improves the odds that, if your first child gets in, your younger children will as well.)

▶ *Geography.* Many districts give priority to children who live nearby. These rules often reflect simple distances rather than attendance district boundaries. For instance, in some districts (like in Buffalo, New York), a student who lives within what is considered "walking distance" (usually half a mile) has a better chance of getting admitted than a child who lives farther away. (Again, this is not always the case, so check the rules in your district.)

▶ *Test scores, grades, and teacher recommendations.* Although the majority of magnet elementary schools admit students regardless of their academic performance, there are some exceptions. The Lubbock, Texas school district, for instance, requires high test scores, high grades, and teacher recommendations for admission to magnet schools. In many districts, admission to "gifted" and "highly gifted" magnet programs requires that applicants score above certain cutoffs on IQ tests or standardized tests. Magnet high schools are also more likely to require tests, a portfolio, or an audition (particularly for arts or performing arts magnets). Again, check with your district and the schools you are considering.

Some districts have additional magnet application procedures, which often make magnet school application more complicated.

♦ *Magnet points.* Some districts, Los Angeles Unified being a prime example, require students to have certain numbers of magnet points to be considered for admission to magnet schools. Parents apply for points *each year* that their child is in the public system (this system prevents students from switching from the private system directly into a competitive magnet school). Students get extra points for attending "predominantly Hispanic, Asian, Black or other" (called PHABO) and overcrowded schools. They get extra points if they have a sibling in the magnet school to which they are applying. Students also get extra points every time they apply to a magnet and are rejected. (Many parents use this process to try to accumulate extra

points—they apply to schools where they stand little chance of admission, in the hopes of gaining more points.) To get into many competitive middle schools, students have to have accumulated points through several of these methods, starting in as early as kindergarten—something that many elementary school parents don't learn until it's too late (much of this information spreads almost entirely through word of mouth). So, although not many systems use magnet points, the lesson to learn from Los Angeles is to ask around and learn everything you can about your district's magnet system as soon as possible. From the time you enroll your child in kindergarten, ask an authority at your child's school (as well as teachers and other parents) if there is something you should be doing **now** to maximize your child's chances of getting into a magnet middle school or high school later on. And, if you know parents who have recently enrolled a child in a magnet school you think you might like your child to attend in the future, try to chat with them and see if they have any advice for you.

To avoid being surprised by unique aspects of your own magnet system, get a copy of your district's magnet school application as soon as your child starts school (many districts offer applications online, but others require you to order them by mail or pick them up at the district office). Even if you are thrilled with your child's kindergarten class and elementary school, the application will clue you into how your local magnet system works and how to be prepared if you want to get your child into a magnet school later on. If anything in the application does not make sense, ask about it now. Then you will be armed with the information when you really need it.

"I would like my child to attend a magnet school, but it's across town. Will the district provide transportation?"

Because magnet schools are supposed to encourage desegregation and because children from different ethnic backgrounds often live in different parts of town, most magnet programs include some efforts to provide transportation for students to get to magnet schools to which they have been accepted. However, some bus rides to and from magnet schools can take hours as they cross town. Before you plan to use district-provided transportation to your child's magnet school, contact the district to find out what kind of transportation they provide, where they would pick up your child, and at what time. This way you can make an educated decision about whether or not the district-provided transportation will solve your trans-

portation problems (for instance, even if there is a bus, it may pick students up several miles from your home two hours before school starts).

Specific Questions about Private Schools

Although this book is geared toward parents of small children, as you read this section you will find that it includes questions about private middle and high schools as well as private elementary schools because many private schools serve students from kindergarten through high school. Other private elementary schools feed into particular private high schools. Thus, when you choose a private elementary school for your child, you should also consider aspects of its upper grades or aspects of the high schools that many of its graduates attend.

"How should I evaluate a private school?"

When you evaluate a private school, follow the same steps listed above for choosing and assessing any school. Private schools should be able to stand up to statistical and "drive-by" scrutiny as well as any public school, with two exceptions. First, some private schools do not make test scores available. You can ask, but some schools won't provide them. This shouldn't necessarily make you suspicious of the school. Because private schools do not report test scores to government agencies, test scores are not public data for private schools. Also, if you do get test scores from a private school, they may not be comparable to those you receive from public schools. Private schools often use different tests than public schools (most prefer tests that can compare their scores to other private schools). Although both kinds of tests are nationally normed, they may have been normed at different times (even years apart), making them hard to compare (see Appendix 5 for more on norming).

Second, meeting with principals and teachers should be much easier at private schools than at public schools. Private school administrators should be eager to meet with you and show off their school. Private schools should all have some kind of open house or orientation for interested parents—if they don't, you should worry about why they don't want you to see the school before you enroll your child and pay tuition.

You should also consider a few more factors when evaluating a private school.

♦ *Is the school accredited?* A number of regional and state associations accredit private schools once they meet certain basic standards in order to ensure quality and accountability. Most

good private schools have accreditation by one of six regional independent accreditation organizations and their seals of approval should help you feel more confident in a private school's legitimacy[2]. There are other numerous organizations that accredit schools. If you are looking into non-religious private schools, I recommend looking into the National Association of Independent Schools (NAIS) (check out their Web site for more information at http://www.nais.org). Most religious schools belong to associations of other schools of the same faith or denomination (e.g., Catholic schools usually join the National Catholic Educational Association; conservative Jewish Schools often join the Solomon Schechter Day Schools Association). If you are looking into religious schools check to see which accreditations and associations that well-reputed schools of your faith usually join (you can look them up on the NCES Web site). You might also ask someone knowledgeable at your church or temple about schools and school associations within your faith. Although there are some very good unaccredited private schools

---

[2] The six regional accreditation associations are: Middle States Association of Colleges and Schools (MSA), New England Association of Schools and Colleges (NEASC), North Central Association of Colleges and Schools (NCA), Northwest Association of Schools and Colleges (NASC), Southern Association of Colleges and Schools (SACS), and Western Association of Schools and Colleges (WASC).

(especially alternative schools and newer schools which have not been around long enough to go through the accreditation process), I would suggest that parents look very closely at any unaccredited school. These schools are more likely to be fly-by-night operations or the types of schools that hire under-qualified teachers.

▶ *How does the school handle transitions from one school level to the next?* One of the most stressful aspects of private schools is the need to keep applying to new schools every time your child graduates. Some private schools have "lower" and "upper" campuses and guarantee that children who attend the lower school (usually grades K-6) will be admitted to the upper school (7-12). Other schools make no such promises, meaning that you have to reapply. Some schools have good connections with other local upper schools, easing the application process. Others do not. As you enroll your child in private school, try to think about his entire educational path and plan accordingly. You do not want to find yourself in the situation of having to put your child through seven years of private school only to find that he cannot gain admission to any of the local private high schools.

▶ *What demands does the school typically make on parents?* This is a question that you might ask an administrator, but you should also put to other parents. Some private schools expect a great deal of support (often in the form of big donations). Some do not react well if you don't comply. Other schools do not expect large donations from all parents. Either way, it's better to know what you are getting into before you enroll your child. Ask the administrator, "What types of support do you typically expect parents to give?" And ask other parents if they have been asked to donate and, if so, how they responded and how the school responded to them.

▶ *If your child plays sports, what league is the school in?* Although this may not apply to all parents, parents whose children are sports enthusiasts may prefer to play in large, competitive public school leagues than in small private school leagues (some private school leagues are quite competitive— this is something you need to investigate).

"I want my child to go to a very selective—ideally an Ivy League —college. Is going to an elite private school the best way to get into one of these colleges?"

Many people think that elite private high schools are the ticket to elite colleges. How true that statement is depends a lot on your child and how well he or she performs academically. Students who attend the best, most elite private high schools gain a number of advantages for college application:

▶ *Rigorous courses.* If your child attends a highly selective private school, chances are the students will be high achievers and the classes will be more rigorous (although possibly not more rigorous than an honors track at a good public school).

▶ *Advanced course offerings.* Most elite private high schools offer a wide range of advanced course offerings, including Advanced Placement (AP) and sometimes International Baccalaureate (IB) courses. These rigorous courses (and the higher GPAs that often come from the weighted grades that children receive from these courses) often help students gain admission to highly selective colleges.

▶ *Advanced supplies and equipment.* Although not all private schools are well-funded, the most elite private schools have big donors and large budgets. This extra money translates into better-equipped science labs, computers labs, and drama productions. For instance, in Los Angeles, Harvard-Westlake, the most competitive private high school, has science lab facilities that rival working labs at UCLA. At Crossroads, another L.A. high school that serves many children of Hollywood actors, directors, and producers, drama productions often use real movie set props.

▶ *Better-connected counselors and more attention from counselors.* Counselors at elite private high schools cultivate relationships with admissions directors at elite colleges. They also spend extraordinary amounts of time crafting highly polished letters of recommendation for students applying to college. This contrasts sharply with college counselors at many large public schools, where one counselor (who typically has few connections) tries to help hundreds of college applicants.

▶ *Reputation.* Many elite high schools have good reputations. If they are known for providing a solid education (and not inflating grades), college admissions committees may be more forgiving of an occasional low grade than if your student came from an unknown school.

Of course, there are also some drawbacks to attending an elite private high school as a means of getting your child into an elite college. You probably won't be able to avoid all of these pitfalls, but you should definitely consider them.

▶ *Cost.* This may seem obvious. But many parents will pay as much for a high school education as they will for a college education. It may not be worth spending your child's college fund on high school if you have good public school options.

▶ *Competition.* Elite private high schools have admissions processes through which they select only the best. This means that your child will go to school with some of the brightest and most motivated students in your area. Many elite colleges only take students who were ranked at the very top (at least top 10 percent, sometimes only the top one or two students) of their high school classes (in 2002, 2,900 valedictorians applied to Harvard—for less than 2,100 slots!). At an elite high school, the competition can be intense. If your child is a very good—but not great—student, a relatively low class rank may hurt his chances of admission to an elite college.

◆ **Difficulty.** Because elite private schools serve a select group of students, they sometimes offer very difficult course material. As a result, a student who might have gotten straight As at the local public school, might get Bs at a highly competitive private school.

Just how all of these factors will affect your child's chances of attending an elite college depend on both your child and the school. Some schools have such strong relationships with some colleges that they can help many students get in. Some schools have such strong reputations that colleges will admit their students even if they are not at the very top of their classes. However, other colleges and universities, especially ones that gun for valedictorians, may overlook a very strong student who is ranked in the middle of the class—even if he has received a better high school education than a valedictorian at a public school.

To assess the possible effects that a particular private school will have on your child's chances of admission to certain colleges, ask the college counselor at the private school. How many of its students apply to the colleges that you are interested in? How many are accepted? And, how many actually attend those colleges? Also, ask what types of colleges kids who are ranked in the middle of the class tend to go to. What about those students in the bottom third of the graduating class? Ask what he or she recommends to students who desperately want to go to a particular school. Although the counselor surely won't make you any promises, his or her answers should help you make an informed decision. If you have your heart set on Brown and the counselor tells you that every year 10 of their students apply to Brown but only the valedictorian or salutatorian gets in, you know what kinds of grades your child will have to have in order to be competitive.

Finally, before you make a decision based on what the counselor said, try to think objectively about *your child*. Although all parents think their child is special, does your child exhibit stellar academic skills? Does it seem like he has the potential to be at the very top of his class at an elite school? Does he seem like he has the personality it takes to withstand the competition at that type of school?

And remember, you are not

locked into a school once you choose. You can always choose again, either when your child graduates to the next school level, or even next school year, depending on how much you dislike your choice. So, talk to as many people as you can, make the best choice you can, and don't be afraid to change your mind and choose again later if it turns out not to have been the best choice.

(One last note about private high schools: the above-mentioned items are just pros and cons about choosing a school *as a vehicle to college*. Many other pros and cons come with elite private schools. For example, they tend to serve wealthy children. This can be a great perk (e.g., if your child gets to go on a European vacation with his best friend) or awful (e.g., if your child feels like he can't compete with his friends' designer clothes and BMWs). Some schools have reputations for being party schools where drugs are easy to obtain. Others provide life-long connections that can be very useful in the business world as your child becomes an adult. When you choose a private elementary school, also consider and investigate these aspects of the private high school your child will likely attend.

"Are religious schools a good choice?"

Many parents send their children to religious schools in order to help them receive a solid religious education and to ensure that their children will have a peer group with a similar religious background. Many religious schools have very strong academic curricula and dedicated teachers. Because religious schools often enforce relatively strict standards of behavior, religious schools are often quite safe and orderly. If you choose a religious school, follow the same process described for public and private schools above. But, also inquire about how much religious instruction children receive. Some schools, for instance, have children spend half of the school day in religious study. If you have a child who struggles academically, she may suffer from spending too large a proportion of the school day on religion rather than basic academic subjects.

Some parents enroll their children in "good" religious schools not of their faith because they believe that that school is "the best" available in their area. If you are considering this type of option, weigh the trade-off between the quality of education provided by the school and the time that students spend in religious study. If the children spend a great deal of time on religion, you may be better off in a public school that is slightly less rigorous but more focused on traditional academics.

Finally, when you inquire about a religious school's "philosophy" also make sure to ask about the school's official religion curriculum. Unlike when you take your child to classes sponsored by the church or temple you attend, you probably won't know the school's religion teacher and won't be able to sense theological shifts through your own experience with sermons and services. Make sure that the school's religious ideals and philosophies mesh well with your own (or, if there are key differences, make sure you know what they are so that you can discuss them with your child at home).

"What about vouchers? I've heard that some parents can get government money to put their children in private school."

Over the past few years several communities, including Milwaukee, Cleveland, and Denver, have offered vouchers for public school students to attend private schools. As a general rule, vouchers provide parents with a set amount of money (often between $1,000-$3,000 a year) to use for private school tuition at a school of their choice (parents have to make up the difference if the tuition is higher than the voucher). Most of the programs offered so far have been experimental or pilot studies. As the debate about vouchers continues, this trend will probably continue, which makes it hard to say which cities will offer vouchers at any given time, or exactly how any particular voucher system will

work. However, because the people promoting voucher systems usually want to evaluate the programs (to see if children using vouchers do better in school than those who do not get vouchers) there is often an experimental component to the programs, meaning that parents have to apply and then enter a lottery to see if they get a voucher or not. Different communities have had different rules about which students qualify to apply for vouchers and whether or not students can apply to religious schools. One common characteristic of voucher programs is that they do not impose rules upon private schools. Private schools retain control over admissions—they do not have to accept a child just because he has a voucher. Also, voucher programs tend to last for limited amounts of times (e.g., three years), so if you apply for a voucher, find out how many years you can use it and assess whether or not you will be able to afford your child's school if the program ends.

Given the constantly changing state of voucher programs, it's hard to give parents much general advice. But two guidelines apply:

▶ *Look into voucher systems if they are introduced in your area.* If you send your child to private school, a voucher could help ease the financial burden. If you send your child to public school, a voucher could provide you with some additional options that you could not otherwise afford. You may not qualify for all voucher programs, but it can never hurt to get the information.

♦ *Follow the same school assessment process with or without a voucher.* Don't let the mere availability of vouchers push you towards private schools. Follow the steps outlined above to assess all schools that you consider, private or public. If you decide that a private school is the best match for your child, a voucher may help you pay for it. But don't choose a private school just because you have a voucher.

"My child is applying for admission to a private school. I have to fill out all kinds of information and write a letter of recommendation for my child. What should I say?"

Many private schools have competitive admissions processes. When older children apply, their grades and test scores come into play. Older children also write admissions essays. When younger children apply, schools usually rely on information about the parents, the family, and letters of recommendation from parents or preschool teachers. There are a few general guidelines that will help make your application look good:

♦ *Be honest.* You may have to do an interview with the school. Your child may have to do an interview. If your child gets in, she will have to attend the school. Don't exaggerate her talents or your family's accomplishments. The truth will come out somehow. Give the school an honest assessment of you and your child and hope that the school is a good match for your child—the honest version of your child.

♦ *Create concrete pictures of your child.* Whether you are writing a letter of recommendation or helping your child write an admissions essay, be concrete rather than abstract. Tell stories. Help the admissions officers envision your child. All parents think that their children are "wonderful," "smart," "inquisitive," "kind," and just about every other positive adjective you can come up with. These words do not convey your child's personality. But if you tell the story of the time your five-year-old was compelled to help a sick gull she found on the beach or the time she insisted on going to the library to learn about space shuttles (tell these stories with details), admissions officers will be able to get a better picture of your child—and hopefully remember her when they discuss which children should be admitted.

♦ *Use the different parts of the application to highlight different aspects of your child.* You only get so many pages to show off your child. Some applications have a form application plus a letter, others might ask for a personal statement from the child. Either way, make sure that each section of your application *compliments* but does not repeat the other. If you highlighted your child's dance talents in the application portion, don't dwell on that in the letter of recommendation—highlight her compassion or her academic prowess instead. Use the application to present a complete and well-rounded picture of your child.

▶ *Explain why the school you are applying to is a good fit for your child.* Schools want to admit children who are going to be happy in their environments. Make sure you explain why the school is a particularly good fit for your child.

▶ *Proofread, proofread, proofread.* Make sure you proofread and spell check all of your admissions materials. Ideally, have someone else read over your materials too. You want to make sure that your letters and essays are clear (even to someone who does not know you or your child) and that there are no obvious mistakes. Nothing turns an admissions officer off more than parents who don't bother to correct their own work.

"I would love for my child to go to a local private school. But I can't afford it. Do they ever give scholarships?"

Actually, many private schools give a lot of scholarships and financial aid. Many schools will be particularly eager to help students who come from underrepresented racial or ethnic backgrounds and students who have special talents (e.g., artistic, musical, or athletic). Don't hesitate to call a private school you're interested in and ask them about the types of financial aid they offer.

CHAPTER 2

Parent Involvement

Y OUR INVOLVEMENT IN YOUR CHILD'S SCHOOL AND SCHOOLWORK IS A CRUCIAL INGRE-dient in your child's academic success. This chapter discusses *why* parent involvement is important and will help you decide just *how* you want to get involved with your child's school (e.g., join the PTA or volunteer in your child's class) and *how much* involvement is enough. This chapter also explains the best ways to interact with your child's teacher and school administrators in order to get them "on your side." There are five general strategies all parents should follow as they get involved in their child's school and schoolwork:

Get involved enough to learn about your child's school and build relationships with school staff.

You can't help your child navigate her school unless you know how the school works. Read school notices to learn about upcoming events and activities. Build a relationship with your child's teacher so you feel comfortable talking with her and asking for help. Get to know the principal and office staff. At least learn which administrators handle which problems (e.g., teacher requests, complaints) so you can direct your concerns to the right people and get answers quickly. You should also know basic information about the school: What resources does the school provide to students with special needs (and how do you qualify for those services)? Which teachers are the most effective for which kinds of students (and how do you request those teachers)? What academic programs does the school use (so you can supplement those programs at home)? And, how does the school organize students (i.e., if the school groups students by academic skill—either into different classes or into reading groups —you need to understand the system to make sure that your child is appropriately placed)? You won't discover all of this information at once, but if you are involved enough (i.e., talk to teach-ers, attend school events, talk to other parents), you will learn it.

Remember that parent involvement serves two purposes: helping your child directly and proving to teachers and school administrators that you care about your child's education.

You help your child directly by working with him. Help with homework. Do enrichment activities. Show him that school is a priority. However, you should also become involved to show teachers and school administrators that you are a "good parent." Teachers and administrators form judgments about parents in two ways. First, they make assumptions about you based on your child's behavior, so make sure your child turns in homework, behaves in class, and acts respectfully. Your child is your representative at school. But, you can also make *your own impression* by talking to teachers and school administrators yourself. Go to conferences and school events. Volunteer at school. These involvement opportunities give you a chance to prove to teachers and administrators that you are a good parent and that they should take the time to work with your child because you will reinforce that work at home.

Advocate for your child.

Although most schools want all of their students to succeed, you care the most about *your* child. You also know your child best. Don't be afraid to talk with teachers about your concerns about your child. Make sure to ask teachers how you can help your child. And if you feel that your child is not getting the help that she needs (e.g., if she is not getting resources she is entitled to or she has been treated unfairly), find out the details of the situation and talk to your child's teacher or principal, if necessary, to remedy the situation.

Treat teachers and school administrators as caring and competent professionals.

Most teachers and school administrators want to do what is best for your child. They are professionals and have been trained to be educators—so give them credit for having expertise. Talk with them respectfully. Ask for advice. Listen carefully to what they say—even if it isn't what you want to hear. Teachers and administrators respond best to parents who interact with them calmly and can talk objectively about their child's strengths, weaknesses, and needs. Over the course of your child's school career, you may meet teachers who do not seem competent or do not act profes-

sionally, but when you first meet any teacher, give her the benefit of the doubt. Even if you don't like a teacher, treating her respectfully will still be the best way to get her to work with you and for your child.

Make sure your involvement benefits your child.

The following sections will help you to think about the kinds of involvement you might enjoy (or at least not hate too much). But, as you get involved, remember that you want your child's teachers to see you as the type of parent *who is supportive of your child's education.* You want teachers to think of you as helpful, supportive, easy to get along with, and interested in learning. Don't let your involvement (either in school politics or in the classroom) turn you into an adversarial parent—that will only counteract what you are trying to accomplish by being involved in the first place.

The rest of this chapter describes specifically how your involvement will help your child succeed in school and discusses dozens of ways to get involved. The following questions and answers will also help you to interact with teachers and school administrators in ways that will push them to work *with you* to maximize your child's school success.

What is Parent Involvement?

"Everyone always talks about the importance of 'parent involvement.' What is it, exactly?"

Parental involvement means taking part in your child's education, both at home (helping with homework) and at school (talking with teachers and helping at school functions). Parents' involvement helps students in three ways.
1. Involved parents *help children with schoolwork directly* by helping with homework, acting as tutors, and providing a stimulating home environment.
2. Involved parents often get *extra consideration from school administrators* because they work hard to help the school.
3. Involved parents sometimes get *special consideration from teachers,* who are often happy to find that they are working "as a team" with a child's parents. When teachers know that parents are involved, help with homework, and want their child to excel in school, they often work harder to help a struggling student.

"What kind of involvement is the most important for helping my child succeed in school?"

The involvement that will most influence your child's achievement is direct involvement with your child. The more time you spend working *with your child,* helping with homework (see Chapter 3), and doing enrichment activities (see Chapter 4 for suggestions), the higher your child's achievement will be. Even if you don't get involved at your child's school, never neglect your direct involvement at home—this is the best way to enhance your child's school success.

"What kinds of involvement will prove to school administrators that I am a good parent?"

You may be able to improve your child's school experience by making a good impression on school administrators. If you participate in school governance, help with fundraising, "pitch in" when the school needs volunteers for events or activities, or donate a lot of money to the school, you will likely be considered "involved" by *school administrators.* Having some leverage (or at least good will) with school administrators may be especially helpful when you ask for favors or if your child is not a perfectly obedient, straight-A student. When you ask a principal for special resources, for a particular teacher, or for special testing, you may get better, faster results if you have a relationship with the principal and you are considered a "valuable" member of the school's community. Many principals worry that parents who do a lot to help the school will leave—enrolling their child in another public school or the private school system—so they may be more willing to go above and beyond to meet the special requests of "valuable" parents.

"What kinds of involvement will prove to teachers that I am a good parent?"

Teachers value a slightly different type of involvement than school administrators. Teachers will consider you "involved" if you:

◆ Send your child to school prepared (i.e., well-fed, dressed appropriately, with the school supplies he needs for the day, and with his homework completed).

◆ Help your child with homework and projects (when he needs help).

◆ Are available if the teacher needs to talk with you (in other words, you come to scheduled conferences and respond to notes or phone calls from the teacher).

◆ Follow through on programs you devise *with* the teacher to help your child succeed in school (for example, if your child is having behavior problems and you agree to withhold privileges if the teacher reports that your child acted up in class, you will be considered a "good parent" if—and only if—you follow through and withhold privileges).

◆ Are easy to get along with. Teachers like parents who are respectful, considerate, and don't make too many demands. This does not mean that you should not discuss problems with your child's teacher. But do bear in mind that no one, including teachers, likes to be criticized all the time. Nor are teachers fond of "helicopter parents"—the ones who are constantly hovering around and interfering.

Although teachers often know when parents are involved in school organizations and have respect for parents who spend a lot of time trying to help the school, the parent involvement that most affects how well teachers can do *their* jobs is the time that parents spend working directly with their children. Many teachers also appreciate parents who volunteer time in more mundane tasks than serving on parental committees, such as those who volunteer to assist on fieldtrips, help in the classroom, or bring supplies for parties.

Teachers often (consciously or subconsciously) give extra help and attention to children whom they perceive to have good parental support. And, they are more responsive to parents with whom they get along. Following the advice in this chapter should help you build strong, comfortable relationships with your child's teachers so that you can work together to form an ideal "educational team" for your child.

"What is the least amount of 'involvement' I can do and still look like an involved parent?"

This chapter describes dozens of ways that parents can get involved. But, please don't think that you have to do *everything*. In fact, if you volunteer for every opportunity at your child's school, you will not only exhaust yourself but probably make people think you're insane. To be "good, involved" parents, you (mom or dad or both) should:

◆ Send your child to school prepared every day (see above for details).

◆ Help your child with homework and projects.

◆ Attend all parent conferences (make sure to call if you *have* to cancel).

◆ Attend Back to School Night and Open House (or at least send a family representative—this can be a grandparent, aunt, uncle, or an adult sibling).

◆ Volunteer to help at least once a year. (You can help in the class, bring treats for a party, help with a fundraiser, or help the class put together a holiday play. The activity doesn't matter, but at least one activity a year shows the teacher that you want to help.)

"Are there any parents who should be extra-involved?"

Parents should not get so involved that they drive teachers or school administrators crazy. But, if you make a lot of demands on a school you should also make yourself especially useful. Teachers and administrators will be less likely to resent your requests if you also make a significant contribution to the school (either in time, effort, or money).

If your child gets in trouble a lot or performs poorly in school, it might be a good idea to be a little extra-involved as well. School administrators and teachers will work harder—even with a difficult child—if they know that that child has strong support at home. Your involvement will help prove that you value education and support the school—even if your child's behavior doesn't make you look like the world's best parent. Just make sure that your involvement does not impede your child's progress (for instance, don't tell your child's teacher that your child could not finish his science project because you were too busy at the PTA meeting to help him—this will not help your cause!).

Getting Information from Your Child's School

"How can I keep up-to-date on what's going on at my child's school?"

It is not always easy to get information about your child's school—especially since schools often rely on children to ferry information back and forth. But, there are some easy things you can do to improve the information flow:

▶ *Read* all *notices that your child's school sends home.* These will tell you about school events, involvement opportunities, and informational meetings (these meetings may contain important information, such as: how to prepare your child for an upcoming test or how to get into a magnet middle school). Even if a meeting or program does not seem relevant to you now (e.g., preparation for fifth-grade graduation when your child is a first-grader), knowing what the school offers "every year" will help you be more aware if your child is NOT bringing information home.

▶ *Find out when you should be looking for notices.* Many schools send all notices home on a certain day of the week. Ask the teacher is there is any particular day when you should make sure to ask your child for notices (or, possibly, go through her backpack).

▶ *Read the bulletin boards at your child's school.* These often note important dates and events.

▶ *Get to know the office workers at your child's school.* The better you know them, the more comfortable you'll feel going in and asking for help or information.

▶ *Talk to your child's teacher.* She can keep you up-to-date on assignments.

▶ *Talk to other parents.* Keep your eyes open for parents who spend a lot of time at the school and become friendly enough to talk with them occasionally. This is a great way to learn about the school (even about unofficial business).

Your school may also have technology that can help you learn about the school. Ask if your school has:

▶ *A homework hotline* where you can call and learn about assignments.

▶ *Voicemail* so that you can leave messages for teachers.

▶ *A Web site* where you can read about school events or your child's assignments.

If your school does not have any of these resources, and you think that they would be helpful, talk to an administrator or a member of the PTA about setting it up (and remember that they will be more likely to act on your suggestion if you also offer to help set up or maintain the new resource).

School Organizations

"In order to be a good parent, do I have to join the PTA or PTO?"

No. Every PTA, PTO, and Booster club needs good parents to serve and help direct the organization. And, ideally every group of parents in a school (i.e., parents of high, medium, and low achievers, parents from all different racial, ethnic, and socioeconomic groups) should have a representative in these organizations. But that does not mean that all good parents take part in these organizations—many do not.

The time may come when you feel that you need to join a parent organization in order to represent parents "like you." However, you need to decide what kind of involvement fits your life, schedule, and personality. Serving on school committees can take a lot of time. Moreover, participation sometimes involves conflict (with teachers or school administrators) that some parents prefer to avoid. Parents who are very involved in these organizations gain a say in how the school spends money, whom the school hires, and how the school organizes itself. However, teachers will not fault you if you do not belong to these organizations. Don't allow others to guilt-trip you into being involved in an organization that you do not want to be involved in. If you do decide to get involved, don't let your involvement (especially arguments within the organization) harm your relationship with school administrators and teachers or take away time you would normally spend helping your child with schoolwork.

"My school has several different parent organizations. What's the difference between the PTA, the PTO, the Parent Council, and the Booster Club?"

Most parent organizations have a similar objective: to give input into the school through an organized structure. But the exact purposes, structures, and histories of the organizations vary.

The PTA

PTA (Parent Teacher Association) is a not-for-profit, national child advocacy group and one of the longest standing parent-teacher organizations in the country. PTA began as the "National Congress of Mothers" in the late 1800s, advocating for better partnerships between mothers and schools and more federal support for children's issues. The PTA continues to send delegates to education conventions, publish a national parenting magazine (called *Our Children*—you can subscribe or read online at www.PTA.org), publish parenting books and videos, sponsor research, and lobby for legislation to help children[3]. Many schools have a local chapter of the PTA. Even if your school does not have a local chapter, your school may solicit "PTA dues" which support the national PTA. According to the PTA Web site, its purposes are:

▸ "To promote the welfare of the children and youth in home, school, community, and place of worship.
▸ To raise the standards of home life.
▸ To secure adequate laws for the care and protection of children and youth.
▸ To bring into closer relation the home and the school, that parents and

teachers may cooperate intelligently in the education of children and youth.

◗ To develop between educators and the general public such united efforts as will secure for all children and youth the highest advantages in physical, mental, social, and spiritual education."[4]

Local PTAs perform many of the same tasks as other parent organizations (fundraising for the school, advocating for school programs, etc.) but are often also involved in state and national issues and contribute to the national PTA. Local PTAs also receive benefits from the national PTA such as: materials, access to PTA workshops and conferences, and access to a network of other PTA members across the country. You can learn how to affiliate your parent organization with PTA by going to the PTA Web site at www.PTA.org.

Parent Teacher Organizations (PTOs)

PTOs are parent-teacher organizations that are not necessarily related to the national PTA. Their dues stay within the group and do not go to national or state umbrella groups. Many PTOs choose to remain independent precisely because they do not want to send money to a national organization (about $850/year for PTA) that they could instead keep for the school[5]. PTO issues tend to be local, centering around one school.

For PTOs that want to be part of a larger organization but don't want to join the PTA, there is the National PTO Network (NPN) which also publishes a magazine (*PTO Today*) and which provides resources for independent PTOs such as: "Expert Guides," group insurance plans, information about how to incorporate, etc. See www.ptotoday.com for more information.

Parent Councils

Councils are advisory committees to schools. Although PTAs, PTOs, and booster groups often advise schools, councils are usually designed specifically to get parent, student, and community input into school decisions. These groups usually spend more time discussing and researching issues than raising money (at private schools, however, parent councils are more likely to also organize fundraising). Although some schools and districts automatically consult councils about major decisions, other councils have to fight for access to budgets or for forewarning when major decisions are about to be made.

[3] National PTA. "A Brief History." Undated. National PTA. 16 April 2004. <http://www.pta.org/aboutpta/history/history.asp>

[4] National PTA. "The Purpose of the PTA." Undated. National PTA. 16 April 2004. <http://www.pta.org/aboutpta/mission_en.asp>

[5] Sullivan, Tim "PTO vs. PTA." August 2002. PTO Today. 16 April 2004. <http://www.ptotoday.com/0800ptota2.html>

Booster Clubs, "Friends," and Other Fundraising Groups

Booster clubs are typically found in high schools and often raise funds for specific teams or activities within the school. Elementary school fundraising groups often do not have the word "booster" in their names. For instance, Main Street School may have a booster club called "Friends of Main Street School" or "Main Street School Parents." The primary purpose of booster clubs is to raise money—and control how that money is spent. Booster clubs often organize fundraisers (that's why when you buy a box of candy that a child is selling for a school fundraiser, you probably make the check out to "Friends of Main Street School" rather than to the school itself).

Money that is donated directly to the school goes into a general fund for school administrators to spend on their priorities. Money that booster organizations raise (or money that is donated to the booster organization) gets spent according to the booster club's priorities. In a perfect world, the priorities of the school and the priorities of the booster organization coincide—but that isn't always the case. Booster clubs tend to attract certain "types" of parents—who then recruit other parents with similar values—which may affect the way the booster club spends its money. Thus, the booster club may choose to hire a music teacher rather than a PE teacher or choose to buy more computers rather than creating scholarships for disadvantaged students to go on class trips. Either way, the booster club's money is the booster club's money.

Booster clubs also decide how to raise money. Many booster clubs rely on sales of magazines, candy, or gift wrap. These sales are relatively easy to organize but often put a strain on parents who don't like to burden friends and relatives with buying everything that their child sells. Other organizations rely more on events that volunteers can staff (e.g., carnivals, car washes, bake sales). These events are harder to organize because they require more parents to volunteer their time, but they do not require students to become door-to-door salespeople. Some booster clubs also throw dinner parties, cruises, and other events to raise money. These events can cost upwards of $50 a head to attend and include events such as auctions and silent auctions. Although these events can be very profitable in affluent communities, they can also create an air of exclusion when all families cannot afford to participate.

Overall, powerful booster clubs maintain a lot of power at schools. They raise money by sponsoring fundraising drives and events that project the school's image into the community. They also decide how to spend the school's extra resources, which can make a school better overall or better for certain students. The extent to which you agree with how the booster club raises and spends money may determine whether or not you feel obliged to join the organization.

Fundraising and Making Donations

"In order to be a 'supportive' parent, do I have to donate money to my child's school and buy all of the things that my child sells to raise money for school?"

Many schools raise money to pay for "extras" that we take for granted. It's very possible that your school's music teacher, PE coach, stereo equipment, field trips, and sports equipment are paid for by fundraiser money (rather than government money). Since your child probably enjoys these services, if you have money to spare, it's nice to either donate money or support school fundraisers. However, donating money and participating in school fundraising is not required. And, aside from the pressure that your child will probably put on you to participate in the fundraisers in order to get prizes, most public schools do not push parents to donate money. Nor will most public schools judge parents negatively

based on the fact that they do not donate money (unless, of course, you are the type of parent who is always demanding more services and can clearly afford to donate more money than you actually do). Donate what you feel you can. And participate in fundraisers you feel comfortable with. Families who donate a lot of money are less common than those who give nothing.

Private schools, on the other hand, are more likely to *expect* donations. Many will hit families up for donations in person—and many will explicitly request predetermined amounts. No family is obligated to donate money to their child's private school (beyond tuition). However, because private schools tend to be smaller than public schools and tend to have wealthier students, if most families at the school donate money, don't be too surprised if you are treated somewhat differently if you do not donate. Also, private school administrators talk among themselves about how "supportive" parents are. The amount you donate to your child's private elementary school will likely be reported to any private high school your child applies to.

"My kids are selling candy (or gift wrap, cookie dough, etc.) as a fundraiser—do I have to let them go door-to-door selling these items?"

I wouldn't recommend allowing kids to go door-to-door selling to strangers. Neighbors, friends, and relatives are fair game (just be prepared to have to reciprocate for their children), but young kids should never go door-to-door alone. If you let your older children go door-to-door, make sure they know to never go into anyone's house. Make sure that they know their safety always comes before a sale—no matter how much candy or gift-wrap a potential buyer promises to buy!

"I just got a new computer. Should I donate my old one to the school?"

Many teachers enjoy having computers in the classroom so that children can learn keyboarding, type reports, and surf the Internet. Most schools also have computer labs (however, because students often don't get to spend much time in the computer lab, many teachers prefer to have classroom computers). Most schools would like more computers than they have. However, before you approach a teacher with your old computer, ask yourself the following questions:

▸ *What is the computer good for?* If it is still good for word processing and playing computer games (most current games are on CD-Rom so a CD-Rom drive would be good—although the school computer lab might have an extra that they could

install) then a teacher might want it for the classroom. The computer should also be Internet ready. The computer may be especially valuable if it is a laptop that can be set up on children's desks so that they can type reports without having to go to a computer station.

▸ *Do you have any serious problems with the computer?* A computer that frequently crashes or shuts down is a bad bet for a classroom. Many children only experience computers in school. Giving them a "buggy" computer will make that experience unpleasant and may turn them off of computers.

▸ Even if you decide that the computer is not worth donating, *do you have any peripherals that might be useful in the classroom?* Teachers might want a monitor, printer, scanner, extra disk drive, printer ink, computer paper, software, or disks.

If you decide that your computer (or a part of it) might be useful to a teacher, ask before you donate it. Be prepared to explain the benefits (and drawbacks) of the machine so that she can make an educated decision. *Do not* bring the machine with you when you ask. This will only put the teacher in the awkward position of feeling like she cannot refuse after you have gone through the trouble of lugging it in.

If the teacher wants the machine, ask if you should bring it to the class or if it should first go to the computer lab (i.e., to be set up for a school Internet connection). If the teacher declines, ask if she can think of anyone else who might want the computer. Another teacher might want it. Or, she might know a student who would like a computer like the one that you are offering. (If the teacher declines, do not be offended. Many schools have grants that have provided them with state-of-the-art computer systems. Other schools have rules that prohibit them from accepting donated computers.)

"Do schools need old TVs, VCRs, or stereo equipment?"

Schools often use TVs and VCRs as learning tools. Some teachers also use stereo equipment, especially for music productions. Some teachers also dub tapes for children to take home (e.g., oral versions of books) so cassette decks with dubbing capabilities might be useful. If you have a machine that you would like to donate, follow the same steps outlined above for computers. Make sure that the machine is in good working order and would be useful in the classroom (rather than something that will just take up space). And again, do not be offended if the teacher declines. The local GoodWill, Salvation Army, or other thrift stores will probably be happy to take your donation.

How to Help Your Child's School by Donating Money or Items

- Give money to the booster club.
- Give money directly to the school.
- Donate money to the school library.
- Give a bookstore gift certificate to stock the classroom library.
- Donate your family's favorite books to the classroom or library.
- Donate reference books (e.g., encyclopedias, thesauri) to the classroom.
- Donate a computer, software, or a computer accessory to the classroom or school computer lab. (See the question above for information on used computer donation.)
- Donate computer supplies such as printer ink or paper.
- Donate art supplies to the classroom.
- Donate play equipment (e.g., handballs, basketballs, jump ropes) to the classroom.

Volunteering at Your Child's School

"I feel like I don't know enough about what my child does in school to help at home—is there any way for me to get to see what the kids learn in my child's classroom?"

One of the best ways to see what goes on in your child's classroom (including her teacher's teaching style, the behavior modification techniques she uses, and the types of homework she usually assigns) is to volunteer in the classroom. Even a few hours a week will give you a glimpse of what your child learns in school and how her teacher communicates information. (This can be particularly useful for parents who struggle to help children with homework because they feel like they don't know how to teach.) As more and more parents work full-time, fewer parents volunteer in classrooms. However, many teachers would be happy to have an extra set of hands for a few hours a week—especially if you can commit to a regular schedule. Bear in mind, however, that some teachers feel uncomfortable being observed and others may want to wait until after the first few weeks of school to give the class time to "gel" before you start volunteering.

If you want to volunteer, ask your child's teacher if she can use the help (sooner rather than later, but it doesn't have to be right at the beginning of the year). Mention that you think you will be able to help your child better at home if you have a better idea of how she learns at school. Be careful not to make the teacher feel you want to scrutinize her.

When you do volunteer, remember that you are a guest in the teacher's classroom. In order to cultivate a good relationship with your child's teacher, act in her classroom the way that you would act in a new friend's home. Follow her cues. If she acts very casually with the children, feel free to do the same. If she maintains a more formal demeanor, do the same. Don't try to chat with the teacher during class. Follow directions. And, if you don't understand a direction that you have been given, wait until the teacher has a break in her lesson and then ask for clarification. Although you may feel entitled to respect because you are a parent and a volunteer, approach the situation as if you were starting a new job and wanted to make good impression on your boss. A strong relationship with your child's teacher can pay off in the same way that a strong relationship with a boss can.

Finally, don't criticize the teacher. If there is something you must talk with her about, speak considerately—after the students have been dismissed. But unless the situation is urgent, don't criticize. Just as all parents raise their children differently, teachers have their own styles. If you were in a friend's home, you would not criticize her parenting unless you saw a serious problem. Follow the same guideline in the classroom.

"What if I see the teacher do something wrong while I'm volunteering in the classroom?"

Teachers are human and they make mistakes. Many teachers are conscious of these mistakes and will correct them. Other mistakes are minor. But, if you witness a mistake, what should you do? First, wait. The teacher may correct the mistake—although she may not realize what she has done until she has a chance to think about it. Once you are alone with the teacher (i.e., during recess), she may explain her thinking process or mention that she has to correct herself when the kids come back.

If the teacher does not correct herself and does not mention the problem to you, you have two choices. If the mistake is minor, you can let it pass. Teachers sometimes state a mistaken fact in an off-hand matter on an off-topic subject. These kinds of mistakes are probably not worth mentioning. But, what if it is an important mistake? What if the teacher is teaching the children to do something wrong? Approach the teacher cautiously and carefully. You might approach the teacher by saying that you have some

kind of expertise in the area (especially if it is an area that she should not have expertise in—for example if you are a nuclear physicist and she makes a mistake in a lesson about atoms).

Or you can ask a question about the lesson to try to prompt the teacher to check herself. For instance, if you see a teacher showing children how to divide fractions and she has them find the reciprocal of the first fraction rather than the second, you might say, "You know, I've always had a hard time with dividing fractions. I can never remember if you find the reciprocal of the first or the second fraction. Is it really the first fraction?" If you're lucky, a statement like that will motivate the teacher to look in the book for clarification. Or you might look in the book yourself and say, "You know, when you started this lesson, I looked in Javier's book to refresh myself on this subject—and it says that you flip the second fraction... would you mind taking a look?" All of these methods make the confrontation less embarrassing for the teacher and should allow you and the teacher to maintain a good relationship (although there will surely be a few uncomfortable moments).

Of course, if you have a strong relationship with the teacher, you may be able to broach a subject like this more directly. But approach it in the same way as you would approach a friend or a co-worker who had made an honest mistake. Approach the teacher humbly and leave her an "out" for why she made the mistake. *Never correct a teacher in front of the children.* She may have to admit to the class that she made a mistake (almost every teacher has had to do this at least once) but she should be able to introduce the correction in her own way, not blushing under your accusations. She should also be given a chance to defend herself—in case *you* are wrong. Or, as is often the case, there are two right answers. I once sat in the back of the room cringing at the way a teacher taught a grammar lesson. She came to me after (probably conscious of the fact that I might think that she was teaching the lesson wrong) and said, "I went on the Internet last night to brush up on these rules and they seem to have changed." She showed me rules about commas and quotation marks from several different writing style Web sites that clearly stated that common usage had changed and that she had taught the students the current, correct way to punctuate. I was very glad that I had not interrupted.

"I'm not really the 'room mother' type—is there any other way that I can be involved in my child's classroom?"

Don't let the old-fashioned notion of a "room mother" who walks around passing out cookies scare you away from volunteering in your child's class-room. Nowadays, many classroom volunteers come in during time off from jobs and careers. And classroom volunteers serve a very wide range of purposes, which they work out with the teacher. Almost all teachers need help making photocopies, grading tests and homework assignments, entering grades in grade-books, and organizing materials. Many parents feel most comfortable with this kind of work—it allows them to see what's going on in the classroom and help out without bearing the responsibility of teaching. This way, they figure, they free the teacher to concentrate on her specialty—teaching.

In other cases, teachers want to take advantage of having another competent adult in the classroom and they ask parents to lead reading groups, work one-on-one with students, or help children when they have questions (e.g., clarifying math problems, helping with research projects, editing reports and stories). While many parents are happy to take on this kind of work, other parents might not feel comfortable teaching. When you talk with the teacher about volunteering be sure to:

◗ Find out what the teacher would like you to do and

◗ Express to the teacher which of those tasks you feel comfortable with.

If you get both of these issues clear before you start volunteering, then there should be no confusion inside the classroom. Nothing is more uncomfortable than trying to explain to a teacher that you don't want to do what she has asked you to do as 30 first-graders look on.

So, if you feel uncomfortable taking on "teaching" tasks, let the teacher know that you would prefer to help out with organizational tasks. Most teachers will respect this request and, if she has work that needs to be done, she will probably take you up on your offer. If, on the other hand, she has aides who do the photocopying and organizational tasks, she might decline your offer to volunteer. If this is the case, don't be offended. Ask if there is anything else that she might like you to do—and if the answer is no, leave your number in case she thinks of something.

If, on the other hand, you feel as if your time would be wasted just making photocopies, ask the teacher if there is anything else that she needs help with—perhaps tutoring or reading stories to the children.

"I don't have the time to commit to being a regular classroom volunteer—is there another way I can help in the classroom and be involved?"

Many parents want to help in the classroom but are too busy to commit to come in every week. Other parents have seasonal jobs which keep them busier in some months than others. Just because you can't commit to being a regular volunteer doesn't mean that you can't be involved.

If you work during the school day, help with evening and weekend events. Most schools have fundraisers (carnivals, carwashes, etc.) on weekends and each class is usually responsible for contributing volunteers. Many schools also have evening events such as talent shows and Open Houses and need parents to help set up, clean up, and keep things organized. Watch for these events or let your child's teacher know that you work but would like to help with weekend or evening events.

If you're a parent who has free time during some weeks of the year, but can't commit to help in the classroom once a week (or simply don't want to spend hours each week photocopying) try to think of a talent or skill that you could share with your child's class. The skill doesn't have to be exotic. I've seen parents come in and teach art appreciation classes and teach the children how to tie-dye t-shirts. You could help the kids grow potted flowers or sew pillows as gifts for Mother's Day. You could help the kids make a piñata for a *Cinco de Mayo* celebration. Taking a few hours to teach children how to watercolor, play the recorder, or recognize the architectural landmarks in your community could make a big contribution to your child's classroom. Anyone who works in the science field can give demonstrations for a class. A biochemist friend of mine visits her mother's sixth-grade class and teaches the children how to make "gak" (and explains the scientific properties of gak). A UCLA professor invites his daughter's class to come on a field trip to his molecular biology lab every year.

If you are good at schoolwork you might offer to tutor occasionally, especially if you are willing to work with a student who is not your own. Or, offer to read to your child's class (even to fourth- and fifth-graders). This experience gives students a chance to learn from a new adult and gives the teacher a break to catch up on grading or administrative tasks. Other parents lead children in discussions. In one school I observed, a retiree came once a week and led the children in various discussions, including one where they brainstormed about what they would do to improve the world if they were given a $1,000 grant.

And don't forget about after-school activities. If your talents lie in sports, talk with the people who run sports programs at your school. Chances are they could use some help. Or see if you can help with a performance or event. I know of a mother who teaches the graduating fifth-graders at her child's school how to do a "choral recitation" which they perform at their graduation ceremony. Another parent helped children paint a mural at their school. Another mother helped teachers sew together quilt squares that the graduating class created as its "legacy." Or, if you have videotaping or photography skills, you might ask the teacher if you could work with the children to create a memory book or memory video of their school year.

If you have a job that you think your child's classmates might be interested in, ask the teacher if they have a career week. If not, ask if she thinks the children might like to hear about what you do. One of the most engaging discussions I've seen in a classroom came about when a child's father, a police officer, talked with the kids about safety, guns, and police. Don't undersell yourself. Almost every job has aspects that will interest kids.

"I want to help in my child's classroom, but I'm shy.
Isn't there some way I can share my talents without having to lead a lesson or work with a lot of kids?"

Yes. For instance, if you are good with computers, you could volunteer to organize the class computers. You could make folders for students to store their work in and make shortcuts to common programs on the desktop so that children can find them. Or spend some time on the Internet "bookmarking" (or marking as "favorites") sites with math games, history resources, biographies, style guides, and other useful sites. Many teachers are not particularly proficient with computers and/or don't have time to organize their computers.

Or, if you are a good bargain hunter and your child's teacher wishes she had a bigger class library, you could spend some time scouring thrift stores and picking up children's books for the class. If you are good at sewing, you could offer to make costumes for a school play.

Other parents wait until parties and other special events. They volunteer to bring in food or napkins or cups or soda. Although this kind of help may seem mundane, it is often helpful to teachers. If parents don't bring treats, teachers have to do it themselves.

"I'd like to volunteer to work with my child's class. How do I sign up?"

If you want to do any of the above activities with your child's class, talk to your child's teacher. See if she likes your ideas and ask her when it would be convenient for you to work with the class. Please consult with the teacher (or school administrators if it is a school-wide project) *before* you begin. Some teachers may feel too pressured to cover their academic curriculum to add extras. Others (not most, but some) might feel leery about relinquishing control of their classroom to others. And when you talk to the teacher, accept her time constraints. Many teachers will appreciate your help putting together the children's holiday performance, but will not appreciate a parent who comes to the class in the middle of year and wants to spend hours working on a play that they did not budget time for. Likewise, many teachers have a specific time of the year when they like to expose children to new careers, or specific times when they cover topics in science. So, go to the teacher, offer up your ideas, but do not force them on her. And again, don't be offended if she declines. Even a teacher who declines your offer will appreciate the fact that you offered to help. That makes you a "good parent" in her eyes. Just don't push to the point where the teacher finds you annoying. Accept the refusal graciously—and offer your ideas to your child's new teacher next year.

"As a father, I would like to be involved in my child's education, but it feels like most of the notes from my child's school are aimed at mothers."

It's true that classrooms are much more likely to have "room mothers" than "room fathers" and teachers are more likely to ask children if their mom helped them with their homework than if their dad did. However, schools' "preferences" for mothers are not an actual preference but a norm handed down from the past, when mothers took primary responsibility for raising children. Now that many mothers work and many fathers either work at home or work in shifts that allow them to be home in the daytime, fathers are a major resource for schools.

Fathers can volunteer in the classroom just as easily as mothers and most teachers appreciate father volunteers as much as they appreciate mother volunteers. Fathers can do any of the activities described above (read the prior sections of you haven't already), even if it is less common. Fathers can, of course, also serve on PTAs, PTOs, and Booster organizations. If, as a father, you feel intimidated by a board that is dominated by women, ask another father to join with you. If a few fathers step up, it will be easier for others.

And, of course, fathers also do a number of more typical "father-type" activities at schools. Almost every school event (e.g., carnivals, plays, car washes) requires some "strong" father types to help set up. Fathers often help with sporting events, do "behind the scenes" work such as building sets for plays, and helping with technology tasks, such as building the school's Web page or running the audio-visual

portion of school performances. But, more and more fathers have been getting involved in the day-to-day activities of school. So, before you decide that getting involved is not "for you," go to the school and see who the major volunteers are. You will likely find that some of them are fathers.

"My child's teacher often asks parents if they can chaperone fieldtrips. I want to but I have a pre-school child and I can't afford a babysitter. Is it OK to bring my younger child along?"

Ask the teacher who is organizing the fieldtrip. Her answer will likely depend on aspects of the fieldtrip, such as admission costs, transportation, and the activity (e.g., she might balk at bringing an infant to a movie). Some fieldtrips are toddler-friendly and sometimes teachers are desperate for any chaperon. If the teacher approves, the trip could give your younger child a head start on learning. But, if you bring another child, remember that the extra child (and any costs or problems he causes) is your responsibility. If the teacher declines, don't be offended. Many issues (e.g., insurance, lack of space) may prevent her from saying yes. Just let her know that you might be available to help in other ways (e.g., it might be fine to bring a younger child when helping with a class picnic).

Ways to Volunteer Your Time

- Share a talent (e.g., teach children to draw, act, juggle, or speak a new language).
- Lead a sports team after school.
- Lead an after-school club (e.g., a chess club, a book club, or even a magic club).
- Talk about your career (children can be fascinated by almost any career).
- Give a demonstration (e.g., science experiments, art techniques).
- Help children make a class remembrance (e.g., a class video or memory book).
- Help students make a craft or project (e.g., gifts for Mother's Day or Father's Day, a piñata for a *Cinco De Mayo* party, decorations for a holiday party).
- Read to the class.
- Help the children organize a performance (e.g., play, musical performance).
- Teach computer skills or help configure computers or computer software.
- Chaperone a field trip.

Parent-Teacher Conferences

"My parent-teacher conference is coming up and I don't know what I'm supposed to say!"

Parent-teacher conferences are the most common way for parents to get information about their child's academic progress. Conferences are crucial for keeping up on your child's education—and they often only last 20 minutes or so. So, make sure that you go prepared. Just as pediatricians recommend making a list of questions before you go to a doctor's appointment, make a list of questions you want to ask your child's teacher before you go to your conference. Take the list out as you sit down and explain that you want to make sure to cover your questions. Don't make the teacher feel like you want to run the conference, just show her that you have questions. That way the teacher will make sure she gives you time to ask questions. Otherwise, she may feel like she needs to fill the time herself and spend most of the conference telling you what she *thinks* you want to hear. By the time she asks if you have questions, you may be out of time. Use your list to signal that you have specific topics that you want to cover.

There are several points you want to cover in the conference:

◆ **Have the teacher explain, in detail, how your child is progressing academically.** Is she on grade level? Which subjects does she excel in and which subjects does she need extra help with? Ask to see the child's grades (if you have not already seen a report card). If the teacher says that your child is struggling, ask to see samples of your child's work and have the teacher show you the skills that your child is having trouble with. Make sure you leave the conference with a concrete idea of how to help and what the teacher wants your child to accomplish.

◆ **Ask the teacher how well your child is behaving.** Ask the teacher to be honest. This will show the teacher that you are concerned about your child's behavior and allow you to stop any problems before they become serious. Although teachers will probably let you know if your child has severe behavioral problems, they may not feel comfortable telling you that your child seems a little lazy, tends to push herself too hard, doesn't interact well with other students, seems too scared to raise her hand, or doesn't pay attention all the time. Although these problems may not seem like huge concerns to the teacher, they are definitely problems you want to discuss with your child and help resolve sooner rather than later.

◆ **Ask the teacher to answer any ques-** **tions that you have had over the past few months (or explain more about projects that you know are coming up).** Perhaps you didn't understand what was expected in a book report that your child got a poor grade on. Perhaps you don't understand the homework system or you are wondering if there is a particular day when you should expect school notices to come home. Ask all of these questions—no matter how minor they seem.

◆ **Ask the teacher if there are any major projects that are coming up that you should be prepared for.** Also, ask if they will be tackling any major subjects that you should brush up on to be able to help your child.

◆ **Ask what you should do at home to help your child.** What books should your child read in his free time? What skills should he be practicing? Are there any workbooks, games, or videos the teacher would recommend? Also, if your child's class reads novels (probably not until upper grades) ask the teacher what they will be reading. (It's a great idea for parents to read the books that their children read so that you can discuss them together.)

◆ **Explain to the teacher what educational activities you do at home and ask if these are the right activities to be doing.** This will allow the teacher to give you some advice. It will also show the teacher that you are trying to provide your child with educationally stimulating activities at home.

▶ *Tell the teacher about any problems that might interfere with your child's academic progress or behavior in class.* Teachers should know if there was a recent death or illness in the family, if you and your child's other parent are going through a divorce, or if your child has any kind of illness (physical or mental) or learning disability. This information may help the teacher understand some of the problems that she has been having with your child.

I sat in on one parent-teacher conference when the teacher expressed extreme frustration about a child who often spaced out, became glassy-eyed, and snarled at the teacher when scolded. The child seemed to have two personalities. The parent snapped that this behavior might be due to the child's hypoglycemia—a medical note that should have been in the child's folder but was hidden amidst other papers. The parent assumed that the teacher knew about the child's condition; the teacher assumed the child was just being difficult. This discussion helped resolve the problem. From that day on, the teacher kept juice in her refrigerator and gave some to the child whenever she got glassy-eyed, which seemed to dramatically improve her performance. The lesson is: never assume that your child's teacher has all the pertinent information she needs to help your child succeed.

"Can my child come to the parent-teacher conference? I really think that we should all talk together about how he is doing at school."

Some teachers allow—or even invite—children into conferences. Others prefer to leave the child out so that they can talk openly with parents. I recommend that you talk with the teacher privately for at least some of the time. You want honest answers about your child's performance—and you may not want your child to hear everything. Moreover, the teacher may not want to be totally honest in front of your child for fear of either hurting his self-esteem or blowing up his head.

However, if you think that your child really should be part of the conference, approach the situation in one of two ways. Try sending a note to the teacher, explaining the situation (perhaps you are struggling to convince your child how important it is to learn to read and you think that you and the teacher can make a stronger case together or perhaps your child is afraid of failure and you think that encouraging words from you and the teacher at the same time will boost your child's confidence) and see what the teacher writes back. Or, since most conferences happen after school with children nearby (usually on the playground), ask your child to stay nearby during the conference. When you begin your conference, explain your situation, and ask if you might call the child in for part of the conference. Again, see what the teacher says. In this case, I would recommend simply going by what the teacher says. If a teacher really objects to including your child, then it's probably best to just relay the teacher's assessments to your child after the conference.

"English is not my first language. Is it okay if I bring someone to the conference with me to translate?"

You should always feel free to bring a translator to a parent-teacher conference (or any other school meeting or event). The translator can be a friend or a relative or anyone you feel comfortable with. Most schools will work to find a translator for you if you do not speak English or feel more comfortable in your native language. Just make sure you ask the teacher beforehand so she has time to find someone.

"I know that teachers usually have conferences when they send home the first report card—but that seems too late. What if my child is already doing poorly by then?"

Most teachers are amenable to talking to parents at times other than conference times. The following section discusses less formal discussions with teachers in depth, but the best thing to do is to make an appointment to talk with the teacher. Although this won't be an official parent-teacher conference, make sure to cover the same points listed above.

Talking to Teachers Informally

"When is the best time to talk to a teacher?"

Often there is no good time to chat with a teacher. Some teachers arrive at school early or stay late, but most use this time for planning or grading. During the school day teachers only have recess and lunch to get coffee, eat, use the restroom, check their mailbox and phone messages, take care of errands, and make plans for meetings. It's often frustrating to teachers when parents show up right before the first bell or during recess expecting to chat or when parents come in unexpectedly and take up time the teacher had planned to use for grading or writing a test. However, most teachers will make an appointment with you at any time in the school year. And, almost all teachers feel more comfortable talking when you have an appointment and they can plan accordingly.

So, how do you make an appointment with a teacher? You can send a note to school with your child. In your note, either ask the teacher to give you a call or note several dates and times that will work for you and ask the teacher to write you back. You can also call and leave a message for the teacher. This is not always a foolproof way of getting in contact with teachers, however, because you will probably have to leave a message with the front office. Finally, if you are on campus, either before or after school (as long as it isn't right before the teacher has to start class) you can go up to a teacher and ask for an appointment. If the teacher seems too busy to talk with you right then, just let her know that you will send a note with your child the next day.

"If I go to the school, will I be bothering the teacher?"

Most teachers enjoy seeing parents at school—they just don't like it when parents expect to have impromptu conferences at inconvenient times. However, do make yourself seen around school—help your child carry in a project or wait in line with your child before school starts. Teachers generally like knowing a little bit about their students' parents and your presence at school will give the impression that you are accessible if they want to talk with you. Remember, though, just because a teacher says "hello," doesn't mean that she has time to talk. If you want to talk about your child, make an appointment.

Also, don't be afraid to pop in (quickly!) to give a teacher a compliment. If, after school, she doesn't seem to be in the middle of anything, stop in to say, "I just wanted to tell you that I really liked the project that you had the children do last week— Kyle found it challenging and I think he learned a lot" or "I'm so glad you're working on geometry, Sarah has been wondering about that and I'm happy you're covering it this year." Most teachers don't get enough positive feedback, but they remark upon it gratefully when they do.

"I don't think that my child is being challenged. Should I talk to the teacher?"

Yes, but make sure that you approach the teacher respectfully. This is one of the most difficult issues to work out between parents and teachers. Parents want their children to be challenged so that they can reach their full potential. But teachers have a room full of students and it's difficult to keep up with the quickest students while keeping others from falling behind. Most teachers recognize the problem of challenging high-achieving students—they just do not always know how to fix it. So, approaching a teacher in an adversarial manner may make the teacher resentful and less likely to try to accommodate you and your child.

But, even though it may be difficult for your child's teacher to challenge your child, you should still talk to her about it. Perhaps the teacher is not aware that your child is bored. Perhaps your child is exhibiting some behaviors in class that make the teacher feel that she is not ready for more advanced work. Or perhaps the teacher has some ideas about how to challenge your child but simply has not had a chance to run them past you. When you talk with your child's teacher follow the following steps:

▶ *Acknowledge work that the teacher has assigned that your child did find challenging.* Mention specific assignments you thought were appropriate.

▶ *Mention, as specifically as you can, why you think that your child is not being challenged.* If your child reports spending a lot of time in free play because she finishes her assignments early, mention that. If your child reports that everything is "so easy," mention that. If the homework that you have seen looks like what your child did last year, mention that. Give the teacher something specific to address rather than just saying, "My child isn't being challenged."

▶ *Ask the teacher for her honest opinion as to whether or not your child is being challenged and* **listen** *to her answer.* Many parents whose child claims to be bored learn from teachers that their child finishes work early because she refuses to do it carefully. Or, the child says that work is "easy" but then does poorly on tests. Or maybe your child says that her work is easy but always takes the easy way out (reading easy books, choosing not to do extra credit, writing short reports rather than more complex ones).

▶ *If the teacher convinces you that your child isn't doing what she needs to do in order to challenge herself, ask the teacher how you can encourage your child to challenge herself more.* See if you can work out a system together. Be sure to say that you are going to talk to your child—and follow through.

▶ *If the teacher agrees that your child is not being challenged, ask her what you can do to create a challenging curriculum.* The teacher may feel constrained by having to present the same material to all of her students. However, she may be able to provide enrichment work for your child to do if your child can demonstrate that she already knows the lessons being taught (for instance if she scores perfectly on a pretest before the teacher begins a math unit, maybe she can work on accelerated math). Or perhaps your child can sit in on classes for the grade above hers for certain subjects. If your child has too much free time, maybe you and the teacher can devise assignments (research reports, creative writing, enrichment math work) for her to do after she finishes her regular assignments.

▶ *Ask what you can do at home to help*

your child realize her potential. What should you and your child do together? What materials should you get (and where can you get them)? Should you get outside help (enrichment classes, lessons, a tutor)?

▶ *Finally, ask if there are any areas in which your child can use some extra work.* Some children who excel in math feel less confident in writing or art. Other children wish that they were better at sports or at public speaking. Sometimes, rather than providing children with enrichment in subjects that they have already mastered, parents and teachers would be better off providing extra help in the child's "weaker" subjects. These efforts may help your child become more well-rounded.

Many children who are not challenged spend a lot of time working on the computer or helping other students. If this is the case with your child, ask the teacher why she thinks this benefits your child. She may have a good rationale for having your child peer tutor (perhaps she feels that your child learns the material better through teaching or that she needs to improve her communication skills) or working on the computer (perhaps the teacher has advanced software).

If the teacher does not have a good rationale, discuss alternate ways for your child to spend extra class time. If the situation doesn't improve or your child exhibits behavior problems because she is bored, consider moving her to a different class or grade, or to a school that has a more challenging program. I worked with one child whose kindergarten teacher felt that she could not challenge him and recommended that the family look into a private school that catered to gifted children. His family found that the private school was a perfect match for their child. Ask around to see if such a program (public or private) exists in your community. If there is a program, inquire about enrollment rules, tuition, and if they have space, and do some research to see if the program is a good fit for your child (see Chapter 1 for more information about choosing schools).

But don't move your child or force her to skip a grade just because she's a little bored one year. Remember that all high achieving children will experience times when they already know what is being taught in class. If your child is not unhappy and isn't acting out, don't overreact. Your child will be challenged in the future—in higher grades, in high school, and in college. And you can make sure to challenge her outside of school. Spending a year or two "less than challenged" at school won't ruin a child. But forcing her to change classes, schools, or grades, can be hard socially. Consider all aspects of your child's development before you make major decisions about schools and grade placement.

"I am afraid that my child is falling behind in class. Should I talk to the teacher?"

Yes, this is the perfect time to set up an appointment with your child's teacher —in fact, your child's teacher may want to talk to you. Set up a meeting and before you go, ask your child the following questions:

▶ What is he learning in school?

▶ What does he understand and not understand?

▶ Does he have a sense of why he has trouble with certain subjects?

▶ Are there any activities that he really enjoys at school?

Then, when you meet the teacher, begin by mentioning some things that your child enjoys and that seem to be working for your child. From there you can segue into your concerns about your child's performance. But, remember that the teacher has about 25 other children with whom she works during the day. Even though your child is struggling, try not to blame the teacher. Try to speak with her with understanding and respect. It may help to follow a few guidelines:

▶ *Explain that your child is struggling with some subjects and that you are wondering what you (both you and the teacher) can do to help.* Make sure not to phrase the comment as an accusation. Explain it as a problem that you would like to solve.

▶ *Listen to what the teacher has to say.* She may have some insights about why your child is struggling or what teaching techniques will work best with your child.

▶ *Ask the teacher if she is trying anything in particular to help your child.* If she is not, ask if she has any ideas about what might be done in the classroom to help.

▶ *Be sure to ask what you can do at home to help your child.* Ask specific questions. What should you do? How long should you work with your child each day? Do you need any special materials in order to work with her? If so, where can you get those materials? Should you seek professional help outside of the school (e.g., an educational consultant, a psychologist, a tutor)?

▶ *If the teacher tells you to do things that do not make sense to you or that you do not know how to do, ask questions and be honest.* Explain to the teacher that you don't understand and ask her to explain it again. Keep asking until you understand. You may worry that the teacher will think poorly of you if you have to ask over and over again. But the teacher will think worse of you if you agree to do certain activities at home but don't because you didn't understand what she wanted you to do.

▶ *Tell the teacher what you honestly think that you can do at home.* Do not promise to do activities that you think you will probably have to skip when you get too busy. If you are constrained by work or family obligations, tell the teacher. Ask if there are alternatives. Try to find a compromise. Overall, make sure that you leave the appointment having agreed to do only what you think you can and will do at home.

After you leave the meeting, do the work with your child that you said you would, and look for improvement. Make sure to report to the teacher if you see improvement or if your work doesn't seem to help. If problems persist, look into tutors, educational consultants, or psychiatrists. Don't be afraid to ask the teacher whether she thinks that your child should be tested for some kind of learning disability. This isn't something you want to jump into, but if your child does have a disability, it's better to learn about it earlier in her school career than later (more about learning disabilities in Chapter 6).

"What are Back to School Night and Open House?"

Back to School Night and Open House are events that allow parents to meet teachers and other parents and see what happens in their children's schools. Back to School Night happens at the beginning of the school year. Teachers often give a short presentation about expectations that they have for students and events and activities that will occur during the year. Teachers often use this time to introduce themselves to parents and set the tone for the school year. Back to School Night is frequently a parents-only event.

Open House tends to be a more casual affair. Many teachers have reports and projects due around the time of Open House so that they can display student work. Open House is a time for parents to see what their children have been doing over the school year and talk informally with their child's teacher (who usually mills around the classroom). Children usually come to Open House and help give their parents "the grand tour."

"I can't make it to my child's Open House (or Back to School Night)—is it OK if I skip it?"

No. Parents should go to Back to School Nights and Open Houses for two reasons:

◗ To show teachers that they care about their children and their children's education.

◗ To show their kids that they value school and care about what they do in school.

Although these events may seem minor (especially if you never get to talk to your child's teacher because she is monopolized by other parents), they are often quite important to kids who want to show off their classrooms and their work (especially if it is posted in a spot of honor).

What if you simply cannot go to Open House or Back to School night? Try to find someone to go in your stead. Although it is nice for teachers to meet students' mothers and fathers, if only one parent can go, he or she should. If neither parent can go and a grandparent, aunt, or uncle is available, someone should go and "represent the family." Since many children attend Open House, if you cannot make it, at least see if your child would like to attend with a classmate and his or her family. And, if no one in your family can go, make sure to explain to your child why you cannot attend and make a special effort to go next year. Children can tell when parents do not make their school events a priority.

"Is there any information I should make sure to get at Back to School Night? Are there activities I should make sure to do at Open House?"

Yes. Whenever you attend a school event try to say hello to your child's teacher. Make sure that the teacher knows you came. They do care! If there is a sign-in sheet, make sure to sign in. Teachers look at these later to see which parents came.

At Back to School Night find out what reports and projects the teacher expects to assign over the course of the year. See if the teacher has recommendations for free reading or at-home projects. Find out what organization system your child's teacher wants your child to abide by. Pick up any handouts that the teacher gives out.

At Open House, make sure to see your child's work! Kids want to show off their work, even if they do not make a big deal out of it. Another good thing to do at Open House is to visit the classroom (or classrooms) that your child might be in next year. Meet the teachers. See what kinds of work and projects they do. This will give you good information about which teacher you might want to request for next year or what work you and your child can do over the summer to prepare for the next year's curriculum.

"During the holidays and at the end of the year, I feel like I should give my children's teachers a gift, but I have no idea what they would want."

Many children bring gifts for their teachers before winter break or before school ends for the summer. Some teachers make a big show of these gifts, opening them in front of other children. Other teachers thank the children and then take the gifts home to open them there. Gifts are always a nice gesture to show teachers that you and your children appreciate their hard work. But what should you get for your child's teacher?

All teachers seem to agree that within the first few years of teaching, they accumulate enough mugs and "#1 Teacher" plaques to last a lifetime. Unless you really know the teacher, clothing and jewelry can be a hard call. Decorative items such as figurines and statuettes often end up in the back of a closet.

So, what do you give? You don't have to get a gift at all. Most teachers appreciate cards and letters from students. In fact, some teachers treasure heart-felt letters from students forever. If you are short on funds or just want to get creative, think about writing a letter or making a special card with your child. If your child likes art, suggest that he draw or paint a picture for his teacher. I know teachers who have kept student art up in their classrooms for years.

If you really want to get a gift, think about something that can be used in the classroom or that will get used up and not have to be stored—including gift certificates, food, candles, and magazine subscriptions. Be careful with food, though. Teachers who live alone or who are on special diets might be overwhelmed by candy and baked goods. The following are good ideas for when you don't know a teacher very well:

◆ Gift certificate to a local bookstore. Many teachers spend a lot of money keeping their classroom libraries stocked. Many also enjoy reading in their spare time.

◆ A magazine subscription (or a kids' magazine subscription for the classroom).

◆ Gift certificate to the local art supply store, computer store, or discount store (such as Target or K-Mart). Many teachers spend a lot of their own money on crayons, paper, computer software, printer ink, and other necessities for the classroom.

◆ Gift certificate to a teacher supply store (or online teacher supply store).

◆ A grade-appropriate educational game or learning tool (especially if you know the teacher keeps games in the classroom).

◆ Gift certificate to a local department store.

◆ Gift certificate to a local restaurant or coffee shop.

◆ Gift certificates to the movie theater (she may enjoy movies over break too!).

◆ Food—especially something that does not have to be eaten right away. One cute gift I saw was a cookie recipe and a mason jar layered with all the necessary dry ingredients that the teacher could save until she was ready to bake cookies.

◆ Items for the classroom, such as computer games, videos, or anything you think that the teacher would enjoy sharing with her future students.

◆ If you must get something decorative, candles and flowers are good bets because they can be used up and don't have to be stored.

If you do know something about what your child's teacher likes, you might consider:

◗ Gift certificates to a spa (if the teacher would enjoy a massage, facial, or manicure).

◗ Gift certificates to a theater or performing arts center (if the teacher enjoys cultural events).

◗ Gift certificate to a local sporting event (if the teacher has a favorite team).

◗ Christmas tree ornaments (if the teacher celebrates Christmas).

"My child's birthday is on a school-day. Can I ask her teacher to have a party for her?"

Many children enjoy bringing cupcakes to share with their classmates on their birthdays. However, some schools forbid parties (and while some teachers in these schools host "cultural celebrations"—such as Chinese New Year celebrations—which are tolerated, they cannot host birthday parties). Other schools do not allow teachers to distribute "unapproved" foods to students. And, even if schools allow both parties and cupcakes, teachers sometimes resent having to take class time to hand out cupcakes and drinks. Overall, birthdays are probably best celebrated

at home, but if you want your child to celebrate her birthday at school, following the following steps.

◗ Talk to the teacher (or send a note). Give her at least a week's notice and ask if it would be okay if your child brought in cupcakes to share with the class.

◗ If the teacher refuses, accept the refusal graciously. This is not important enough to risk hurting your relationship with your child's teacher.

◗ If she says that cupcakes are okay, ask when you should bring them and if you should plan on staying to help pass them out and/or clean-up. (Some teachers will expect your help. Others would prefer that you don't hang around.) Also be prepared for a teacher to tell you that you may bring a treat but that she will simply hand them out before lunch so that they don't waste any class time.

◗ If you bring a treat, make it a modest one. Don't burden the teacher with party hats, juice, or gift bags. Bring cupcakes, cookies, or something that can be passed out easily (rather than a cake that needs to be cut).

Dealing with Problems at School

"My child got in serious trouble at school—how do I handle this?"

If your child gets in serious trouble at

school (e.g., for fighting, cheating, threatening another child), you will probably get a phone call from the school. If this call comes, *you must resist* any instinct to immediately defend your child or deny that he "did it." Many parents automatically deny that their child could have been involved in any kind of trouble. Since you do not yet know all of the facts, this is absolutely the worst response you can have. This response will lead teachers and administrators to assume that your child got in trouble precisely because you are "the type" of parent who believes your child can do no wrong. Although it is always possible that your child is innocent, you must have all the facts—from more people than just your child—before you voice that conclusion. (I have actually seen children sneer at teachers who threaten to call their parents, saying, "So what? I'll just tell her I didn't do it and she'll believe me.")

What do you do if you get that phone call? If the situation warrants it, make sure that your child is OK. That should be your first concern. Then ask whoever is making the phone call what they want you to do. They will likely want you to come in for a meeting. Try to accommodate this request. If you can talk with your child and the teacher or principal (and any other children who were involved), you have the best chance of getting the full story and being able to explain to your child why he was punished.

When you meet with the principal or teacher, remain calm. Ask the adult what happened. Ask as many questions as you need to in order to understand the situation. Ask your child if this sounds like what happened. If your child is guilty he may admit it and then you can proceed to figuring out an appropriate form of discipline. If, however, your child says that that is not what happened, ask if your child can tell his side of the story. Listen to both sides and try to think objectively about the situation. Does this seem like something your child would have done? Does your child change stories when caught doing something wrong at home? Does your child often do things that he knows he shouldn't do? Bearing all of this in mind, try to reconcile the adult version of the story with your child's. If your child claims that other children were involved, most teachers or principals will also call in those children to explain the problem. If they do not and you believe your child, ask that the other children be called in. That way, you'll hear every side of the story.

After the story has been sorted out, you and the teacher or principal will have to decide on some type of discipline. First, you want to clearly understand the school's rules. For instance, your child may think it's unfair to get in trouble for fighting if someone else swung first. However, many schools have a zero-tolerance rule about fighting, which means that any child caught fighting gets punished, no matter who started it. If this is the rule at your school, there's no point arguing about who started the fight. Simply accept that your child broke a rule and will receive some kind of punishment. Parents who insist on arguing about clear-cut rules will find less lenience when it comes to future problems.

Like the zero-tolerance rule, your child's school may have set disciplinary actions (for instance, they may suspend all children who get involved in a fight). Although you can discuss with the principal whether or not these punishments are fair, remain calm. And, if the teacher or principal shows no sign of letting up, it is probably wisest to accept the punishment and hope that your child learns a lesson from it. Parents who fight administrators after their child has admitted guilt or when the evidence against him is clear only get a bad reputation for being uncooperative. And, arguing with the school administrators sets a bad example for your child.

If, however, you feel that your child has been unfairly accused, then you have to make some decisions. If your child is not too upset and the discipline is not too harsh, in some cases it may be easiest to accept it and explain to your child that sometimes people make mistakes, sometimes we are in the wrong place at the wrong time, and next time he should try his best to stay away from kids who are getting into

trouble. In other cases, however, you may need to fight the punishment. In these cases, it is probably best to talk with the principal (or take the situation to the principal if the principal is not already involved) without your child present. You may even need to take the situation to district officials if the punishment seems truly unfair. But before you go that far, try a sincere, one-on-one discussion with the highest official at the school.

One more point: If you child is in trouble, you may be asked to pick him up. When you get to school and see your child, don't scream at him and don't cause a scene. Anything negative (or too positive) that you say to your child will become fodder for office gossip. If you scream at your child, school administrators might presume that your child is a troublemaker because you are abusive. If you are too nice to your child, they might assume that you are too permissive and do not discipline your child. The best thing to do is take care of any administrative things you need to do, meet with the teacher or principal if that has been arranged, apologize for any inconvenience, and take your child home.

Finally, if your child gets suspended, don't let the suspension become a vacation. Make sure you pick up assignments for the days he misses at school and have him complete homework. Also make sure that he has special chores or tasks to accomplish at home. Don't reward his misbehavior at school by letting him watch TV for two days.

"My child's teacher wrote me a note saying that my child is misbehaving in class—how do I handle this?"

Some teachers send lots of notes home and others never do. Some teachers threaten to send notes home—and rarely have to—but will if a child misbehaves too often or continues to misbehave after she has been warned. Most teachers use notes home as a high level of "punishment." Most children don't want to get in trouble with their parents (the worst that the teacher can do to them is make them stay in at recess or go to detention—parents, on the other hand, have many more forms of discipline available to them).

View notes from the teacher as a source of information. If your child is talking too much in class, not paying attention, or talking disrespectfully to adults, you want to know. Most teachers will ask you to sign the note (to prove that you read it) and have your child return the note to class. You should:

- *Read the note* and either sign it and send it back with your child, or send a note of your own acknowledging the note.
- *Talk to your child.* Find out what she did wrong and how she intends to remedy her behavior. (Most children will admit their misbehavior—though they may add that the teacher was in a bad mood or that they were unfairly picked on.)

- *Discipline your child.* Make the punishment fit the crime (e.g., loss of TV, video game, or telephone privileges). But do be stern with your child. Most teachers do not send notes home unless they are very frustrated with a child or the child has repeatedly committed the same offense. Because many teachers threaten to send notes home when children misbehave, you want to discipline your child enough that she does not want to risk getting another note home in the future.

- *Consider having your child write a note to the teacher,* apologizing for her behavior and explaining what she is going to do in the future to keep herself "on track."

- During parent-teacher conferences, *ask explicitly about your child's behavior.* Make sure that she has improved. If she has not, you need to continue to talk with your child about how she can improve her behavior. You might set up a system in which the teacher can regularly report your child's behavior to you.

Don't worry too much about an occasional note home. But, if you receive a lot of notes, make an appointment to talk with the teacher. If your child has ongoing behavior problems you want to deal with them as soon as possible. Teachers get less and less forgiving as children get older.

"I feel like my child's teacher doesn't think that I'm doing my job as a parent—but I help my child with his homework every night!"

Teachers often don't know the parents of their students very well. So, they tend to make assumptions about parents based on their child's school performance and behavior. Teachers may presume that you are not being a "supportive" parent for a number of reasons, including:

◗ Your child isn't turning in homework regularly.

◗ Your child blames his family for incomplete or incorrect homework (e.g., "I had to go shopping with my mom" or "My parents wouldn't help me").

◗ Your child loses books or comes to school without materials he needs. (If your child wears eyeglasses make sure he brings them to school every day!)

◗ Your child goes to school hungry or tired.

◗ Your child is frequently absent or late.

There are two primary ways to remedy a teacher's misimpressions about your "parenting skills." First, talk to your child about acting responsibly. Make sure that he does his homework and brings completed homework to school. Talk with your child about making sure he turns homework in (if need be, check his folder when he comes home to see if the homework from the day before is still in there—you would be amazed at how many children do homework and then forget to turn it in). Create a system with your child to make sure he brings all of his materials to school every day (see Chapter 3). Make sure that your child is on time for school and try not to keep him home unless he is ill.

Second, form a relationship with the teacher so that she does not have to make assumptions about you. Let the teacher know who you are from her contact with YOU, not from the assumptions she makes based on your child's behavior. Make sure the teacher knows that you help your child with his homework and that you support his education.

"I really hate my child's teacher. How can I get my child moved to a different classroom?"

Throughout your child's school career, she will have teachers you love and probably some you dislike. What remedies you have available when you truly dislike a teacher depend on your school's policies and the principal's discretion. However, before you make any moves, make sure you understand exactly why you dislike this teacher—

and make sure that a frank conversation with the teacher will not change your opinion.

1. Write down exactly what you dislike about the teacher. Think rationally about whether these are good reasons for disliking a teacher.

▶ *Are there specific reasons?* Or, does the teacher just give you a vague "bad" feeling? If it's just a "bad" feeling, consider that it might simply be a personality conflict. See if you can observe in the classroom for a day (or for a few hours). It's possible that the teacher interacts better with children than with adults and that seeing her interact with the class will put your mind to rest.

▶ *Do you dislike this teacher because your child complains about this teacher more than she has complained about other teachers?* Talk honestly with your child about the teacher. What does she like about her? What would she change about her if she could? If the good aspects outweigh the bad—or if they at least balance each other out— you might leave well enough alone and hope for a better teacher next year. Also, be critical of your child's reasons. For example, some children dislike teachers who challenge them too much. However, if the bad characteristics outweigh the good, you are ready for step two. (But, think hard before you take this next step—you are not assured of success and you may create some very hard feelings at the school.)

2. Take your list to the teacher. Your list should be specific. Comments like "she's mean" are hard to cure. Specific comments (with specific examples) are more useful. For instance, maybe your child feels that the teacher only calls on boys, or only calls on "smart" children and ignores her. Or, maybe the teacher screams at the children and your child comes home crying and frightened. Or, maybe your child consistently comes home having learned lessons wrong.

▶ *Approach the teacher respectfully.* There is likely another side to the stories that your child has relayed to you. Explain your concerns to the teacher, but give her ample opportunity to explain her perception of what is going on in the classroom.

▶ *If the teacher seems reasonable, see if you can find a solution to the problems.* If, however, the teacher is not responsive and either denies all of the problems (and you have reasonable proof that they are real problems) or refuses to change her behavior, it may be time for step three.

3. Take your complaint to the principal. Remember, schools resist parent complaints about teachers because there is very little a school can do to get rid of bad (but tenured) teachers. The principal will be reluctant to change your child's class because then he will likely have a torrent of other parents who want their child moved to another class as well. But if you have very serious complaints about your child's teacher (and I wouldn't suggest going this far unless the complaints *are* very serious), go to the principal and advocate for your child.

▶ *Compile a second list.* This list should explain why the problems you have with the teacher are specific to your child. For example, you might argue that, because your child is behind academically, learning lessons wrong is especially detrimental. Or you might explain that your child has recently experienced a trauma (e.g., the death of a loved one) and his nightmares are exacerbated by the teacher's rants. Reasons that are particular to your child will provide the principal with an excuse for moving your child and not other children. If the teacher had an inappropriate response to your complaints or the solutions that you offered, include these in your list.

▶ *Speak rationally at all times.* The principal will be most apt to respond to careful reasoning (not hysteria).

▶ *Although you should be respectful, also be an advocate.* When schools have bad teachers they often put children with non-confrontational parents in their classes. Don't conform to their expectations. Stand up for yourself and your child.

▶ *Also, offer other solutions to the problem.* Suggest that your child be pulled out of that class for certain portions of the day (going, perhaps, to another teacher for math). Suggest extra tutoring, extra counseling time, or extra resource help. Ask what kind of help is available for the teacher to help her to improve her skills. Can she team-teach with other teachers? Can she get extra aides? Can she get counseling? Can she be reprimanded for the harsh punishments that she is meting out? Can all of you sit down and have a conference and talk about your child's placement?

▶ *Make sure that you leave the principal's office with an agreement and make sure to follow through on that agreement.* Even if you are unsuccessful in getting your child moved to another class—make sure that the principal sees you as a force to reckon with. If you do, he will probably make sure that your child does not get the worst teacher in the future.

Good Teachers

"Can I request a particular teacher for my child?"

Some schools permit requests and others do not. Some do not allow official requests but will consider unofficial requests. If you want a particular teacher:

▶ *Start with the front office.* Ask what the procedure is to request a teacher for your child for next year. If there is an official procedure, find out what it is, and follow it. You may be asked to write a letter to the principal or fill out a form.

◆ *If the office says you cannot request teachers, ask around.* Ask other parents if they know anything about teacher requests. You will probably hear that some parents do succeed in having requests granted. You will probably also hear reasons about why those parents succeeded while others failed (perhaps the successful parents are very involved in school activities, are very difficult or demanding parents, or are friends with the principal).

◆ *Talk to your child's current teacher.* Sometimes teachers put together the classes for next year (for instance, the second-grade teachers might get together to assemble the third-grade classes for the next year). Thus, your child's teacher might consider your request even if the principal will not officially consider it.

Once you have gathered your information, there are several ways you can increase your chances of having your request granted.

◆ *Make your request to as many people as possible.* If the school accepts requests, make an official request. Talk to your child's current teacher and the teacher you want your child to have next year. You might as well make your request heard. After all, some children will get the teacher you want, and if everyone knows you want that teacher, they may just decide to make your child one of the "lucky ones."

◆ *Be very specific about why you want the teacher you are requesting.* Do not simply say that she is the "best teacher." All parents want the "best teacher" for their child—why should you get her rather than someone else? Explain why that particular teacher is a good match for your child. Perhaps your child needs a firm teacher to keep her on track. Perhaps you already have a strong relationship with that teacher because an older sibling had her. Perhaps the teacher has a gift for working with struggling readers and you think your child will benefit from that expertise. Perhaps your child's current teacher told you that she thinks that it would be a good match. Write a letter that makes a strong case that the principal can use to justify placing your child with the teacher you want, even if he does not honor another parent's request for the same teacher.

◆ *Be courteous.* Neither principals nor teachers like feeling as if parents are bullying them around. Be careful to explain that you understand the complexities involved in placing children in classrooms and that you appreciate their consideration.

"I really love my child's teacher. What's the best way to show my appreciation?"

Teachers rarely get compliments on their work. They almost never get monetary bonuses to reward good work and, unless they want to become administrators, they never get promoted. So, expressing your appreciation is one of the nicest things you can do for a teacher. If you think that your child's teacher did a really good job, write a letter praising her work and describing the impact you feel she had on your child. Send a copy of the letter to the principal and, if you know who they are, to some of the local school board members or the superintendent. (You can use a business format and "cc:" the letter to the "higher-ups" or just send a copy of the letter with a note or post-it explaining that you thought that they would like to know how wonderful one of their teachers is.) I have seen teachers express deep appreciation for notes of thanks they received from parents and students. Some even copy them and show them off to other teachers and administrators.

CHAPTER 3

Helping with Homework

M OST KIDS WISH THEY DIDN'T HAVE TO DO HOMEWORK. MANY PARENTS WOULD rather their kids didn't have homework too—especially when they constantly have to nag their kids to get it done. But, however inconvenient it may be, homework serves several important purposes. Homework allows kids to practice lessons and concepts that they learned in school and drill new techniques into their minds so that they become second nature. Homework allows teachers to move through curriculum faster. When children can show—with correctly completed homework—that they have mastered skills, teachers can stop teaching those skills and move on to new and more interesting material. Homework also gives parents a glimpse of the subject matter their children are studying. And, how much your child struggles with homework will tell you if your child is being challenged in school. If your child persistently has homework that is impossible for her, you will know that there is a problem—either with your child's class placement, her listening skills, her processing skills, or the way that the teacher explains new concepts and assignments. Just knowing that there's a problem gives you an advantage—you can begin to search for a solution before your child falls too far behind. Try to keep the following principles in mind when helping children with homework:

Help your child build homework habits for a lifetime.

Children who learn how to get organized, budget their time, and follow good study skills in the first grade are often well-prepared to handle increasing workloads as they get older. When your child starts school, help her to get started on the right foot. If you take the time to help her get through her 15 minutes of kindergarten homework efficiently, you will help her build great work habits that may last a lifetime. You may also save yourself a lot of "homework nag" work in the future! Although many of the tips in this chapter seem time consuming, most children outgrow needing a lot of help if they receive firm guidance early on.

Think of homework as practice.

Although homework assignments can be fun, they are often tedious. Doing two dozen long-division problems is not fun for anyone. So, why do teachers assign them? They assign repetitive homework so that your child will learn to do problems well enough to do them in her sleep. Once your child learns a concept cold, she can move on to more complicated problems (e.g., long-division with decimals), will understand abstract problems (e.g., how to divvy up $150.98 among 3 people), and will still remember the concept next year. While some teachers do assign busywork, most try to assign homework that is relevant to recent lessons. And, almost by necessity, homework is duller and more repetitive than classwork. Most teachers don't rely on parents to teach *new* concepts at home; they assign homework on concepts that they taught in class. If your child finds homework boring then, hopefully, that means that she has mastered the concepts.

Remember that you *can* help with most of your child's homework—even if it looks unfamiliar.

Most elementary school homework comes with directions. And, most can be done with the help of a textbook. Don't be intimidated just because your child is studying a topic that you are not familiar with or don't remember. When he has to answer questions on Ancient Mesopotamia, the answers are likely in his social studies book. When he has to label the organs of the body, he probably has a book or handout with all of the necessary information. If you can't remember how to multiply fractions, look in his math book. You will probably understand the explanation even if your child claims to be completely lost. Children sometimes have homework that parents can't figure out (either because the directions are unclear or because children don't bring home the necessary information), but don't be afraid to try to learn *with* your child as you help with homework.

Help your child think of homework as his job.

When kids get home, they want to relax, play with their friends, watch TV —do anything but schoolwork. But impress upon your child that doing homework must be his priority because school is his job. In many ways, school is preparation for life. Children learn not only math and reading but also how to keep organized and how to act responsibly. Your child must develop an organization system to help him keep track of his assignments, stay on top of his class material, and use his time wisely. Although your child may need (a lot of) your help to develop his "system"—ultimately, he must take charge of keeping himself on track. Your child must also be responsible for making sure his job—his homework—gets done. Don't make excuses for your child. Don't let your child tell you "it's not important." It is extremely important that your child does his homework every night and that he does it well (even if the teacher does not correct it). But, like any other job, he can ask for help if he needs it. He may ask you about an assignment and, if you and your child are truly puzzled, he can take it in the next day and ask the teacher (if this happens too many times,

however, your child may just be using misunderstanding as an excuse to get out of work).

Different children work best with different work styles.

The styles that work for your child may not be the styles and practices that worked for you. Not every technique in this book will work for every child. Some children will only need one memorization tip to ace their tests. Other children will need to work through every memorization tip they can find. But, as long as your child is getting good grades, is learning her school material, and (according to you and her teacher) is working up to her potential, let her work the way she feels comfortable. Don't fight with your child unnecessarily. Be interested and concerned. Be vigilant and look for any problems or potential problems. But, as long as she's succeeding—also let her take responsibility for her "job."

Getting Kids Organized

"My child keeps telling me that he doesn't have any homework but then his teacher tells me that he never does his homework— how can I find out the truth?"

Almost all information from schools passes to parents through kids—which means that parents are often left in the dark about what they need to do to help their kids succeed in school. Sometimes kids forget what homework they have to do, other times, they just don't want to do it. No matter what the reason, schools have been moving toward making information more accessible to parents. For starters, find out if your school has either a *homework hotline* or a *homework Web site* where you can get information. If your school does not have either of these services, you might want to mention it to your child's teacher, the principal, or the PTA.

But, of course, you and your child cannot rely on the school to keep your child organized. Your child must develop an organization system to keep track of his assignments and make sure that he has the materials that he needs to complete his assignments. You may need to help your child develop his "system." But you must also insist that your child take on these tasks himself. If you take on the responsibility (e.g., nagging your child constantly, driving him back to school every afternoon to pick up forgotten books), your child may still need you (or a personal secretary) in high school and college. Work with your child to create an organization system that works *for him*. But remember, different children need different amounts of structure. If a system works for your child (in other words, he does his homework without you nagging him, he gets good grades, and

his teacher is happy with his performance), let him use his system until you see evidence that it is not working.

There are a number of steps that you can take to help your child get organized.

▶ *Have your child pick out an organizer, planner, or agenda book.* Some schools provide their students with a calendar that goes throughout the school year. If your child likes the one that the school provides, go with that. But sometimes children feel more motivated to use their calendars when they choose the book themselves. So, if you are having trouble getting your child to use an organizer, make a special trip to the office supply store and ask him to choose an organizer that he likes—it's worth the investment. If none of the organizers seem quite right, you can also try making your own pages (either handwritten or with the computer) and keeping them in a binder or folder that your child chooses. When choosing or making a planner, think about how big your child writes. If you need to make page-a-day agenda pages for your first-grader, do it. He can have his own special homework binder. (If you make up some planner pages that you and your child particularly like—show them to the teacher, she may have other students who would enjoy using them too.)

▶ *Ask your child to write down his homework for every single subject every single day.* If you have to, pre-

Monday	
Tuesday	
Wednesday	
Thursday	
Friday	

A page-a-week page you might find in a fifth-grader's homework planner.

Homework for Monday

A page-a-day page you might find in a first-grader's homework planner.

write the name of each subject on each day. This "writing-it-all-down" system will force your child to either write down an assignment or write down "none" or "nothing" if no homework is assigned in a particular subject. This way he (and you) will know that there actually is no assignment and that your child didn't simply forget to write it down.

▶ **Ask your child to check the agenda book each afternoon before leaving school to make sure something is written down for each subject.** If he misses something, have him ask the teacher what the assignment is for that subject.

▶ **Check the homework book with your child every evening before he starts his homework.** If he needs help, assist him in making a plan for the evening so that everything gets done—even the long-term assignments such as "study for spelling test on Friday."

▶ **Have your child check off each assignment as it's done.** Some kids like using highlighters to color finished assignments. Many kids get a sense of satisfaction out of crossing out assignments and then seeing that everything is done.

▶ **Create a special place for your child to put his homework when it's done so that you can make sure that it gets to school in the morning.** And make sure the calendar goes into the backpack as well!

If your child has been having trouble getting homework turned in, make sure that you let his teacher know about your new system. She may be able to help make the system a success and she will surely appreciate your efforts to help get your child organized.

"I've tried to get my child to write down her homework, but she either forgets or she writes it down wrong. No matter what I do, she seems to be missing homework assignments!"

For many children, putting together a "writing it all down" system will solve homework organization problems. Other children need a more strictly monitored system. If your child has a particularly bad homework problem (or if the organizer alone doesn't work) try the following ideas:

▶ *Enlist the help of your child's teacher.* Explain the system to the teacher and ask if she will quickly check your child's homework book after school each afternoon and make sure that your child has written down all of her assignments. Ask the teacher to initial each day if it's correct.

▶ *Reciprocate the teacher's help and check your child's completed homework each evening.* Use her list (which has been initialed by the teacher) and check off that your child completed each of her homework assignments. If she did, you initial the book as well. If there was a problem with an assignment, write a note to the teacher and put it in the book—she will see it when she checks in the afternoon. Beware, however, of making too many excuses for missed assignments. Teachers will be most likely to spend the time helping your child if they feel like you are exerting every effort to make sure that homework gets done.

▶ *Develop consequences for not getting homework done.* Ask your child's teacher if she imposes consequences on students who do not do homework. If she does not, explain that you would like your student to have some consequences for not turning in homework. Discuss the possibilities of consequences at school versus the teacher letting you know when homework is missing so that you can discipline your child at home. Whatever consequence you decide on, make sure that it's realistic and stick by it. Teachers are often willing to go the extra mile (e.g., calling parents to report on homework) but get frustrated when parents do not follow up.

▶ *Ask the teacher not to give your child any special consideration for missing homework.* If your child does not do her homework, her grades should reflect that. Ask the teacher to explain to your child the role that missing homework played in her low grade. You should also explain to your child how her homework completion problems affect her grades.

Of course, punishments are not the only way (or necessarily the best way) to push children to do homework. Punishments merely show children that their irresponsibility has consequences. Also encourage your child to do her homework.

▶ *Try to make homework fun.* Sit down

with your child, read with her, and talk about what she's learning. Make sure to point out the useful aspects of the assignments that she's doing (e.g., how she needs to use math to figure out how much candy to buy for her birthday party)—and try to build on her interests to fuel her enthusiasm (e.g., if she wants to be a veterinarian explain how important biology and anatomy will be when she is treating sick animals).

▶ *Praise your child for doing homework.* When you initial her book, tell her how proud you are that she finished all of her work. Don't bribe your child, but do, occasionally surprise her with a treat or a reward for work well done. Perhaps a fun activity on the weekend after a full week of perfect homework.

▶ *Point out improved grades and test scores to your child as she begins doing more and more homework.* The best reason for your child to do homework is to improve her academic performance—make sure she sees the improvement and feels proud of herself.

Although all of these systems require a lot of work from parents, once your child gets into a routine and starts seeing the benefits of doing homework (e.g., more praise from you and the teacher, better grades, better understanding of schoolwork), she should be able to work more and more independently. If you start working with a good system right when your child starts

school, you may well be able to prevent problems from beginning at all.

"My child usually knows what he has to do for homework but he often does not bring home the books, papers, or other supplies that he needs."

Some schools (and some teachers) will let children bring home a "home set" of books so they will always have books at home. If forgetting books at school is a persistent problem for your child, it may be worth asking your child's teacher if she has an extra set.

However, most children overcome this problem simply by becoming more organized. While most children can look at their planner, see that they have to do "math, pages 23-24," and bring home their math book, other children need to explicitly list—and check off—the books they need to bring home. Make sure that your child has a planner with plenty of space to write. Then have him divide each day's space into two columns. In one column he should write each assignment. In the second column, have him write every book or supply he needs for that assignment. He should write down the supplies *when he writes down the assignment* (if he waits until later, he may forget an important component). Have him check the list each day as he packs his backpack to go home. With practice he may even be able to outgrow this system. But some people continue these kinds of list-making systems into adulthood just to make sure that they do not forget anything.

Here's an example of how to help your child organize his calendar:

Monday, April 26	**Materials:**
Math—pages 23-24, #1-25 odd	Math book
English—final draft of ghost story	Ghost story rough draft
Science—chapter 9 review—all	Science book
Social Studies—none	Nothing
Tuesday, April 27	**Materials:**
Math—pages 25-26, all	Math book, math notes
English—read *Sounder*—chapter 4	*Sounder*
Science—none	Nothing
Social Studies—chapter 11 worksheet	Social studies book, worksheet

The When, Where, and How of Homework

"My child has a desk (that she insisted we buy for her) but she refuses to use it. She insists on doing homework in the living room or flopped on her bed. How can I force her to use her desk?"

You may not need to force her to use her desk. And, as you probably already know, forcing her is the best way to make her really hate her desk. As you negotiate with your child about where she should do homework, remember that people have different approaches to learning and learning environments. Some people learn best in a neat and orderly setting (e.g., using a

What Every Successful Student Needs

- *A binder with an organizational system.* Some teachers ask students to divide binders with "subject tabs" (inserts with colored tabs that children can label "math," "reading," etc.). Other students prefer to use colored folders inside their binders to keep papers together. Wait until your child begins school to put together the binder. Many teachers will send home instructions about how they want binders organized.

- *A calendar, organizer, agenda, or homework book.* Use one from school, one you bought, or one you made. Just make sure that each day has enough space for your child to comfortably write all of her assignments (remember, first-graders write big).

- *A place to put her backpack.* Have your child make a commitment to put homework, books and binders into her backpack every night before bed (or, ideally, as soon as homework is finished) and put the backpack in the same spot every night. This will eliminate early-morning searches for materials.

- *A backpack without loose papers* (and a parent who spot checks to make sure that it stays that way). Sometimes teachers don't collect homework every day, but if your child keeps her assignments neatly in her binder, she will have them when they are collected. Loose papers may also be fliers that your child was supposed to bring home to you.

- *The phone numbers of friends or responsible classmates to call to find out about homework assignments.* When your child desperately needs to talk to a classmate, it will be too late to gather the phone numbers. Let her keep a list and keep a copy for yourself.

- *A book or magazine to pick up when bored.* Kids are least likely to read if they have to hunt down reading materials.

- *A good dictionary.* This doesn't have to be a massive hardback volume. A child's picture dictionary will work well for a young child. An older child may like having a small paperback she can leave on her desk.

- *Reference materials* (e.g., encyclopedias, almanacs, CD-Roms, Internet access) or a plan for how to access reference materials. Keep these materials handy not just for homework but to help your child answer everyday questions (e.g., if she's watching the news she may want to know where a country is or what alligators look like). You can feed her curiosity easily if you have reference materials at hand.

From the book *School Sense: How to Help Your Child Succeed in Elementary School* by Tiffani Chin, Ph.D. (Santa Monica Press • 800-784-9553). © 2004 by Tiffani Chin.

clean desk) while others learn best amidst mild disorder. (See Markova & Powell's *Learning Unlimited* (1998) for an in-depth look at different learning styles.) Some people need complete silence while doing homework, while others need some background noise. Some people need to sit up at a formal desk, others prefer more comfortable study positions. Although these differences are mere differences in opinion and style, they can be very frustrating when parents and children have contrasting work preferences. But, if your child is getting her work done, doing her homework correctly, and learning the material she needs to learn—don't fight with her about the desk. At some point almost all children insist that they need a desk that they will never use. Let it go.

However, if your child is not getting her work done, is not doing her work correctly, or is not mastering her material, then you need to figure out a better way for her to work. The best way to handle arguments about how to do homework is to work *with* your child. Let your child understand that you will be flexible about where she chooses to work, as long as she gets her work done correctly and efficiently. However, if you think that she could improve her homework quality, enlist her in a little experiment in which she tries out different positions. Ask her to switch off for a week: one day doing homework your way (say, at the nice desk you just bought her), other days doing homework another way (say, sprawled out on her bed with her feet in the air). She might even spend a day or two trying some kind of compromise (maybe sitting on the bed with a lap desk). Ask your child to cooperate fully and promise that when you finish the experiment, you will stop nagging her. Time how long homework takes in each position, and check to see how neat her homework is. Check for correctness and discuss your child's reading with her to make sure she understands. Watch your child work, note how much she fidgets, how focused she seems, and how often she needs to get up (walk around, get a drink, etc.). Each day, have your child write a list of the pros and cons of each position.

At the end of the week (or two weeks if you have several positions in rotation) sit down with your child and ask her which position *she* thought was the best. Explain which position you thought worked best for her (remember—NOT the one that you personally prefer but the one that worked the best for her). Use your notes to show her why you think she worked best in different positions. Even if she preferred working on her bed, if you show her that she worked twice as fast at the desk (and thus, could spend an extra 30 minutes on the phone), she might more readily agree to work at the desk.

Then, make an agreement about

how she will work in the future. You may decide on a hybrid choice—doing math at the desk and reading on the bed. You must both agree that she will do her homework in the positions in which she worked "best." And as long as her work gets done, keep your promise and do not nag.

"Is it OK for my child to do homework in front of the TV or with the radio on? He insists that he 'needs' it."

As a general rule, most children do not do homework efficiently in front of the television. Television is a distraction and even if your child does complete his homework (and does it correctly) it's probably taking him longer than it should. Some children (and some adults) do, however, work better with background noise. That background noise can come in the form of music, other people's chatter, or even TV. (Again, see Markova & Powell's *Learning Unlimited* (1998), for a more in-depth discussion of learning styles.)

To assess whether or not your child works better with or without background noise, follow the same routine suggested above. Have your child alternate between doing homework with or without the radio (or TV, or being in the same room as his siblings) for a week and make an agreement to abide by the results. Time how long it takes him to complete his work,

check for incorrect or sloppy work, quiz him for comprehension (especially if he claims to be able to read in front of the TV). Keep track of the quality of work and the time it takes him to complete it. Have him write down the pros and cons of working with the TV or radio on or working with the TV or radio off. At the end of the week, decide *together* which system is better. (Depending on your child's preferences, you can also experiment with different volume levels or different types of music. While your child may be distracted by high-volume rap music, lower volume or non-vocal classical or jazz might provide the perfect amount of background noise.)

If you find that your child works more efficiently without the TV or radio on, try to help him enjoy the extra free time he will earn by working with the TV or radio off. Make sure he does something that he enjoys with the time he saves by finishing homework faster (e.g., go to the park, or let him go to a neighbor's to play ball). Also make sure to point out the extra time and encourage him to decide to turn the TV off on his own.

And, of course, if your child works better (or just as well) with the TV or radio on, keep your end of the bargain and stop nagging. If, at a later time, the quality of his work goes down or he seems to take much too long with homework, try another experiment.

"I wish my child would do homework in the afternoon rather than waiting until evening, but she insists that she needs time to relax. Can I force her to do homework immediately when she gets home from school?"

Most parents prefer to have children do homework right when they get home from school. Some children learn to prefer this system, too. When children have a lot of homework, starting right away is the best idea—that way they won't run out of time. However, some kids do need a chance to relax after school. If your child is very active, fidgety, or really struggles with schoolwork, sitting through the school day can be very tiring and frustrating. Having to sit right down to do homework may be more than she can stand. If your child manages to take a break and still complete her homework without you nagging her and without pushing back her bedtime, allow her to schedule herself. Some children are very good at self-regulating and know how much of a "break" they need to take before they can get to work.

If, however, your child is not finishing her homework, does not start her homework unless you bug her repeatedly, or constantly needs your help with homework late in the evening when you have other things to do or are too tired to help, you need to help her stick to a better

schedule. Figure out how much homework she usually has (timing her for a few days will give you a better idea than just asking her). Then give her a range of options. For instance, if she gets home from school at 3:30, you eat dinner at 6:30, and she typically has an hour of homework, decide together on a designated homework hour between 3:30 and 6:30. If she needs some time to unwind but loves to watch a TV program at 5:00, then you might decide to start work at 4:00. Promise not to nag her to start earlier and have her promise to start precisely at 4:00. Make sure she keeps to her schedule—but do it in a way that reminds her that she agreed to this schedule as well (and if she starts late, she should have to work during her TV program (TV off, of course)—do not let her delay the work until after dinner).

Also, decide what to do on days when she has a lot of homework. Decide if she should start work early, work more after dinner, or skip her TV program. How to arrange extra homework will depend on your family's schedule. But be sure to reach a firm agreement and stick to it. When your child gets home from school, ask if she has "a normal" amount of homework or "a lot" of homework and remind her of your schedule.

Overall, the best way to get your child to work efficiently and on schedule is to give her a large role in determining the schedule. As long as she sticks to it, don't harass her. However, if she does not stick to the schedule, impose consequences (missing the favorite TV program or skipping play dates in favor of doing homework are appropriate consequences). Hopefully, seeing that poor scheduling results in losing fun time (just as it does for adults) will help her realize the value of her schedule.

"I'm not home when my child gets home from school. How can I force him to stick to a homework schedule?"

If you are not home when your child gets home from school, you must encourage him to implement a homework schedule system himself. Get him a timer and have him track how long it takes him to do his homework assignments. (Check his time when you get

---

How to Minimize Arguments over Homework

- *Allow your child to have her own preferences, techniques, and schedule as long as she completes her homework correctly.* Everyone works differently. Some people require complete silence while others need background noise. Some like to get all of their work done in one sitting while others take breaks. As long as your child is getting her work done—and doing it right—don't nag her.
- *Don't be a dictator.* Show your child that you are willing to consider her wishes. Experiment with different homework schedules (e.g., doing homework right after school or right after dinner) and styles (e.g., doing homework at the desk or on the couch). Have your child compare how well she does her homework under different conditions. Try to decide *together* on the best methods *for her.*
- *Consider bringing in backup.* Sometimes an outside party (e.g., a friend or relative) will be able to work with your child under less emotional circumstances than you can. If you have limited time or tend to fight with your child over homework, consider hiring a tutor (even a local high school or college student) to work with your child on homework.
- *Allow your child to fail if she insists on failing.* You can't force your child to be a straight-A student. She needs to learn that not completing homework can hurt her grades. She needs to learn that it can be embarrassing to go to school without homework. If she refuses to do homework, allow her to suffer the consequences.

home—as long as he is doing his work correctly and completely, encourage him to work swiftly and efficiently.) Then, help him decide how to schedule his homework time (see question above for details). Hold him accountable for having his homework done by the time you get home from work (or at least with enough done so that he can eat dinner and go to bed at his normal bedtime if you decide on a schedule that allows him to do some of his work in the evening). If he does not have enough work done by the time you get home, do not let him do anything fun (e.g., TV, playing, etc.) until his homework is complete.

"I don't get home until late so by the time I can help my child with homework, she's already tired. What can I do?"

Most children can complete a lot of their homework without help. Work with your daughter on scheduling (see questions above). Ask her to try to finish all of the homework she does not need help with before you get home. Hopefully, by the time you get home, she will only have a few questions that you can work through relatively quickly.

If, however, your child needs a lot of help, you might look into getting someone to help her. Many schools have after-school programs that provide homework help (the quality of this help varies considerably, however, so make sure you check the program out before you enroll your child—see Appendix 1). You might also consider hiring a tutor for your child. If your child struggles especially with a particular subject, make sure you hire a tutor who specializes in that subject. Since tutors can be very expensive (especially if you want them to come to your house—they may charge as much as $50 an hour), sometimes a good alternative is to hire a local high school or college student to come over and work with your child in the afternoons. You could probably negotiate a much better pay rate with a student and most high school students with A or B averages would be able to help an elementary-school student with homework.

"My child never gets her homework done. Even though she starts working when she gets home from school, by bed-time, there is still more to do. She's just a little kid. Why does she have so much work?"

OR

"My child gets way too much homework. What can I do?"

Does your child have too much homework or is she just working inefficiently? Some children daydream between every math problem. Others spend more time watching TV and talking on the phone than working on homework (even though they have their books open). Try working on homework with your child for a few days. Examine how she works:

♦ *Does your child seem focused?* Is she working continuously? Or, does she stare into space and take long pauses? If she pauses a lot, ask her what she is doing. She may admit that she's daydreaming or she may tell you that she's thinking. Ask her what she's thinking about. Try to assess if she's really thinking about her work, or just spacing out. If she is just spacing out, encourage her to work faster. Time how long it takes her to do an assignment when she spaces out, compared to when she is focused (even if you have to keep reminding her to be focused). Do fun activities in the time that she saves when she works quickly. Try to convince her to work efficiently by showing her the benefits of getting homework over with so she can move on to more fun activities.

♦ *Does your child seem to struggle with particular aspects of her work?* Many children take a long time to do homework because they lack some of the necessary skills to do the work efficiently. For instance, by the time teachers start teaching long division (usually in third or fourth grade), they expect students to have memorized the multiplication tables. Any student who does not know the multiplication tables will struggle with long division—and spend twice as long on any long division assignment than they should. Watch your child while she works. Is she struggling with a particular skill? If she is, find a way to help her develop that skill (e.g., quizzing her with addition or multiplication flashcards). If you are not sure how to help, make an appointment to talk with the teacher. She will probably have some suggestions and will appreciate your insights into your child's difficulties.

♦ *Does your child struggle with all of her work?* If it seems like all of your child's homework is too difficult, make an appointment to talk to the teacher. Your child may have a learning difficulty. Or she may not be paying attention in class. Or the class may be working at too fast a pace for her. Either way, you must have a conference with the teacher.

♦ *Does your child seem to work efficiently but still have to work for hours to complete homework?* If your child is working hard and working with focus and still works for hours, make an appointment with the teacher. On an average day, most elementary school students should not have more than an hour or so of homework (although days before tests and days before projects are due may require more work). If your young child (first or second grade) consistently has a great deal more than an hour of solid work or your older child (third, fourth, or fifth grade) consistently has more than 1-2 hours of work, you need to have a parent-teacher conference.

If you go in to talk with the teacher, follow the guidelines for parent-teacher interaction in Chapter 2. Remember to approach the teacher respectfully and considerately. Do not use an accusatory tone. Do, however, bring in your records (e.g., notes of how long it took for your child to do different assignments, notes on which assignments seemed particularly long). Before you talk to the teacher, you might also try to talk to other parents to see if their children also struggle to complete their homework. This will give you more background on the problem (and whether the problem lies with your child or the assignments). The teacher (or the school) may firmly believe that children should have two hours of homework a night (if this is the case, you may want to consider if this is the right school for your child). Remember, as you talk to the teacher, that your child may just work very slowly or your child may be more meticulous than the average student. Even if this is the case, a frank conversation with your child's teacher may help you devise a system whereby your child can get the full benefit of homework but does not have to spend hours and hours a night working on assignments.

"I've looked at my child's homework and she seems to get way too many 'busywork' worksheets that don't seem to teach her anything. What can I do?"

Make sure you understand what the teacher wants your child to learn from her homework. Sometimes long, tedious assignments are honest attempts by a teacher to help children memorize an important fact or process. Also, make sure that you give the teacher the benefit of the doubt. Sometimes they do send home busywork assignments just to keep children working. If it happens only occasionally, don't worry about it.

However, if it happens too frequently, make an appointment to talk to the teacher. Again, follow the guidelines for parent-teacher interaction in Chapter 2. Be respectful and courteous but ask what the teacher hopes your child will learn from her homework assignments. She may be able to explain something that you didn't see. If the homework is just plain busywork and the teacher has no good rationale, this may be a good time to talk to some of the teachers your child might get next year. If all of the teachers in the school agree that busywork is useful homework, it might be time to consider switching schools. As for this year, explain to your child that homework is her job, even if it does seem a little pointless, and help her to work through it efficiently. Hopefully next year will be better. (If the problem is really serious, you might also consider talking to the principal—see Chapter 2 for steps to follow when complaining about a teacher.)

"My child is supposed to read for 20 minutes every night. I am supposed to sign his reading log. But, he usually just asks me to sign it in the morning before he goes to school and I'm pretty sure he has not actually done the reading. I don't want to sign but I don't want him to get in trouble either. Should I just sign it?"

No. If you sign a reading log without seeing your child read, you teach him that reading isn't important and that it is OK to get credit for homework he has not done. Teachers often assign free reading as homework. Since children don't have to show any tangible proof that they did the reading (such as a worksheet or page of math problems), they often don't read. And, many children learn at an early age that their parents will sign just about any school form without really looking at it. Don't get into this habit. Read every form that you sign. And, if you did not see your child read, don't sign his reading log. Your child *should* get in trouble if he did not do his homework! If you are not home while your child does his reading, ask him to summarize what he read for you. If you suspect that he is not being honest with you, skim his free reading book. This may seem like a lot of work for you, but you don't want your child to learn that he doesn't really have to do homework that he doesn't physically turn in. You also don't want him to learn (especially this early in life) that his parents are easy to manipulate. (And, as a bonus, a lot of children's books are actually quite good. If you read the books your child reads, you will be that much more prepared to discuss them with your child, which is a great enrichment activity—see Chapter 5 for more details.)

"My child and I constantly argue over small issues. Should she use a pencil or pen? Should she print or write in cursive? Does she have to write out the whole problem for math work or just the answer? No matter what I say, she says her teacher has a different rule. How can we resolve these problems?"

If your child is doing assignments incorrectly, her teacher is probably taking points off of her assignments. If your child receives good grades, let her do her work *her* way. To give you peace of mind, you can also ask the teacher yourself during parent-teacher conference. But, since the teacher is not around while you are arguing at home, the arguments are fruitless. Drop them until you have proof (either in the form of your child's low grades or directly from the teacher) that *you* (and not your child) are correct about the teacher's rules.

However, if your child's grades are low, ask your child to see the corrected assignments that get handed back to her and see if her teacher has made any notes about her work. You may well see that the teacher is taking off points for the exact reasons that have been provoking your arguments at home (e.g., not writing out math problems, not working in cursive). Use these assignments to explain to your child why it's important to follow the teacher's rules (even if she thinks it's a waste of time to write out math problems).

If your child does not have any corrected assignments, make an appointment to talk with the teacher (or try to contact her by phone or email). When you talk with the teacher, ask her directly about how your child should format her assignments. Also ask to see your child's corrected work. Explain to the teacher that you feel like you can help your child better if you see her corrected work. Your child may have a packet of corrected work that you can pick up or look through. If the teacher says that she hands work back to the children (but your child does not seem to actually bring it home), have a talk with your child about making sure she brings graded work home to show you.

"My child and I always fight over homework. He refuses to do it. He refuses to listen to my advice. We spend more time arguing than working."

If you have already tried the other methods in this chapter to alleviate fights over where and when your child should do his homework and you still fight constantly, it might be time to bring in a tutor. Some parents find that, no matter how good a relationship they have with their child, when it comes to homework they battle constantly. I once tutored a young boy from a close-knit family that had a lot of fun together. But, the moment they tried to do homework together, they began to shout. I, on the other hand, came for two hours every night, and we almost never fought. I even helped him with French homework even though his mom spoke French fluently and I had never studied it at all. The system worked because tutors have several advantages over parents:

▶ *Tutors don't bring "baggage" to the homework environment.* You may have fought with your child earlier in the day. You may be extremely worried about his academic performance. These stresses create tension before you and your child even begin homework. Tutors, on the other hand, have a clean emotional slate.

▶ *Tutors don't have to live with the child after homework is finished.* A tutor can drive your child as hard as she needs to in order to push him to get the work done. She doesn't have to worry about the child giving her the silent treatment over dinner.

◗ *Children see tutors as "experts."* Although children often have a hard time believing that their parents "could know anything," they see tutors as teachers. They trust that tutors know what they are talking about.

◗ *Tutors have experience teaching.* When a tutor comes to work with your child in geometry, she won't be trying to learn it *with* your child. She probably knows the material like the back of her hand. This makes her more relaxed and more confident. She may also know more "alternative" techniques for doing the problems your child is struggling with.

Of course, not everyone can afford to hire a tutor. If you can't afford a high-priced private tutor, consider hiring an older student whom your child looks up to. Or, see if your child's other parent, a grandparent or other relative, or family friend has more luck. Sometimes children just need a change of scenery. If a tutor of any kind is out of the question, try your best to imitate a tutor. Set aside special "tutor time" with your child. Explain to your child that you are going to try to set aside non-homework related problems while you are doing homework and that you are going to try to forget about home-work problems once you finish. And,

keep your word. Don't nag him about homework over dinner!

"How do I find a good tutor?"

Word of mouth is usually the best way to find a good tutor. Ask your friends and your child's friends' parents to see if they have heard of any good local tutors (or good high school or college students who do tutoring). Ask your child's teacher (or previous teachers). Even if people can't recommend a good tutor, they may be able to recommend a good tutoring company or another friend who has a good tutor. Any kind of recommendation is better than nothing. If you can't get any leads, put up flyers at the local college or high school, place an ad in the local college newspaper, or go and talk with some teachers or counselors at the local high school—they may be able to recommend a bright, responsible student. If you know any older students, ask if they tutor or know any friends who tutor. There are also some Internet sites cropping up that refer tutors across the country (www.tutor2000.com, www.hireatutor.com, and www.aplus4you.com). Although these companies aren't as good as getting a personal referral (and they don't have great datasets for all areas), they may give you a start.

Before you hire a tutor, talk to him. Ask him about his experience and his qualifications (e.g., How long has he tutored? How many students (of what ages) has he worked with? What relevant classes has he taken? What grades did he get in those classes?). Have your child talk with him and see how they interact. And, once you hire a tutor, look for results. Does your child like the tutor? Does he feel like he understands concepts better? Is he finishing his homework? Are his test scores going up? This won't all happen at once (especially rising test scores). Please don't expect miracles from a tutor who comes for an hour once a week (even if you are paying a lot of money for the tutor). But if your tutor is good, your child should very quickly feel like he understands his schoolwork better.

High school and college students will probably charge between $15-$30 per hour. Private tutors may charge between $30-$60 per hour (fees will depend on your location). Expect higher fees from tutors who work with tutoring companies.

"My child will not do her homework—I always end up doing it for her. Is this OK?"

No!

Parents often feel that their child's homework *must* get done, no matter what they have to do in order to get it done. But, doing your child's homework will only cause more problems. Your child will learn that she does not have to do homework—that you will come to her rescue. She will learn that she does not have to face the consequences her teacher gives to students who do not do homework, and that she can get good grades without putting forth any effort. And, if you do your child's homework, the teacher will almost certainly know (teachers know your child's writing and also what level of work your child is capable of)—and this will make the teacher think less of you and your child. In fact, if you do your child's homework, her teacher will assume you are actually undermining your child's learning rather than helping.

So, what should you do if your child refuses to do homework?

▶ *See if there is a reason why she refuses to do the work.* Many parents struggle and fight with their child, assuming that she has an "attitude problem," only to find out that she is struggling with a fear or learning disability that is preventing her from doing her homework. Talk with your child. Ask her why she does not want to do the work. Is the teacher too harsh with her? Is she afraid of making mistakes? Does she not know how to do the work? Is she afraid of getting a bad grade? Do some work *with* your child. Does she seem to be struggling a great deal? Are certain activities (such as reading or writing) extremely hard for her? If she seems to be struggling too much, talk to the teacher. The teacher may be giving her assignments that are too difficult. Or, your child may have a learning disability. Either way, talk to the teacher and try to find a solution. Most children do not refuse to do work that they feel capable of doing. If there is a problem at school, talk to your child and make an appointment to talk with her teacher.

◗ Do some work with your child. Work together. Read with her (taking turns), talk about the material, work through problems together. Do not do the work for her, but sit with her while she works, encouraging her and helping her. By watching her, you may find that she is struggling exorbitantly with the work. You may find some subjects you want to work on together—or get some extra help with. Or, you may find that she just has trouble concentrating. You may also find that she likes the attention from you and actually enjoys doing the work while you are there (if this is the case, try to plan fun activities with your child, and push her to start doing homework on her own so that the two of you can do fun things together after the homework's done).

◗ Explain to your child that you consider homework (and schoolwork) to be the most important thing that she does. Prod her along. Encourage her to keep going. Praise her for work well done. Encourage her to finish so that she can move on and do something fun (e.g., read, watch TV, play with her friends or siblings). Let her know that,

since homework is the priority, she won't do anything fun until the homework is completed. (Be reasonable about breaks and snacks, however, and give your child a chance to relax a little after school if that seems to improve her attitude towards homework.) Push your child to finish her work (push as hard as you can without nagging her to death). If your child absolutely refuses to finish her work, pack up and move on with your evening. Do the necessities: have dinner, brush teeth, choose clothes for school the next day, go to bed. No playing, no TV, no fun. If your child complains, explain to her that if she is too tired to do homework, she must be too tired for anything else. If she explains that she is not too tired, ask if she got her second wind and would like to take another stab at the homework. If so, great, pull it out and try to get it done. If not, proceed with the evening's necessities and then to bed. Try the same technique the next evening, and the next. Be consistent. No fun unless homework gets done. If she persists for an entire week, give her the weekend to rest and regroup. But if she continues to refuse to do homework the next week, explain that she might have to do work over the weekend to catch up. Then start taking away weekend activities. Again, be consistent and follow through. Your child must learn that there are consequences for not doing work—and it's better to learn this earlier rather than later.

◆ *Don't be afraid to send your child to school without her homework completed.* Doing homework is your child's responsibility, not yours. If she refuses to finish her work then she must accept the consequences of going to school without work. Some teachers take away privileges (such as recess or PE) when students don't turn in their homework. Many children feel a great deal of pressure from their peers to do work and get answers right when they correct homework during class time. You do not, however, want your child's teacher to think that you are the type of parent who does not try to help your child complete her homework. So, when you first send your child to school with unfinished homework, send a note to the teacher (if you do not think that your child will bring it to the teacher, drop it off at the office and they will put it in the teacher's box). Explain that you are struggling with your child to get homework done and you worked with her for some time (say how long) the night before, but that she refused to complete her homework. Explain that you withheld your child's privileges the night before and you hope that the teacher will institute any consequences she usually gives to children who do not do their homework. Explain that you are hoping that your child, with your support, will learn that responsibility pays off. Give the teacher a phone number or e-mail where she can contact you if she wants to talk or make an appointment to meet. But explain that you very much hope that you can work together as a team to help your child understand the importance of doing her work.

All of these steps probably seem much harder than just doing the homework for your child. You can do the work in five minutes—while helping your child could take hours. But the sooner your child learns to take responsibility for her homework, the easier the process will be. And, if you want her to succeed in school, she *must* learn that she has to do her homework herself.

"My child is involved in a lot of extracurricular activities (e.g., sports, drama, dance, etc.) and sometimes we don't have time for homework. Should I write a note to the teacher?"

No. Your child is responsible for completing her homework every night. She may have to work harder or more efficiently on days when she has extracurricular activities, but she is responsible for getting the work done—or cutting back on her extra activities. Remember that school should be your child's first priority.

Some parents may decide not to make school their first priority (if, for instance, they have a child who is particularly talented in sports or drama and aiming for a career in movies or professional athletics). However, if you do decide that school is not your first priority, you will also have to accept that your child may not excel academically. If she does not do homework several nights a week, it may be impossible for her to get As or Bs. It may also be hard for her to keep up with her classmates. And, if her film and or athletic career doesn't pan out, it may be too late to get your child back on the "academic track."

"We had a family emergency and my child did not finish his homework. Should I write a note to the teacher?"

Yes. Again, your child is responsible for completing his homework every night and he should try, to the best of his ability, to do it even if there is something going on in your family. However, if it was absolutely impossible for your child to do his work, do write the teacher a note. Explain briefly what happened (you do not have to go into personal details but write enough so the teacher understands the nature of the family emergency). Also explain what the teacher should expect in the near future. Will your child be making up the work that he did not complete? Will your child be missing a day of school (e.g., for a funeral)? Will it be difficult for you to help your child with homework over the next few days? Might your child be especially emo-

tional over the next few days? Try to give the teacher all the information she needs to work well with your child during and after the emergency.

Helping with Assignments

"Sometimes when my child asks me for help on her homework I have to look in her book for the answer and I feel so stupid."

Never feel embarrassed if you have to look up the answer to a child's question in a book—even if it is your child's textbook. Answers come from books and one of the best skills you can teach your child is that she can find the answers to almost anything in a book (and she can especially find the answers to her science questions in her science book). The best thing about looking in the book for answers is that you get to teach your child *how* to find answers in her book.

One of the greatest advantages that you have—as an adult—is that you can read faster than your child. You probably also know how to navigate a book better than your child. So, when your child asks for help finding the answer to a question in the science book, you will, more than likely, be able to find the answer more quickly than she can. Most adults have learned how to skim and how to use headings to find relevant information. This gives adults an advantage. And, children who know how to do these things well usually won't ask for help—they will find the answer for themselves.

So, when your child asks for help, sit down with her. Look over the chapter she has just read or the information she is learning. Find the answer to her question for yourself (and don't be afraid to tell her to wait a minute while you look). In all of my years of private tutoring, I have frequently found myself flipping through my tutees' textbooks, finding answers (which I often did not know beforehand) and then helping to guide the child to the right answer. I have never had a child criticize me for this practice—in fact, they were usually impressed that I could find an answer that they could not and they often asked how I found it "so fast." (And, of course, I taught them how to efficiently find information for themselves, too!)

What Parents Should Do to Help with Homework

- *Check to make sure your child has completed all assigned work.* If your child is not always honest with you, check his work against his student planner or calendar.
- *Review math problems.* Spot check at least 25 percent of the problems to make sure that your child understands the procedures he has executed and is not making too many careless errors.
- *Proofread essays.* Sit down with your child and go over spelling, punctuation, and grammar mistakes together. Make sure that he learns from the corrections you make.
- *Work together on difficult assignments.* If your child struggles with reading, read with him. If he can't do a math problem, try to work it out together.
- *Be available to study for tests.* Many children need an audience when they study for tests. Some like to be quizzed. Others like to explain concepts and processes to someone. Try to be available as a tester or sounding board.
- *Be available to talk about new and interesting information that your child has learned.* Homework shouldn't be completely tedious. Talk with your child about interesting facts that he is reading about in science and history. Let him show you new math techniques he has mastered or share a funny part of the book he is reading.

From the book *School Sense: How to Help Your Child Succeed in Elementary School* by Tiffani Chin, Ph.D. (Santa Monica Press • 800-784-9553). © 2004 by Tiffani Chin.

"My kids sometimes bring home math, science, or social studies worksheets and ask me for help and I can't figure out how to help them!"

One of the hardest parts about worksheets is that they usually don't come with books attached, which means that parents and tutors lose their most important resource. Sometimes teachers have seen the same types of worksheets so many times, they no longer seem confusing. Other times teachers copy off homework in a hurry and they forget to make sure that the instructions are clear. Either way, some worksheets are almost impossible to complete if your child does not bring home explicit enough directions or enough background knowledge. But there are a number of strategies you can try:

▶ *Read the worksheet carefully.* Sometimes worksheets have enough background information in the directions to help parents guide a child through the worksheet.

▶ *Ask your child to call a classmate.* Another student may be able to provide the "missing piece" of information that makes the assignment doable.

▶ *Ask your child to bring home any book that is related to worksheets he has for homework.* So, if he has science homework, have him bring home the science book, even if the homework is not directly from the book, so that you can help him look up answers in the book.

▶ *Ask your child to bring home any handouts the teacher gives out in class or any notes that he takes during lessons.* Homework often draws directly on what children learned in class. All children should get in the habit of bringing home class notes and handouts for reference and study.

▶ *Keep some reference books at home.* A good encyclopedia set, or even a child's one-volume encyclopedia, can be handy. So can almanacs. Even good dictionaries can sometimes help you out with a science or social studies worksheet that requires knowledge that you don't have. The Internet can also be quite helpful.

However, children should be able to do their homework without their parents doing a great deal of extra research (many children require help but they should not require their own personal reference librarian). If your child continually comes home with worksheets that lack enough information for you to help, and the textbook from school does not help, you must go and talk with the teacher. When you meet with her, politely explain that you have been trying to help your child with her homework but that you are struggling because you don't remember enough about the subject matter to help. Explain that you have had your child bring home his textbook, notes, and handouts but they do not seem to help. The teacher may respond in several ways:

♦ *Be prepared for the teacher to tell you that your child is not doing his share*—that he is not taking down class notes or other information given out in class. If the teacher tells you this, try to work out a plan with the teacher to keep your child on track and make sure to talk with your child about paying attention and taking notes in class.

♦ *Your comments may surprise the teacher.* She may not realize that she is handicapping parents and preventing them from helping by sending home assignments without complete information. Try to explain, in as much detail as possible, what kinds of information would be helpful to you.

"Sometimes my kids bring home math homework and when I try to help them they tell me that I'm doing it wrong and that their teacher insists that they do it her way—but I don't know how to do it that way!"

Although almost every elementary school math problem has only one right answer, there are often many ways to get to that right answer. Almost any parent or tutor can tell a story of helping a child with a common arithmetic problem (e.g., adding or dividing fractions) and having the child explain a bizarre method of solving the problem. Very often the child can only explain a small, vague portion of the technique, but insists that her teacher will only

allow her to solve the problems using this technique. It's one of the most frustrating aspects of helping any child with homework. And it's not at all uncommon.

The problem arises because you and your child's teacher are a "teaching tag-team"—the teacher teaches your child at school (with the techniques that *she* finds most effective) and then she hands off to you to reinforce that teaching at home. But, when your child cannot explain to you what she learned in school, you may find yourself at a loss. If the teacher uses techniques that you do not know and that are not in your child's textbook, you may find yourself at a double loss. How can you teach something that you don't know? You can't. But you don't have to throw up your hands either.

♦ *Ask your child if she has a book that shows the technique or any notes or examples from class.* If she does, you may be able to figure out the technique the teacher used. (Sample problems are key—many teachers have students write out samples in their notes.)

♦ *Ask your child to show you everything she does remember*—again, you may be able to figure out what's going on by combining what your child shows you and the technique you remember for doing that kind of problem.

If you cannot get any good information from your child but you do know how to do the math problem with some technique of your own (please make sure that your technique is correct!) then:

▶ *Explain to your child that you don't really understand the technique she is trying to show you, but that you know a different way to do the problem.* Tell your child that you are going to show her your way, just to see if it is easier. (There are many ways to solve math problems—some ways work for some people and some ways work for other people. Often when kids can't remember a technique they learned in school, they don't understand that method very well. In this case, your way may be easier for her.)

▶ *If your child does think that your way is better, then teach your child your method.* Then write a note to the teacher explaining that you did not understand the technique that your child learned in school and your child did not seem to fully understand it either. Explain that you taught your child the method that you learned in school and you hope that that is OK with the teacher. Add that if the teacher really wants your child to learn her approach, you would appreciate it if she would send home a book or worksheet explaining that approach. Write out a demonstration of your technique so that the teacher will understand your approach. As long as your child can do the problems correctly, most teachers will allow her to use whatever

technique works for her.

▶ *If your child looks at your technique and insists that the technique that she learned in school is easier, send a note to the teacher.* Explain that you did not learn the technique that she taught the children and your child could not explain it sufficiently. Explain that you tried to show your child another technique but that your child preferred the one that she learned in school. Ask the teacher to work with your child on the concept and to please send home a book or worksheet explaining the technique that she is teaching so that you can help your child in the future.

If you have this problem frequently, talk with the teacher. Explain to the teacher that you really want to help your child but are unfamiliar with the math techniques she is using. Ask if there is a book that you can borrow or photocopy, or worksheets that she can send home to teach you. Most teachers should be happy to help you help your child.

"My child often insists that she was taught to do math problems a certain way, but her answers are all wrong. What's going on?"

Sometimes teachers teach math techniques wrong. More often, children misinterpret lessons but then adamantly insist that they're right. If your child is following a technique that you don't understand, watch her work.

1. Try to see if she's making careless mistakes. She may be using a viable technique but miscalculating somewhere.

2. Check the textbook. Does her method seem similar to the one in the textbook? If it does, check to see if she is following the textbook method but just making some kind of mistake.

If your child is just miscalculating, work with her and encourage her to work more carefully.

If, however, she does not seem to be using a correct technique, try one of the following solutions:

♦ *Teach her the method in the textbook.* Although children often get attached to the lessons they learned (or think they learned!) in class, they may be persuaded by the black-and-white proof of the textbook to concede to learn "another" method.

♦ *Teach her a method that you know.* See the answer to the previous question for how to teach a child a new method.

♦ *Write a note to the teacher.* If you do not have a textbook, do not know another way to do the problems, or simply cannot convince your child that she is wrong, stop your child from working on the assignment (there's no point in having her practice problems incorrectly) and write a note to the teacher explaining that your child is unclear on how to do the problems. Explain that you could see that she was doing the work incorrectly, but that you were unable to teach her another method. Explain that you would appreciate it if the teacher could look at your child's work and re-explain the process. You might also ask for the teacher to write out (or photocopy) an explanation of how to do the problems for you to look over at home. Read the letter to your child so she understands why you are not having her finish her homework and so she knows why she is supposed to give the teacher the note (you don't want your child to think that you are "telling on her"). (Don't give your child the impression that you are blaming the teacher. Make sure she understands that you are just asking for extra help.)

No matter which route you choose, follow up. Make sure that your child can do the problems tomorrow. And, continue to monitor her work to make sure that she doesn't backslide into the incorrect method.

"The books that my child has to read for homework are too hard for him and I don't know how to help!"

The first thing you need to do is talk to your child's teacher. Your child may need extra help at school or he may be placed in a class or a reading group that is too difficult for him. Talk to your child's teacher as soon as possible. But there are also some techniques that you can use to help your child make it through difficult reading material (many of these techniques will also improve his comprehension):

◆ *Read with your child.* No child is too old to read with an adult. By listening to your child read, you can coach him through difficult words and passages. By listening to you read, your child can enjoy the story without struggling over words and pronunciation. A good technique is to take turns—have your child read one page, you read the next, and so on. I have even read aloud with middle school students. A few years ago, I was depressed to see that one of my tutees was reading *Watership Down*, a book I had hated as a child. But, as we read together, I found that I actually enjoyed the story. Even more importantly, my student proudly told me that he was the only student in the class who thought the book was interesting!

◆ *Talk with your child about what he is reading.*

- This is especially easy when you read together. You can talk about the material as you read it— explaining things he doesn't understand, predicting what might happen on the next page, speculating on why characters act as they do, etc.
- When you do not read together, try to spend some time skimming the material that your child has been assigned to read. Then you can talk about it later to make sure he understands what happened in the story.
- If you cannot read with your child, still try to talk with him about what is going on in the story. Try to make sure that he understands. If it seems like he's confused (or just keeps repeating one part of the plot that does make sense to him) then you need to sit down together and go over the story again.

◆ *Pull out vocabulary words that your child doesn't know.* Look them up and define them together (if there are a lot of words, don't make him look up all of them, tell him some so that it does not become too tedious). Make a word list or vocabulary cards that you can work on for a few minutes a day. This will improve his reading. And don't wait for your child to tell you that he does not understand a word. Just because a child can read a word, does not mean that he understands it. Choose words from the text and ask your child if he knows what they mean. If he doesn't, put them on the list.

◆ *Go to the bookstore or library and get some books that are at your child's level for him to read in his free time.* He will only improve his reading skills if he reads a lot—and books that are too hard will not encourage him to read. Make sure that he sees the good side of reading by reading books at the right level and that contain information or stories that he is interested in.

"The answers to my child's math assignments are in the back of the book. She says that it's OK for her to look. I call this cheating. Who is right?"

There are two legitimate reasons for looking at answers in the back of the book:

1. To check work. Math books put answers in the back of the book (usually only for the odd problems) precisely so that children can check their work and make sure that they are figuring problems out correctly. So, if your child is just checking her work, she should be allowed to look in the back of the book.

2. To try to learn how to do a problem. Sometimes children can figure out how to do difficult problems by working backwards from the answer. If your child looks in the back of the book occasionally in order to learn a process, that's fine.

However, no teachers allow children to simply copy answers from the back of the book. In fact, most teachers make a point to assign odd *and* even problems for homework explicitly so that children cannot copy all of the answers. Teachers also make children "show their work" (this means that they have to write out the problem and the work that they do to find the answer) so that they cannot simply copy answers. If your child is copying answers directly from the back of the book, she is cheating.

"My child says it is OK for him to write 'I don't know' or put a question mark next to problems he doesn't know how to do. Is this OK? What if he does it for half of the problems on his homework?"

Some teachers allow students to write "I don't know" next to problems they don't understand. Thus, your child's grade isn't hurt if he leaves a problem or two that he didn't understand undone. However, children should be forced to think and challenge themselves. If your child writes "I don't know" every time he finds a problem difficult, he is taking the easy way out and cheating himself of the learning process. Encourage your child to do all of his problems. If he gets really frustrated with a problem, work on it with him—try to sort through it together. If, after all of this work, he still cannot find the answer, allow him to write, "I don't know." But follow up. The teacher will probably walk the students through the problem in class the next day. If she doesn't, your child should specifically ask for help on the problem that he could not do. Either way, your child should be able to explain the answer to you tomorrow night.

Checking and Correcting Homework

"When my child writes an essay or report, am I supposed to correct her spelling and punctuation or is this cheating?"

Unless the teacher explicitly tells children not to get help (and, if this is the case, she will probably require students to complete the essay in class), you can help your child fix spelling, punctuation, and grammatical mistakes. In fact, you should. However, do not simply act as your child's editor. When you correct your child's written work, you must work together. You should also make sure that your child does her own proofreading before you take over. You don't want to encourage her to be sloppy because, "My dad will take care of it." So, when your child finishes her report, follow these steps:

1. Ask her if she proofread for spelling, punctuation, and grammar mistakes. If she has not, have her do it, including running spell-check if she used the computer to type the essay.

2. Take a quick look at the paper. If it contains obvious mistakes that you know your child should have caught (e.g., forgetting to put periods at the ends of sentences, misspelling her teacher's name), give it back to her and tell her to proofread it more carefully.

3. Sit down with your child to look over the paper together. Point out mistakes as you read. Have a dictionary nearby to look up words (although, if there are a lot of spelling mistakes, don't look up words you know—it will take too long—just tell her the correct spelling). Have your child correct misspellings (do not write for her!). Talk about changes in phrasing or grammar. Discuss the punctuation she uses incorrectly before you have her fix it.

4. Hold her responsible for remembering grammar and punctuation problems you have discussed in the past. The main reason for going over the work together is so that she can learn and improve her writing skills. Make sure she is not just relying on you to do her work for her.

5. Don't rewrite the essay for your child. It should sound like her work. Fix spelling and punctuation mistakes. Try to eliminate run-on sentences and sentence fragments (make sure to explain why she is fixing these mistakes), but don't try to teach your second-grader how to use semi-colons if she is still learning how to use commas and periods. If you are unsure of how sophisticated your child's writing should be, when you go to your parent-teacher conference ask to see samples of "good" and "bad" writing from children in your child's class. The teacher should be able to point out the skills that children in your child's grade should know. She may even be able to show you her grading rubric (or grading standards) so you can judge your child's writing yourself. For more details, look up your state's grade-specific writing standards (these will probably be on the Internet or you can ask the teacher if she has a copy). These standards will show you how well your state expects children to write at different grade levels. Although you might have higher expectations for your own child's performance (particularly if she is a very advanced writer), the standards will at least give you an idea of how hard you should push her to master difficult grammatical rules and concepts.

"Should I check my child's math homework and make him correct items that are wrong? Is that cheating?"

Do check your child's math homework, but do not correct problems for him. Mark the problems that are wrong and have him rework them. Don't feel obligated to check every single problem in his homework, just check enough problems so that you can tell if he understands the work and is working carefully (a child who makes too many careless errors is doomed to do poorly on tests—it's a habit he needs to break).

Ideally, you should peek over your child's shoulder *while* he's working to make sure he's doing the work correctly as he works. Nothing is more frustrating to a child than learning that the work that he has just spent an hour

on is completely incorrect. Try to catch problems before he has practiced an incorrect technique too many times.

Preparing for Tests

"What's the best way for my child to study for tests? How can I help?"

The very best preparation for tests is to do all of the work leading up to the test (e.g., assigned reading and homework assignments) carefully and thoroughly as it is assigned. Although there are many studying strategies that children can implement, the very best preparation for a test is actually learning the material. And, most elementary school tests are based on material that children have learned in class and practiced in homework. So, encourage your child to pay attention in class, do homework, and do assigned reading— this will dramatically cut down on the time she has to spend studying the night before a test.

Especially encourage your child to read carefully. Many children learn at a very early age that they do not need to read (either literature, or assignments from science and social studies books) in order to complete worksheets or answer review questions. They just skim assigned pages looking for answers in order to complete classwork and homework more quickly. Although this strategy is expeditious when it comes to completing assignments, it can prevent children from learning the material. Encourage your child to do assigned reading and occasionally quiz her (the way a test might!) to make sure that she understands what she is reading.

"My child has a test tomorrow. What's the best way for her to prepare?"

If your child has been doing her work and studying all along, she shouldn't have to do too much extra on the night before a test. But there are a number of review strategies that she can work on to make sure that she understands important concepts and has memorized key facts. The following are a number of suggestions for possible review techniques. Most children do not have to use all of these techniques. Help your child find the strategies that work best for her.

◆ *Do chapter reviews and chapter tests in the textbook.* Most textbooks have sets of questions at the end of each chapter (sometimes even at the end of each chapter section). Your child should be able to answer all of these questions.

◆ *Do practice problems.* Children often need to have someone else (usually an adult) make practice problems for them. You can quiz your child orally or write down a set of problems for

her to work through (you probably have to write problems for math).

◆ *Make vocabulary lists or flashcards and study from them.* English, science, social studies, and even math tests, often test vocabulary. In your child's textbook, vocabulary words may be in bold or listed in the chapter review. Or, the teacher may have handed out a list of key vocabulary words. Making a word list or flashcards is a crucial studying step—many children learn through writing, so don't make the flashcards for her.

◆ *Write out math facts, formulas, important dates, and important facts.* Writing out facts can often help children memorize them. I often have children write out multiplication facts 50 times just to imprint them in their brains.

◆ *Write practice essays.* If your child can write a practice essay, she probably knows the information she needs to know to write a real essay.

◆ *Explain information to a parent, sibling, friend, the family pet, or stuffed animals.* Many children learn through talking and explaining. Let your child learn difficult concepts (such as how chemical reactions occur) or historical processes (such as the factors that contributed to the Civil War) by explaining them to someone else.

◆ *Reread important chapters and passages.* Simply refreshing her memory by rereading can help a child prepare for a test.

◆ *Go over assignments, homework, classwork, and quizzes.* Most teachers base tests on work that children have already done. If your child reviews the work that she has done, she will likely review many of the topics that the teacher considers important. Also, previous tests will tell you and your child something about future tests. Go over old tests. Does the teacher emphasize vocabulary? Names? Dates? Formulas? Try to understand her priorities and use those priorities to set a study-agenda.

"My children have a lot of material that they need to memorize for tests and I cannot seem to help."

There are dozens of different techniques for memorizing materials. As much as some children hate memorization, it is a fact of life for many school children. And it's something that many require help with. How can you help your child memorize material more easily?

◆ *Work on the timing.* Although some children can sit down with information for an hour or so and memorize a great deal of material, most children memorize better in small bites. Almost any material can be memorized over a period of time in which you spend 10 minutes a day. Experiment with different amounts of time at a sitting and see what works best for your child.

◆ *Start early.* There are limits to how much a person can memorize in a night. Begin memorizing material well before the test.

◆ *Find a format that feels comfortable for your child.* Many children like to use flashcards. Others prefer to work from a list. Others like to be surrounded by the material that they need to memorize (e.g., they like to put post-it notes on the bathroom mirror and leave lists on their nightstand).

There are also many memorization techniques that you can try:

◆ *Speak and repeat.* People need to hear things many times before they remember them. Children who learn through listening and/or speaking often have a lot of success repeating facts over and over out loud.

◆ *Write.* Many people learn better when they write information. Have your child write out facts repeatedly. However, don't have him write mindlessly. He must think and pay attention as he writes in order for the writing to impact his memory (explain that he is not writing as punishment but rather to help him remember).

◆ *Touch.* Some children learn best through their sense of touch. Have your child write facts with his finger on sandpaper or in the palm of his hand.

◆ *Quiz.* Many children need to be pushed to recall facts. Try quizzing your child on the facts he needs to know. You can even create a "Jeopardy!"-like game of it.

◆ *Create rhymes, songs, and funny facts.* It doesn't matter how silly your memorization techniques are—as long as they work. For instance, a child learning the periodic table (for basic chemistry) might remember that the abbreviation for helium is HE because when he sucks helium from a balloon it makes him laugh, "He he!" When I am drawing a graph, I remember that the x-axis is the horizontal axis because the horizontal axis looks like the ground and an "X marks the spot" on the ground. Encourage your child to come up with tricks to help him remember facts that are particularly hard for him. Make a game of it!

"My child learns what she needs to for tests but doesn't seem to retain what she learns."

Many students—young and old— "cram" for tests. They sit down the night before and desperately try to memorize all the material they need to know for a test. Although this technique has gotten many students through exams, it has been shown to be a poor method for long-term learning. Although people often think of cramming as something that high school and college students do, many young children do it too—and they often do it with the help of their parents. Many, many parents have tight schedules and, like their children, put off studying until the last moment.

Then, the night before a test, they find themselves desperately quizzing their children to help them memorize what they need to know. Not only is this stressful and detrimental to long-term learning, but it teaches kids that cramming is the right way to study for a test.

So, how can you prevent cramming and help your child retain what he learns?

◆ *Teach your child to master material as it is assigned.* When he has to answer questions at the end of a history chapter, do not encourage him to just skim the chapter for the answers to the question. While this technique *will* get the assignment finished faster, it puts off the task of actually reading and understanding the chapter. Make sure your child does assigned reading (and ideally discusses what he read with you, a friend, or a sibling) when it is assigned. Many students find that if they do this, they eliminate a great deal of studying or cramming time.

◆ *Take a long-term approach to studying for tests.* Very few tests come as surprises. With the exception of pop quizzes (which teachers usually only assign to test whether children did their reading homework), children know about tests at least several days in advance. Ask your child to write down the dates of upcoming tests and include studying for that test as part of each night's homework until the day of the test. If your child has a spelling test every Friday, study the spelling words a little each night (your child can either choose to learn a few every night or go over all of them each night—depending on which style works best for your child). If your child has a history test coming up, make sure he begins the studying he needs to do (whether it be outlining, drawing, talking with you about the material, re-reading the chapter, doing the chapter review, or reviewing vocabulary) as soon as he knows that a test is coming up (and, if he has been mastering the material as they have been covering the chapter, much of this studying work will be easy).

▶ *Help your child apply what he is learning to real life.* Children retain what they learn better when they care about what they learn. Good teachers try to make obvious the reasons why children should care about what they are learning. But sometimes teachers fall short of this goal. Other times, the teacher's reasons will not be salient for your particular child. (For instance, your child's teacher may always relate math to science, which is great for children who want to become engineers. But if your child is more interested in cooking, try to integrate his math lessons into the work you do in the kitchen.) Talk with your child about what he is learning and how the material relates to his interests and *his* life (e.g., how an astronomy lesson relates to his favorite cartoon, which takes place on Mars, or how learning new

vocabulary words will help him to beat his sister in Scrabble).

"My child seems to be able to memorize material, but she does not seem to understand it very well—how can I help her really learn the material?"

Many people have trouble really understanding material after just reading a book or completing a worksheet. Sometimes children (and their parents) have to go an extra step to make sure that they actually learn the material they are working on. You can go that extra mile in several ways—and you'll probably find that some techniques work better for your child than others.

▶ *Discuss the material and try to apply it to other, different scenarios.* For instance, if you are studying science, see if your child can apply the new concepts to processes beyond the assignment. If she is studying the different states of matter (e.g., water (liquid) can be converted to ice (solid) or steam (gas)), have her tell you the state of objects around your house and how they might change from state to state (e.g., What is the couch? Her juice? The air?). If you are studying a concept in history, the American Revolution for instance, have your child explain different points of view. What did the Americans want? What did the British want? Whose side would your child have been on? Who was being unreasonable and why? Even if you don't know the material, you can probably learn enough to discuss it with your child by skimming the chapter yourself.

♦ *Have your child explain the material to you.* Explaining is one of the best ways to really learn something. Have your child explain the concepts to you. If you don't understand (or think that she is wrong) then go over the materials together. Read it together (you read part, have your child read part), talk about it, make sure the pictures, illustrations, and diagrams in the book make sense to her.

♦ *Encourage your child to try out several different learning techniques.* Some people like to talk to themselves. Others like to draw pictures or charts to clarify concepts. Still others outline or write summaries in order to understand and remember. Some people actually like to teach—a friend of mine who was a pre-med student in college used to set up a white board and explain biology concepts to an audience of stuffed animals. Experiment with different techniques and see which ones seem to resonate best with your child (and remember—these techniques may not be the techniques that work best for you!).

"My child gets very nervous before tests. Is there anything I can do to ease his test anxiety?"

Being well-prepared for a test is the best cure for anxiety. Help your child develop a study schedule so he studies a little every night (and keeps up with assigned classwork and homework). Then, by the time the test comes around, he should know the material very well and not have to be nervous about the test. Cramming often increases children's sense of panic because by the time they start studying and realize how little they know, it's too late to master the material—they are flying by the seat of their pants and they know it. You can also help your child calm his anxiety by helping him to stay organized, have his materials ready for school before he goes to bed, and make sure he gets up early enough so that he does not have to rush in the morning (especially on test days).

As a parent, you should be careful about how you express your expectations for your child's test performance. Make sure your child understands that you think he's smart. Also make sure he knows that no grade—on any test—will determine his entire future or indicate how intelligent he is. Help him work hard to prepare for tests and then remind him of how much effort he has put in. Stress the fact that, even if he does not do as well as he would like to on one test, you will help him work on new study strategies so he does better on the next test.

There are several tips that you

can give your child in preparation for tests:

♦ *Think positively.* Children often get bogged down in negative thoughts, which hurt their confidence and their test performance. Remind your child how well he did when you quizzed him and how well he understands the material. Encourage him to think positively and try to nip negative comments in the bud.

♦ *Take a deep breath and relax as the tests are passed out.* Have him practice clearing his head of other thoughts (especially negative thoughts) as the test is passed out. Work with him on taking a moment to become relaxed and calm.

♦ *Read directions carefully.* Many children find tests confusing because they expect to understand exactly what to do without even reading the directions. Make sure your child takes the time to read the directions. Explain that it is okay to ask the teacher for clarification if he does not understand the directions on a test.

♦ *Take tests one question at a time (and don't get bogged down on really hard questions).* Many children stumble across one very difficult question on a test and either waste all of their time on that question or get so frazzled that they cannot complete other, easier questions. Make sure your child understands that missing a few questions on a test is normal, that some questions will probably seem hard, and that he should not allow one or two hard questions to break his concentration.

If your child continues to struggle with test anxiety, you can try a few other strategies:

♦ *Make practice tests part of your studying routine.* Help your child to write practice tests (ask the teacher for samples if you are not sure what her tests look like) and have your child take practice tests for several nights before a test. That way he will get used to the format of the test and having to recall information.

♦ *Help your child practice working under time constraints.* Many children get freaked out during tests because they have to complete their work in a short amount of time. Use a kitchen timer and give your child set amounts of time in which to complete homework assignments or practice tests. At first, give him ample time—just to let him get used to doing work with a ticking clock nearby. Then shorten the time intervals so they challenge him a bit more (don't make it impossible—that will only increase his anxiety—but give him time limits so he will have to pace himself a little). If he has trouble finishing, help him to identify questions that he knows the answers to, so he does them before the more challenging problems. If your child is daydreaming, help him to stay focused by reminding him that he has to finish the work in a set amount of time.

● *Practice with non-school tests and quizzes.* Have your child take quizzes from magazines, books, and on the Internet. Make up little quizzes for him about television shows or hobbies that he's particularly interested in. Through practice, your child will learn that tests and quizzes are a normal part of life—and not something he should get too anxious about.

● *Teach your child some test-taking skills.* There are dozens of books that teach test-taking skills. Most are geared toward standardized tests such as the SAT and have very useful tips that children and adults can use when taking tests (e.g., the best ways to eliminate answer-choices and make educated guesses). Read some test preparation books and then teach your child the tips and tricks that seem most applicable to him. The tips may help him increase his test scores as well as feel more confident about his ability to approach a test smartly.

If your child's anxiety persists despite all of the above suggestions, you may want to consider professional help. You have three options:

● *Test preparation tutors.* A tutor who specializes in test preparation may be able to teach your child specific test-taking strategies that will be particularly good for him. Most tutoring agencies have tutors who specialize in test preparation.

● *Test preparation classes.* Not only

will your child learn test-taking tips, but he will also learn that other children struggle with tests as well. Most major test preparation companies (such as Princeton Review and Kaplan) have courses for children. Your local community college or recreation department may also have test preparation courses for kids.

● *A therapist or counselor.* If your child is suffering from severe anxiety, his feelings may stem from more than just his fear of tests. It may be worth it for him to talk with a therapist and try to get to the roots of his anxiety. A therapist may also be able to suggest some relaxation tips that will help your child deal with test-induced stress.

Extra Credit

"What is extra credit work?"

Extra credit work is usually optional work (or an optional portion of an assignment) that children can do to get extra points. Some teachers figure out grades on a point system and assign a certain amount of points to each extra credit assignment so that a child can raise his grade. Other teachers just give students' grades a little boost if they do extra credit. But, no matter how it's graded, extra credit is always optional.

If your child is very far behind in class (but is motivated to improve his grade) you and he might ask his teacher if there are any assignments that he can do for extra credit. Even teachers who do not regularly assign extra credit might allow a child who has "turned around" (and become more motivated) to do extra work or an extra report in order to raise his grade before the final report card.

"My child's teacher often assigns extra credit homework or problems. Should I make my child do the extra credit?"

Not unless she really needs to boost her grade. As a general rule, optional work should be optional. And, ideally, every child will find some optional assignments that she really wants to do. However, not all extra credit assignments will appeal to everyone—and since they are extra credit they are probably not central to the curriculum. You should encourage your child to do extra credit, especially if the assignment is something that aligns with her interests or talents (e.g., if your child is a talented artist and there is an extra-credit assignment to draw an ocean mammal the class is studying or if your child wants to become a chemist and the school is hosting an optional science fair). And, it's always good to discuss optional or extra credit work with your child—she might not realize how fun it could be until you talk about it. However, because extra credit is optional, children should be able to make their own decisions about whether or not to participate.

The exception is if your child has a very poor grade in the subject in which the teacher offers extra credit. In that case, your child should not view extra credit work as optional but rather as something that she *must* do in order to raise her grade to an acceptable level. Teachers often give extra credit precisely in order to give children who have fallen behind a chance to catch up. Doing extra credit shows that a child who fell behind (for whatever reason) is willing to try and work hard. Doing extra credit shows that your child is not "lazy." Explain to her that the extra credit is required *for her* because of her low grade and praise her for doing extra work to raise her grade.

CHAPTER 4

Helping with Reports and Projects

HELPING WITH CHILDREN'S PROJECTS AND REPORTS CAN BE PARENTS' HARDEST SCHOOL-work. Many parents confess that they end up doing most of their children's projects for them—just to survive. Even when children do most of the work themselves, parents often feel overwhelmed by how much effort it takes to make sure children don't leave projects to the last minute, coordinate all of the partners in their child's "work groups," gather resources and materials, and find out how to format various aspects of the project (e.g., the bibliography, the display). As you and your child embark on reports and projects it will help to keep three principles in mind:

The point of all projects and reports is to learn.

Teachers assign reports and projects to help children experience science, history, literature, and other subjects in in-depth, tangible ways. Science projects help children understand the process of assessing scientific evidence. Research allows children to "discover" new information. Book reports teach children how to critique literature. Doing reports teaches children research, writing, and organizational skills. Long-term projects help children learn to budget time. Working in groups helps children learn how to delegate work and cooperate. When you work with your child on projects, focus on making sure she *learns* from the experience. Your child should be able to discuss her subject matter in her own words. She should be able to execute and understand her own science project. Projects and reports are only pointless torture when your child doesn't learn from them.

Your child's project should represent your *child's* work, not yours.

Make sure your child turns in projects and reports that reflect her interests, knowledge, and skills. When you go to Open House at your child's school, you will see projects that no child could have possibly made on his own. Many parents obsess over making their child's projects perfect—even if it means that *the parents* do most of the work. If this is your impulse, resist it! Children's projects should demonstrate what children know, what they can do, and what they learned through the process of writing the report or putting the project together. Teachers know what children are capable of (they see your child's schoolwork every day) and are rarely fooled when parents do their children's work. In fact, teachers often give extra credit to students who obviously do their own work, even if their products are less polished than those of their classmates. Your child's project should also represent his vision. If your child has his heart set on a certain type of display, let him try it (even if you suspect that it won't work). Give him a chance to try his idea and learn from his mistakes; just encourage him to start early enough to have time for "Plan B" (in case he fails utterly). In the end, he may surprise you.

Your child's projects are your *child's* responsibility.

As an adult, you should do what you can to facilitate your child's work (e.g., drive her to the library, wield the x-acto knife so she doesn't cut herself, check her spelling). But, it's your child's responsibility to listen to her teacher when she explains the project, to stick to her deadlines, and to execute the project. It is your job to help, but it is not your job to make the project happen. If your child does not do "A" work, she does not deserve to receive an "A" on her project just because her parents stayed up all night finishing it for her. The only way your child will learn to be responsible for her own achievement and proud of her work is for her to do the work and earn her grades herself.

The first part of this chapter addresses research reports in general. Sections on book reports and science projects follow. As you read the last two sections, remember that many of the tips for research reports apply. Although most teachers have specific rules for how reports and projects should be done (and you should consult with your child's teacher whenever your child is unclear about the requirements for an assignment), this chapter provides general guidelines that will make writing reports and doing projects a better (and less frustrating) learning experience for everyone in your family.

Research Reports

"My child often has to do research reports but I'm not sure what they should contain or how they should be organized."

One of the most common problems with reports and projects is that while teachers expect projects to be done at home, they do not always convey to parents what they should look like. But teachers do usually give *their students* information about how reports and projects should be done. So, if your child comes home saying that he has to do a report or project, ask him if his teacher gave out an explanatory assignment sheet. If not, ask if the teacher had him write down requirements for the project. If your child denies getting instructions, *talk to the teacher.* She should not only be able to provide you with explicit instructions, but she should also be able to tell you if she explained the requirements to the class. If she did, you need to have a chat with your child and explain to him that he *must* take notes when teachers explain assignments. Teaching your child to write down assignment requirements will not only make *your* life easier but will teach him a crucial skill that he will need in high school and college.

When teachers send home directions about reports and projects (or give students instructions to write down), they ideally include the following (if you do not receive all of this information—either have your child ask the teacher or ask the teacher yourself):

▶ *What is the assignment—exactly?* If your child comes home with some nebulous notion of having to write a report, he might not have gotten all the facts. You do not want to begin working until you know exactly what the assignment is—slightly different prompts can make for very different reports. For instance, children often write reports about famous people (e.g., presidents, famous African-Americans, or scientists). Sometimes teachers want reports to be biographies—chronicling a person's life. Other times teachers want students to make an argument (e.g., why the president they chose for the report was a great president). Sometimes teachers want students to discuss just one aspect of a subject's life (e.g., a president's major accomplishment or how a scientist overcame adversity). Each of these prompts will lead to a drastically different essay and writing the wrong report can result in a low grade. Help guide your child to write to the assigned prompt.

◗ **What should be included in the report?** Teachers who assign reports often have key ideas that they want covered. For a biography, for example, a teacher may want five sections: early life, education, challenges, accomplishments, and legacy. For a report on a state or country a teacher might also want five sections: history, resources, culture, economy, and future. For a science project, most teachers want students to cover all of the steps of the scientific method (question, hypothesis, procedure, results, conclusion) and provide background information about the subject and any scientific principles

tested in the experiment (e.g., if your child tries to test whether ants like sugary or fatty foods better, he should also include background information about the diets of ants). Your child's teacher will likely grade his report on how well it covers all required topics.

◗ **How long should the report be? How should it be formatted (printed, cursive, typed, single-spaced, double-spaced, etc.)?** Some teachers balk at this question. They may say that they don't care about length—they just want the report to contain all of the relevant information without extra wordiness. If you get an answer like this, ask again, explaining that you really don't have any idea what children of this age are capable of and would appreciate a page range—is it supposed to be a 1-2 page report or a 5-10 page report? Most teachers will give you a range.

◗ **Besides information, what should the report include?** Many teachers like children to include pictures or drawings. Sometimes they require maps, models, or other visual displays. Science projects often require a backboard displaying information.

◗ **What are the minimum requirements for a passing project?** What "extras" are required to get an A? Some teachers require students to go above and beyond for an A. They may want students to bring in props to use during their oral reports or ask them to wear costumes. Pictures may be *optional* for a passing grade but required for an A (this is why you should be skeptical when your child tells you about "optional" parts of assignments). Some teachers have grading rubrics that they follow. (If your child's teacher has a rubric, ask for a copy, explaining that you want to make sure that your child is doing the best work possible.)

▶ *Is there an oral component of the report?* If your child must present his report to the class, make sure that he practices it. He should be able to fluently pronounce all the words and read it slowly and articulately. Have him practice reading the report while holding it in front of his chest so that the report does not block his face (and his voice). If your child is shy and doesn't want to practice in front of you, let him practice in front of a mirror, the family dog, or a sibling. But, once he is more comfortable, encourage him to use you as an audience. You are probably better equipped than the dog to correct his pronunciation of unfamiliar words and names. However, if your child simply refuses to perform for you, ask if he will sit down and quietly read the report to you (no performance anxiety) so that you can make sure he knows all of the words.

▶ *How many sources (e.g., books, magazines, encyclopedias, the Internet) must your child consult and what kinds of sources are acceptable?* Teachers often require students to use three (or four or five) different sources (e.g., a book, an encyclopedia, and a Web site).

▶ *Does the teacher want the bibliography in a particular format?* Ask to see a sample.

"What is a bibliography? How do you make one?"

A bibliography goes at the end of the report and lists all of the books, articles, and Web sites that the author used to write the report. Different disciplines, publishers, and teachers use different formats for bibliographies but they all contain the author, title, date, publisher, and place of publication of each reference. Each type of reference (e.g., book, encyclopedia, newspaper, Web site) has its own bibliographic format. Your child's teacher may ask students to format bibliographies in a particular way (which she will probably demonstrate). But the following formats follow Modern Language Association (MLA) guidelines and are commonly used in elementary schools. (Note that the first line of each entry is not indented but subsequent lines are. On your computer this may be called a "hanging indent." Also note that underlining and italicizing perform the same function.)

For a book:

Author (last name, first name). <u>Title (underlined)</u>. Publication place: Publisher, publication date.

For example:
Dahl, Roald. <u>Charlie and the Chocolate Factory</u>. New York: Random House, 1974.

For an encyclopedia entry:

Author (last name, first name; encyclopedia entries are usually followed by the author's name in small type—if no author is listed begin the reference with the title). "Title of the Entry (in quotes)." <u>Name of the encyclopedia</u>. Edition date.

For example:
Kent, James. "Elephants." <u>World Book Encyclopedia</u>. 1999 ed.

For a magazine or newspaper article:

Author (last name, first name). "Title of the Article (in quotes)." <u>Name of magazine</u> (underlined). Date of issue: Pages.

For example:
Walters, Elaine. "Understanding the Science of Sports." <u>Sports Illustrated for Kids</u>, June 1998: 27-28.

For a Web site:

Author (Last name, first name; author may be listed at the top or bottom of the article—if no author is listed, begin the reference with the title). "Title of the Web page (in quotes)." Date Web site posted or revised. Name of organization/institution affiliated with the Web site. Date you accessed Web site. <Complete Web site address (in angled brackets)>

For example:
Long, Julia. "The Mysteries of Hawaii's Active and Dormant Volcanoes." 11 Feb. 2001. Science Hawaii. 22 Jun. 2002. <http://www.scihawaii.com/volcanos/mysteries>

"The reference materials I have are too hard for my child to understand. What do we do?"

Before you dive into adult-level materials, look for kid-level materials. There are many kid-level references available. For instance:

♦ *Encyclopedias* written for kids. These usually have simpler language than "adult" encyclopedias and include a lot of pictures.

♦ *Almanacs* designed for kids. These have many tidbits of information—from short biographies and histories of nations to statistics and maps.

♦ *Short, easy to read non-fiction books and biographies* that are written explicitly for children. Some of these books are very easy to read (and include a lot of pictures) while others are chapter books, geared more towards pre-adolescents and teens.

Look for children's reference materials:
♦ *At the public library*—help your child look for resources in the *children's section*. Going to the library and using reference materials is a great skill to teach your child. (See the tip box on

the Dewey Decimal System in the next chapter for help on finding books on your child's report topic.)

♦ *At your child's school library.* Unfortunately, teachers often assign similar reports to all of their students at the same time, so it might be hard to find the books you need.

♦ *In the children's section of your local bookstore.* You will likely find a reference section for children and possibly a section devoted entirely to biographies written for children. If your town lacks a good bookstore, check out online booksellers (e.g., www.amazon.com and www.barnesandnoble.com), which often have customer reviews to help you choose. Some online stores sell used books at cheaper prices (see www.bibliofind.com and www.alibris.com).

♦ *On the Internet*—either from home or from computers at the local library. Some search engines such as www.yooligans.com, look explicitly for children's sites. You can also try general search engines (such as www.google.com, www.yahoo.com, www.metacrawler.com). Enter the report topic along with the word "children," which will often bring up kid-friendly Web sites. You can also find online encyclopedias and almanacs designed for kids on the Web (e.g., www.factmonster.com).

"What if I don't have time to find materials designed for children?"

It is possible to help a child write a report using materials that are too difficult for her to read on her own. You just have to help her decode the information. When children write reports using resources that are too hard for them, they often end up copying their sources word-for-word. If you tell them not to copy, they change only a few insignificant words. (For example, they would change the previous sentence to, "So when you tell them not to copy they change a couple of not very important words.") By changing a few words, they are not copying directly, but they are still committing plagiarism (see question on plagiarism later in this section).

How can you make sure your child does not plagiarize and learns good research skills? Sit down with the information (which, hopefully, is not too long—if you are using a long book, skim it and find groups of pages that are applicable to your child's report topic). Then, follow the one-sentence-per-paragraph note-taking rule (see tip box for a demonstration of how to apply this rule). The one-sentence-per-paragraph note-taking rule is a great way to break down dense information to make it palatable for a child's report. Here's the one-sentence-per-paragraph note-taking process:

♦ *Read the first paragraph of your source material* (article, encyclopedia entry, book section) together. Let your child read what she can. Help her with

153

words that she doesn't know and explain concepts that she doesn't understand (even if you have to look up some of the concepts yourself, explain them as simply as possible).

▶ **Talk about the information,** what it means, and how it relates to your child's report. For instance, if she is writing about how Ronald Reagan was the U.S.'s best president and you read a paragraph about the STAR WARS defense system, talk about the defense system, what defense is, the role a president plays in the defense of the country, and the technology used in STAR WARS. After you cover the *meaning* of these concepts, discuss whether or not Reagan's defense policy was one of the things that made Reagan a "great" president. If she thinks it was, she should include it in her report.

▶ **Have your child write down a single sentence that summarizes the paragraph.** This one-sentence-per-paragraph note-taking rule ensures that your child's notes will be in her own words (she should know the meaning of every word and concept that she writes). It also condenses the information since children's reports should contain only a fraction of the information that an encyclopedia entry would contain. The thought and discussion that go before writing down that single sentence help your child to think about her argument before she actually writes the report.

If your child is using a book that does not need to be condensed quite as much as a difficult encyclopedia entry, your child can follow a *two*-sentence-per-paragraph rule. Even a two-sentence rule will force your child to read and process the information that she reads before she summarizes it in her own words.

"My child needs pictures, maps, and other visual displays for his report. Where do I find these things?"

Nowadays, one of the most common ways to get pictures or illustrations is to use the Internet. Color inkjet printers have become fairly inexpensive and children can print out pictures easily and quickly (but keep extra ink cartridges handy—printing pictures uses a lot of ink). If you don't have this technology at home, your school, and possibly your child's classroom, likely does. Ask your child if he is allowed to surf the Web at school and look for pictures. You may even be able to accompany him to the school computer lab. There are also low-tech ways to get "visuals."

▶ **Draw.** Teachers will never discount a child's work because he drew rather than printed pictures off the computer. If your child does not feel that he draws well, have him try tracing, which works especially well with maps. He can use tracing paper or tissue paper (glue tissue paper to thicker paper to include in the report) or shine a light up through a glass-topped table to make an ideal tracing desk.

▶ *Photocopy pictures from books.* Black and white photocopying is inexpensive and available at office supply stores, many libraries, and even some drug stores. Color photocopying is usually available at copy stores, and usually costs about a dollar a copy.

▶ *Scour second-hand stores* for old copies of *National Geographic* magazines which often have great photos. Sometimes old reference books have outdated information but good pictures and can be purchased cheaply and cut out.

▶ *Old postcards, snapshots (e.g., from vacations or the zoo), calendars, and pamphlets (e.g., from museums, historic buildings, tours, etc.)* can make great visual displays. Also, many bookstores have calendars at extreme discounts in February and March (for a few dollars you could pick up calendars with 12 wild animal pictures, 12 famous women pictures, or even 12 pictures of famous buildings in your state). When your child tells you he's supposed to pick a report topic, make

---

Turning in the "Perfect" Report

- *Follow the teacher's criteria.* Use a checklist (make one if you need to).
- If your child uses a computer to write the report, have him use the *spell check* function. Every child should know how to use this function of his word processor.
- *Have your child proofread his report.* Have him read the report out loud, moving his finger across the page. Have him read each word out loud as he touches it. This process makes it easier to find words that he might have inadvertently left out.
- *Proofread the paper with your child.* Read it together. Talk about mistakes and discuss changes. He can learn from this process as well as create a perfect paper.
- Have your child *practice oral reports* until he can say them smoothly and confidently.
- *Buy plastic report covers* (they don't have to be expensive) for your child to put his finished reports in. Although most teachers don't care if students put their reports in covers, most kids love report covers (if yours doesn't, skip this step). Just putting a report in cover can help kids feel like they have accomplished something.

sure he knows what materials you already have (e.g., pictures of the Alamo from a visit to Texas, brochures of the White House from Grandma's trip to Washington, D.C., photos of dolphins from a visit to the aquarium) so he has the option of choosing a topic that he's prepared for.

"When my kids write reports I tell them that they can't plagiarize but I don't know how to prevent them from only changing a word or two from what it says in the encyclopedia."

Plagiarism is a huge problem in schools (even at universities). One reason it's such a big problem is that many students don't know what plagiarism is or the best ways to avoid it. So, even if they feel that plagiarism is wrong, they find it difficult to avoid copying.

First of all, what is plagiarism? Although many people think that they are guilty of plagiarism only when they copy someone else's writing word for word, the Oxford English Dictionary's definition of plagiarism is "to take and use as one's own the ideas or writings of another."[6] By that definition, changing a few words of a sentence from a reference book and writing it in your own report is plagiarism. And, according to the official policies of many universities (including Georgetown University, the University of Indiana, and the University of Washington) students must reference their sources whenever they use *an idea* that is not their own—even if they substantially change the words that they use to express that idea. The only exception to this rule is "common knowledge," such as the fact that that sky is blue or that the world is round. Of course, for children, citing all new knowledge would be daunting. Almost every report that they write is based on knowledge that comes from someone else and most elementary school students are too young to deal with numerous footnotes or in-text citations.

So, how can your child avoid plagiarism? First, anytime a student quotes someone else directly she should put the quote inside quotation marks and acknowledge her source. There are several ways to acknowledge a source. Older students may want to use footnotes (put a number next to the sentence that contains the quote, put that number at the bottom of the page, and write the bibliographic information next to the number—for an example, see footnote 6 after the dictionary quotation above). Footnotes are especially easy with word processing programs such as Microsoft Word, where you can click "Insert footnote" and the program

---

6 "plagiarized, n. 1." *Oxford English Dictionary,* 2nd Ed. Edited by J.A. Simpson and E.S.C. Weiner. Oxford: Claredon Press, 1989. OED Online. UCLA Young Research Library, Los Angeles, CA. 16 April 2004. <http://dictionary.oed.com/>.

will automatically put in the "little number" and then allow you to insert the bibliographic text in the footer of the page. However, for younger children, it may be easier to simply name the source in the text of the report. For instance, a child might write:

According to the White House Web site, Abraham Lincoln "had to struggle for a living and for learning."

Or

In Dr. Seuss's book, *Green Eggs and Ham,* the main character says, "I do not like them, Sam-I-Am."

Both of these excerpts tell the reader where to find these quotations. Whether she uses footnotes or refers to her sources in her report, your child must mention her source when using direct quotations. Anything less is plagiarism and may qualify the student for suspension or expulsion from school.

Second, everything your child writes, that she does not quote and cite, should come from her head. Your child should read about her subject, take notes, and then formulate her own ideas for the report. The following tips will make this easier:

♦ **Get materials that are at a suitable reading level for your child.** If she can read and understand her materials, she will be much more likely to think about the information before writing it down than if she doesn't understand the source book.

♦ **Push your child to condense or summarize information in her own words.** A good way to do this is to follow the one-sentence-per-paragraph note-taking rule. For each paragraph your child reads in a source book, she writes only one sentence on her outline, notes, or index cards. That sentence should summarize the paragraph and be entirely in her own words (she should know the meaning of *every* word she uses in her report). If your child struggles with this process, do it with her. Read paragraphs together. Talk about what they mean. Explain things that she does not understand. Then ask her to write down one sentence that summarizes the paragraph (cover up the source material if that helps her use her own words).

♦ **Once your child has finished her notes, put source materials away.** Have your child write the report based on her notes. Then her final report will truly be hers.

♦ **Encourage your child to use footnotes or in-text cites when the facts that she is writing are not "common knowledge."** Of course, it would be ridiculous to have a child footnote every fact that she didn't know before she began the research. If she did, a two-page report about George Washington would have more footnotes than text. Lots of the facts in children's reports could be considered common knowledge: that George Washington was the first president of the U.S., that he was a general in the Revolutionary

War, that he was married to Martha. *A good rule of thumb, for elementary school reports, is for your child to cite any information that she does not read in more than one source.* Thus, since every book and encyclopedia entry about George Washington probably mentions the year he was born, consider that common knowledge. However, if only one author goes in-depth into George Washington's mixed feelings about the war, and your child mentions that in her report, she should probably reference her source. Few elementary school teachers will punish children for not having footnotes—and you might decide not to include them. But using footnotes is good practice for the future and helps children distinguish their own ideas from ideas they need to give others credit for.

▶ **Make sure your child lists ALL sources in her bibliography.** Even if your child's teacher says that footnotes are unnecessary, your child must list every book, article, and Web site she read in preparation for the report in her bibliography.

▶ *Remember that your child does not need to cite her own opinions.* If your child writes a report arguing that George Washington was the best presi-

---

Reference Terms

- *Bibliography*—a list of references at the end of a report, article, or book.
- *Endnotes*—notes at the end of a report that provide additional information or references. All endnotes are numbered and correspond to a superscript (small, and set above the regular type) number in the text. Some people use footnotes instead of endnotes.
- *In-text citation*—a shortened reference to source material (including just the author's name and publication year) that is placed within the body of the report. For instance, if you quoted this book you would cite it as: (Chin 2004).
- *Reference*—an entry in a bibliography, footnote, or endnote that provides bibliographic information (author, title, date, publisher, place of publication) about source material so that a reader could find that source.
- *Footnote*—a note at bottom of a page in a report that provides additional information or a reference. All footnotes are numbered and correspond to superscript (small, and set above the regular type[7]) numbers in the text. Some people use endnotes instead of footnotes.

---

[7] The small "7" in the text refers to this footnote—footnote 7.

dent ever, that statement and her reasons for making it are her own (as long as she is not copying someone else's essay that makes the same argument).

Third and finally, skim your child's source materials and final report and look for similarities. Although sources and reports will have the same information, no sources are written by 8-year-olds and your child's report *should* sound like it was written by a child. When a child can write a report that does not sound like the source material, you know two things: One, your child has mastered the material well enough to write a report. Two, your child has not plagiarized anyone else's work.

"How should I help my child organize his thoughts when he's trying to write a report?"

Although some teachers ask children to organize their thoughts in particular ways (e.g., in clusters, outlines, or note cards), there is no one way to organize information. Each system has pros and cons.

▶ *Bubbles or clusters.* With this method, a child writes a topic in the center of a piece of paper and then creates "offshoot" bubbles containing subtopics. Offshoots contain increasingly precise information. Many children learn to use bubbles in school and feel comfortable with them. This method lets children write information in a casual format and graphically link this information, which can be useful for children who think spatially. Clusters are good for kids who are intimidated by blank pages (they start by simply writing their main topic in a big circle in the center). The main drawback of clusters is that they can be hard to organize. But they are good for brainstorming and can later be transferred into an outline or note cards.

Here is how a student might begin a cluster about the American Westward Movement:

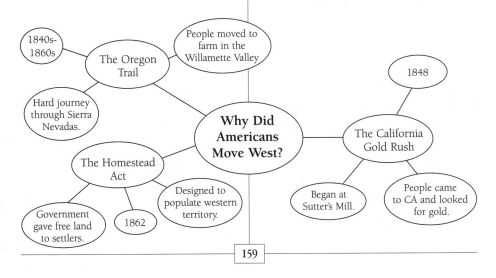

A student making this cluster would fill in more details about why, when, and how Americans moved west. She could also add sub-topic bubbles (for instance, branching off of the "People came to CA and looked for gold" bubble, she might write about the techniques people used to look for gold).

▶ *Outlines.* Outlines are the neatest way to organize information. When done well, children only need to fill in a few sentences to turn outlines into full reports. It can, however, be difficult to add information to outlines because you never know how much room to allow for each section when you start. It's also difficult to reorder outlines without rewriting them. Outlines work well as an intermediary step between clustering and writing.

An outline with the same information as the cluster above (along with some additional facts about how people looked for gold) could take two forms, a numbered outline (example A) or a bulleted outline (example B):

EXAMPLE A:

Why Did Americans Move West?
1. On the Oregon Trail
   a. Heavy movement on the Oregon Trail from the 1840s to the 1860s.
   b. Required settlers to make a treacherous journey through the Sierra Nevada Mountains.
   c. Settlers came to farm in the fertile Willamette Valley.
2. During the California Gold Rush
   a. Began at Sutter's Mill in Northern California
   b. Gold was discovered in 1848.
   c. People came to find gold and get rich.
      i. Many panned for gold in streams, which was a very slow process.
      ii. Some used sluice boxes to sift through sediment more quickly.
3. Because of the Homestead Act
   a. Law signed by Abraham Lincoln in 1862.
   b. Designed to populate western territory.
   c. U.S. government gave free land to settlers who lived on the land for at least 5 years.

OR

EXAMPLE B:

Why Did Americans Move West?
● On the Oregon Trail
  – Heavy movement on the Oregon Trail from the 1840s to the 1860s.
  – Required settlers to make a treacherous journey through the Sierra Nevada Mountains.
  – Settlers came to farm in the fertile Willamette Valley.
● During the California Gold Rush
  – Began at Sutter's Mill in Northern California.

– Gold was discovered in 1848.
– People came to find gold and get rich.
  ♦ Many panned for gold in streams, which was a very slow process.
  ♦ Some used sluice boxes to sift through sediment more quickly.
● The Homestead Act
  – Law signed by Abraham Lincoln in 1862.
  – Designed to populate western territory.
  – U.S. government gave free land to settlers who lived on the land for at least 5 years.

♦ **Note cards.** Note cards embody some of the best features of outlines and clusters. Like clusters, note cards are casual and less intimidating (your child can write a topic on the top of each note card to fill the blank space). They are also expandable. So, if your child finds more information after she fills a note card on a topic, she can make a second card for that topic (or a third or fourth). She can also move the cards around to change the order of her topics. As your child gets older and uses many sources, she might even write bibliographic information for sets of facts on the back of each note card. The main drawback of note cards is that they are easy to misplace. (If your child loses note cards easily or writes large, try having her use the

note card process but writing on pieces of paper rather than note cards).

Note cards with the same information as the cluster and outlines above might look like this:

The Oregon Trail
● Heavy movement on the Oregon Trail from the 1840s to the 1860s.
● Required settlers to make a treacherous journey through the Sierra Nevada Mountains.
● Settlers came to farm in the fertile Willamette Valley.

The California Gold Rush
● Started at Sutter's Mill.
● Started in 1848.
● Came to CA to look for gold.
  – Some panned, some used a sluice box, some mined.
  – Most did not find gold.

The Homestead Act
● Law signed by Abraham Lincoln in 1862.
● Designed to populate western territory.
● U.S. government gave free land to settlers who lived on the land for at least 5 years.

Any note-taking system will work as long as it forces your child to stay organized and requires her to put information into her own words. One caution: typing notes directly into the computer may not be a great idea

The One-Sentence-Per-Paragraph Note-Taking Rule

The following paragraph is from the White House Web site, which has biographies of all U.S. presidents. While it has a lot of good information, it is too detailed for a child's report:

> From 1759 to the outbreak of the American Revolution, Washington managed his lands around Mount Vernon and served in the Virginia House of Burgesses. Married to a widow, Martha Dandridge Custis, he devoted himself to a busy and happy life. But like his fellow planters, Washington felt himself exploited by British merchants and hampered by British regulators. As the quarrel with the mother country grew acute, he moderately but firmly voiced his resistance to the restrictions.
> (source: www.whitehouse.gov/history/presidents/gw1.html)

To sum up this paragraph in one sentence, a child might write:

"Washington liked living on his farm, Mount Vernon, but he got frustrated with British rules and started to speak out against them."

Or
"Washington liked living at Mount Vernon but finally joined the fight against the British."

Or
"Although he eventually went against the British, Washington did not really want to disrupt his happy life at Mount Vernon."

Obviously there are dozens of "summaries" a child could write. But, whatever your child writes in his notes should be in his own words (note: the words "exploited" and "hampered" don't appear in the summaries!) and come from his own understanding of the paragraph.

The one-sentence-per-paragraph rule is easy to follow. All *you* need to provide are:

- Reference materials at his reading level, OR
- Your help (or another adult's help) in reading and understanding the source material.

because it makes it too easy to copy source material word for word (or copy and paste it from Internet pages). Whatever system your child chooses, try to help her to incorporate the following:

▶ *Follow the one-sentence-per-paragraph rule and write down each sentence in an organized fashion.* She can make a cluster, outline, or index cards. Sometimes the format of the report will dictate the system. For instance, if the student has to write a report on France and include sections about its agricultural products, languages, and history, she may find it easiest to have a note card for each topic and take notes from each source onto the appropriate cards.

▶ *If your child is going to use footnotes, make sure she notes which source each of her facts comes from (it may be impossible to retrace her steps later on).* One way to do this is to write down the bibliographic information for each source on a piece of paper. Then number each source. Then each time your child writes down a sentence (or a group of sentences), she can write the number of the source next to it. She can then use those numbers to fill in the footnote references in her report. Another way to do this is to write down all the information from each source together—creating an outline for each source—and then integrate the material later.

▶ *Keep notes together.* Keep papers in a folder and/or rubber-band note cards together so they don't get lost.

(If you find the source material too difficult, enlist the help of another adult. Ask a friend to work with your child or, better yet, ask a librarian or bookstore clerk to help you find books at your child's reading level. If you can't find suitable materials, talk with the teacher. She may have some resources or may help your child choose another topic.)

The passage about George Washington that I used here comes from an excellent resource, but given the difficulty of the passage, most children would need to read this paragraph with an adult and discuss the meaning before they could come up their own summaries. If you simply left a young child with this document and some note cards, he would probably just copy down the words because he wouldn't understand it well enough to do otherwise.

From the book *School Sense: How to Help Your Child Succeed in Elementary School* by Tiffani Chin, Ph.D. (Santa Monica Press • 800-784-9553). © 2004 by Tiffani Chin.

"My child needs a 'visual display' for his report—what supplies do I need and what counts as a visual display?"

Although some children will undoubtedly bring in elaborate "visual displays" that have clearly been constructed by an adult, most teachers don't expect museum quality dioramas when they assign visual displays. Usually, they just want students to do hands-on activities that will help them understand their topics. For instance, a child might use clay to make a three-dimensional map of the state he wrote a report about. A map of California would reveal how geographically diverse the state is and why its economy is so varied. On the other hand, if a student were doing a report on the Oregon Trail, she might present her report dressed in a long skirt and apron to demonstrate the clothing women wore in the nineteenth century. Or, if your child is writing a report on a "hunting and gathering" society, he might construct a "spear" to demonstrate the weapons they used to hunt. The process will help him appreciate how hard it is to attach a stone to the end of a stick.

Any tangible item or outfit that your child has assembled neatly will qualify as a visual display. The visual display should be something that a child can make on his own (or with minimal adult help), and remember, it doesn't have to be perfect. It just has to represent clear effort by your child to create a useful visual display that adds to his report.

"My child always tells me about her projects or reports the day before they're due—how can we do these projects well in just one night?"

Do not let your child fall into the habit of waiting until the last minute for long-term assignments. Help your child get organized so that this does not become a chronic problem. You need to make sure that you know about projects sooner and your child starts working on them before the last minute. As children get older they will be expected to do more and more long-term projects, which require planning and time management. If she does not learn these skills now her grades may suffer in high school when the work becomes too difficult for her to write a paper or do a project in just one night. (See Chapter 3 for ways to help your child organize her assignments and plan her time.)

"My child just told me about a project—and it's due tomorrow! How do we get it done?"

Most parents will have this experience at least once in their child's school career. Often, you will be able to help your child put together something that is at least passable.

▶ *First, have your child bring you ALL of the information that he has about the assignment.* You need to get all of the information about the project requirements (see the answer to the first question in this section for a list of the information you should have). If some information is missing, have your child call a friend *immediately* and ask if they have the information—by the time you realize you have a question, it may be too late in the evening to call another child.

Ideas for Creating Visual Displays

- *Make a poster:* Get a large piece of poster board and glue pictures, maps, and drawings to it (include captions). If a plain white poster board looks too dull, buy colored poster board and use construction paper to make contrasting backings for the pictures and their captions—you can even cut the backings out in shapes that relate to your topic (for example, the shape of the state you're writing about). Use the computer to print a title or use a stencil to write a title neatly across the top.
- *Make a diorama (a 3-D model of a scene or habitat):* Cover a shoebox bottom with tin foil, wrapping paper, or brown paper. Place the box on its side so it creates a "cave" in which you can construct a little world (e.g., an animal habitat, a battle scene, or a historic town).
- *Create a model:* You can buy a model if something appropriate exists (a covered wagon, a space shuttle) or you can build something yourself.
- *Draw a map:* Draw or trace a political map or make a 3-D map with salt, flour, and water or with clay. Children can also devise their own types of maps (e.g., one that shows the battles that George Washington won or lost; a map showing where Native American Indian tribes moved as settlers moved into the American West; a map showing where different animal habitats are located).
- *Illustrate:* Draw a portrait of the subject of your report or draw pictures of the clothing that people wore in the area or era you are writing about.
- *Make a timeline:* Draw a line several feet long (tape several pieces of paper together or use a long piece of butcher paper). Along the line, mark years in which important events happened for your subject (significant events in a subject's life or a state's history). Then use pictures, drawings, and captions to visually depict the history of your subject.

From the book *School Sense: How to Help Your Child Succeed in Elementary School* by Tiffani Chin, Ph.D. (Santa Monica Press • 800-784-9553). © 2004 by Tiffani Chin.

Materials for Visual Displays

- Use small figures (army people, dolls) for people. If you need a particular kind of plastic figure, try your local bakery—they often use small figures to decorate cakes.
- Use old shoeboxes or cereal boxes for rectangular shapes (the base of a car or covered wagon) or cut them up and use the cardboard to form other shapes.
- Glue dirt or grass to paper or cardboard to make things look earthy. At arts and crafts stores you can buy dried flowers and artificial grass. A local florist might give your child some trimmings or leftover flowers and greens.
- Use cotton balls for snow.
- Use clay or play-dough to shape people, animals, or landscape (hills, rivers, etc.)
- Use toothpicks or Popsicle sticks to build houses or fences.
- Use combinations of Styrofoam balls and pipe cleaners to make figures of animals or people. Clothes made from paper or cloth, feathers, or fur can make them look more real.
- Use old building blocks to form buildings.
- Clay makes good mountains and volcanoes. Or, take a piece of heavy paper, roll it into a cone shape, and glue on dirt and grass to make it look like a mountain.
- Play-dough also works well for sculpting faces.
- Use a blown up balloon as a base for a round or oval model. Sometimes kids want to use clay or papier-mâché to sculpt a face or a planet. But solid balls of clay and papier-mâché are heavy and can take forever to dry. Blow up a balloon to approximately the right shape and size for the model, then put clay, play-dough, or papier-mâché on the balloon. When it dries, the center of the model will be hollow.
- Tin foil often looks like water.
- Saran wrap or cut up plastic baggies can look like glass or ice.
- Use your yard: weeds can be vines, leaves glued together look like bushes or trees.
- Toilet paper, paper towel, and wrapping paper rolls come in handy for all kinds of projects. You can slice them to make round wheels. You can use the tubes as tunnels. Cut them and the bottoms can be the bases of huts, silos, or other round buildings (a cone of paper will make a nice roof).

From the book School Sense: How to Help Your Child Succeed in Elementary School by Tiffani Chin, Ph.D. (Santa Monica Press • 800-784-9553). © 2004 by Tiffani Chin.

▶ *Second, gather any work that your child might have already done.* Many teachers give children time in class to do work on projects and your child may have already started. Make sure you gather any library books he might have checked out or Internet pages he might have printed in the computer lab.

▶ *Third, get to work.* Choose the easiest of the references and read them together. (If your child does not have any references from school, hopefully you have some at home or can print something from the Internet. If you do not have access to references and it is too late to go to the library or the bookstore you probably have to accept the fact that your child cannot turn the assignment in tomorrow. Read on for how to handle that problem.) Help your child outline the basic requirements of the report. Do not let your child do the fun parts (drawing, cutting out pictures, surfing the Internet, etc.). Instead, sit down with the information that you have (or can get quickly) and work on the "meat" of the project.

Most children's reports can be finished in an evening, although they won't be as good as something that they had worked on longer—nor as fun. Try to help your child put together a report that hits the key requirements and is passable. And don't feel guilty about making him work longer than he wants to. As you work remember a few key points:

▶ *Don't strive for perfection.* You probably don't have time and, frankly, you don't want your child to get an A on a project he waited until the last minute to do—that only teaches him that procrastination pays off.

▶ *Do not do the work for your child.* You will probably feel more pressure than he does to do the report and to do it well—but don't let him manipulate you into doing the work. You can and should help, but he should be doing the reading and the writing. Remember, the point of all projects is for your child to learn something.

▶ *Don't let him cheat or cut corners.* It does not become okay to copy the words straight from a book just because you're running late. If you can't get it done in the time you have, it's better not to finish than to resort to plagiarism. Children will not forget if their parents lower their ethical standards "when it's really important."

▶ **Absolutely** *do not stay up all night finishing the report or project for your child while he sleeps.* Encourage him to do his best on the basics. If it is impossible to get the report done, give your child a choice: turn it in late (and work hard tomorrow) or turn it in incomplete. Your child needs to face the consequences of waiting until the last minute. If you do the report for him and he gets a good grade, he will learn that waiting until the last minute is a great strategy. Most children are embarrassed when they do not turn in their projects on the due date (and most everyone else has theirs), and they feel bad when they turn in a substandard report and get a low grade. Take advantage of this. It's much better to let your child fail once or twice in elementary school than to enable him so that he goes to middle school and high school without the skills he needs to budget his time.

Most of all, do not let waiting until the last minute become a habit for your child. Explain his responsibilities and make sure he has a system for keeping track of long-term projects (see Chapter 3). While he is fine-tuning his system, keep in touch with his teacher. Find out for yourself when projects are due, talk with your child about how to plan ahead, and help him break work down into daily steps so that the project seems more manageable.

"My child did not finish her project which is due today. She's begging me to let her stay home from school to finish it. Should I let her?"

The day may come when your procrastinating child cannot finish a project before it is due. *Do not* keep your child at home on the due date so that she can work on the project. Do not write your child's teacher a note saying that she was sick. If your child does not have the report done, then she goes to

school without a complete report. She may get a bad grade. She may get scolded. She may feel embarrassed in front of her classmates. These are consequences she may have to experience in order to remember that she cannot wait until the last minute to work on projects.

"My child didn't tell me about his project until the night before. We didn't have any books and the library was closed so my child went to school without his work. His teacher must think I'm the worst parent in the world. Should I hide from her for the rest of the year?"

No, you *must* follow up with the teacher. You can't just hide—even though you will probably feel embarrassed. If your child turns in an incomplete report or project (or doesn't turn one in at all), make an appointment to talk with the teacher *as soon as possible*. Unfortunately, most teachers come to two conclusions when a child doesn't turn in a report or project. First, they conclude that the child was too lazy or irresponsible to do the work. Second, they assume that the parent was too lazy or irresponsible to help the child do the work. The first conclusion is correct. Your child did act irresponsibly. However, in order to maintain the support of the teacher, you must prevent her from reaching the second conclusion. Let her know that you are trying to teach your child a lesson—that you were not being lazy, you just refused to do your child's work for him. *NO* teacher expects you to do your child's work. Most will respect you for not doing the project for the child and not making excuses. But, unless you talk to the teacher, she may assume the worst.

Here are some guidelines to follow when you talk with your child's teacher:

♦ *Tell the teacher that you realize that your child did not turn in his project.* Also tell her that your child did not tell you about the project until the very last minute.

♦ *Don't make excuses for your child.* Just explain that he waited until the last minute to start and you decided that he should learn the consequences of that.

♦ *Explain your plans for trying to make sure that this doesn't happen again.* Tell the teacher what you told your child about the consequences for not doing work and not telling you about work that he needed help with. Describe the system that you are considering for helping him keep track of his deadlines (see Chapter 3 for possible systems). Ask her for any suggestions for improving your plan.

♦ *Ask if your child can turn the work in late for partial credit.* By offering to do the project, you show the teacher that you are willing to work, you just

need more time. By asking for partial credit you show that you understand that late work does not get full credit.

If you follow up with the teacher, she probably won't fault you for sending your child to school without his project—and she certainly won't fault you nearly as much as she would if she saw your child's report written in your handwriting (and yes, they can usually tell).

"My children's teachers keep assigning group projects and coordinating meetings with the other kids is always a disaster!"

Group projects can be very frustrating—for children and for their parents. Teachers assign group projects for many reasons. Sometimes they assign projects that are too big for one person to do alone. Other times they want children to learn how to work together—as they will likely have to in the working world. Either way, throughout your child's school years, you will probably experience more than a few group projects. There are several ways to minimize the problems that sometimes come with group projects:

♦ *Talk with your child about which partners she should choose.* Children usually work with their friends (and teachers usually let them because it is easier for them to get together outside of school). Talk with your child about which of her friends are responsible, and live close enough to meet with. Try to discourage your child from working with students who have been irresponsible in the past or who tend to have trouble getting together (because of parents' work schedules or any other reason).

▶ *If the teacher assigns groups and your child has had problems with a particular child in the past, write a note to the teacher requesting that your child not work with that child again.* Explain the reasons for your objection (for instance, explain that you live too far from the other child for them to meet, or explain that the other child refused to contribute the last time they worked together). Do not simply write that your child does not like the other child. This sort of excuse would not sound professional to an employer and will not sound reasonable to a teacher.

▶ *Make sure that your child gets the phone numbers of each child that she works with so that they can contact each other on weekends and in the evenings.* If you know that your child will work on group projects during the school year, it might be a good idea to ask the teacher for a class roster at the beginning of the year—that way you will be armed with everyone's phone number. (The teacher will probably be most amenable to putting together a roster if you offer to type up the names and numbers once they are collected.)

▶ *Talk with your child about maximizing in-class time that the teacher gives them to work on the project.* Most teachers give the children time at school to work on group projects. Some children use this time as social time. Stress the importance of making good use of class time when the group members are all together.

▶ *Talk with your child about dividing the work among group members.* Help her figure out how to divide the labor so that every member of the group can do some work independently. Children often think that every child must jointly do every bit of research and writing. It's often better to split up the project (i.e., if they are writing about the solar system, each child could be responsible for three planets; or if they are writing about a Native American tribe, one student could work on food, another on housing, another on language, and another on customs). Try to split up the project, so that each child has a defined contribution that includes most components of the project (e.g., each student could research, write up, and draw a picture for his or her section of the report). This way, students will need to spend less time together. Obviously, they still need to meet at the end to compile, edit, and finalize.

▶ *Understand that group projects get group grades and that picking up the slack for other members of the group is sometimes a "necessary evil" that comes with group projects.* If your child wants a good grade on a group project and ends up doing all the work, accept that. Support her and help where you can. And discuss the ramifications of this problem and how it should influence her choice of partners in the future. However, make sure your child has given the other children the opportunity to help out. Sometimes children take everything upon themselves and then complain about the burden. When children "take over" they not only end up doing too much of the project themselves but they prevent other group members from learning from the project. However, if you feel that your child has truly done most of the work because the other students did not complete their tasks, a note to the teacher (respectful, of course), would not be inappropriate. Although you should not expect your note to affect your child's grade (or the grades of the other children), it may encourage the teacher to ease up on group projects or help your child choose better partners. (In fact, many teachers will prevent children who have not worked well together in the past from working together in the future.)

▶ *If you feel that your child is doing less than her share of projects, talk to your child.* Find out why. Does she feel pushed out of the process? Is she relying on "one of the smart kids" to do all of the work? If the former is true, ask her to assert herself and if

that is unsuccessful, write a note to the teacher. You do not want your child missing out on the learning process or being penalized for "not doing her share." If you learn that your child is simply taking the easy way out, insist that she complete her share of the work (or take on a share of the work, if none has been assigned to her). You do not want your child to learn that the best way to get a good grade is to join "smart" groups and then do nothing. This attitude will make other children resent her and will also cheat her out of any academic benefits of the project.

Book Reports

"I never know what books my child should read when her teacher assigns book reports."

Make sure your child knows her teacher's rules or guidelines about choosing books. Some teachers have specific books that they want the children in their classes to read. Others assign genres (such as historical fiction or fantasy). Some teachers disqualify certain books (i.e., many teachers do not allow books if they have been made into a movie). Make sure your child follows her teacher's guidelines when choosing books.

If the teacher does not tell children which books they should choose,

How to Be Prepared to Help Your Child with Reports and Projects

- *Stay on top of dates and deadlines* (even if you have to check with the teacher until your child perfects an organization system). Don't let your child surprise you the night before something is due.
- *If you can, invest in a computer* with a word processor that has a spell check function (new computers usually come with these programs and older computers often have them).
- *Always have on hand:*
  - ♦ Extra printer ink and paper. Printers always seem to run out of ink when you are printing the final version of a report.
  - ♦ Poster board, glue sticks, colored pens or pencils, construction paper in various colors, tracing paper (or sturdy tissue paper), and report covers. Not having to run to the store in the middle of the night will make last minute projects less daunting.
  - ♦ Basic supplies for your child's visual display of choice (e.g., clay, play-dough, ingredients for papier-mâché, Styrofoam balls, pipe-cleaners, old shoeboxes, etc.)
  - ♦ A camera and film (or better yet, a Polaroid or digital camera, for instant developing). Kids often need to take before-and-after photos for science projects.
  - ♦ Some reference tools: encyclopedias or an encyclopedic CD-Rom, almanacs, science books, and history books. You can save a lot of time and aggravation if you don't need to go to the library for all of your information.
- *Save:*
  - ♦ Old magazines (or articles from magazines) that contain pictures and information about the types of topics you think your child might have to write a report about (famous people, science topics, famous places).
  - ♦ Odds and ends, such as the plastic characters that come on birthday cakes, army people, and other small toys. These sorts of things come in very handy for models.
  - ♦ Outdated encyclopedias or reference books. If you see cheap reference books with good pictures at garage sales, pick them up. Facts may change over time, but many historical pictures don't. Your child can cut pictures out of these old books for reports.

here are some pointers for choosing book report books:

▶ **Make sure that your child can read and understand the book that she chooses.** Although many parents are thrilled when their child picks challenging books, I have seen many book reports that showed that the child barely understood the plot of the book. Once your child picks a book, have her read a few pages to you. If she stumbles over more than two or three words on a page, the book is probably too hard. Even if she can read the words fluently, ask her what some of the harder words mean. If she doesn't know the meaning of more than two or three words per page (and can't guess by looking at the context), the book is probably too hard.

▶ **Make sure that the book is not too easy for your child.** Don't choose books that are much easier than the level of the textbook that your child is reading at school (unless that textbook is much too hard for you child).

▶ **Let your child choose the book, with your help.** Go to the bookstore, library, or your child's own bookshelf together and choose a book that she wants to read.

▶ **Try to estimate how long it will take your child to read the book.** If the book report is due in a week, make sure that

---

  ◆ Old calendars with pictures of animals, art, historic places, or famous buildings. These can make great report illustrations.
- **Gather information when you see it:**
  ◆ When you go on vacation, gather up pamphlets and handouts.
  ◆ Buy postcards. The postcards and pamphlets you picked up while visiting grandma in South Carolina may form the background of your child's state report on South Carolina or her history report on the Confederacy. The pictures you took of the lava fields in Hawaii might look great on a science project backboard. So, when you know your child has to pick a character or place for a report, consult with her about the materials you already have (perhaps from a trip to Washington, D.C.). Encourage her to choose a topic you have some information on.
- **Use free resources.** For instance, many states and historical sites will send you pamphlets, pictures, and information. If your child is doing a report on Thomas Jefferson, she could write to the Jefferson Monument and request some brochures to use in her report. (Remember, however, that you need to do this well in advance of the project's due date.)

From the book *School Sense: How to Help Your Child Succeed in Elementary School* by Tiffani Chin, Ph.D. (Santa Monica Press • 800-784-9553). © 2004 by Tiffani Chin.

your child can read the book in three days. If the book report is due tomorrow, make sure she can read the book in half an hour. For older children (fourth-grade and up), teachers usually expect children to read chapter books. If your child is an accelerated second- or third-grader, the teacher might expect chapter books from her, too.

♦ *Look at the suggested reading age on the books you are considering.* Some books specify an age on the cover. Other books indicate a reading level on the back. Look for something that says, "R.L. 11," which indicates that the book is for 11-year-olds. (Beware: these numbers are publishers' best guesses but may not suit your child's reading level. You should know from the teacher if your child reads at grade level or not.) Most bookstores also divide books up into general age categories (e.g., Beginning Readers, Ages 5-8; Intermediate Readers, Ages 9-12).

If you are unsure about the book you and your child have chosen, ask your child to bring it to school and have her teacher "approve it" before you begin. Her comments on the first report of the year should give you a sense of the books she thinks your child should read.

"What are the main parts of a book report?"

Different teachers have different ideas of what should go into book reports.

But, there are several key components that most teachers require:

♦ Plot—what happened in the book?

♦ Characters—who were the main actors in the story, what were they like, what did they do in the story?

♦ Setting—where did the story take place? In what time period did it take place?

Many teachers also require some or all of the following parts:

♦ Opinion or Review—your child's opinion about the book, would he recommend it to someone else? Why or why not?

♦ Genre—what type of book is it (e.g., science fiction, historical fiction, adventure)?

♦ Theme, moral, or lesson learned—What did your child take away from the book that resonates with his life or taught him something that he did not know before?

Your child's teacher should tell him exactly what components she expects book reports to have. If your child claims not to know, have him call a friend and ask. If he still doesn't know what components to include, make sure he asks his teacher.

"My child HATES book reports; what can I do to make them more fun?"

Book reports are a way for teachers to

force children to read outside of school. Unfortunately, they sometimes make children dislike reading. There are several ways to try to make book reports more enjoyable (and less tedious).

▶ *Let your child choose a book that she wants to read.* If she cannot think of anything, search for books that align with her interests (the librarian might be able to help). Also ask her friends' parents if their children have particularly enjoyed any books. Your child might be more willing to read a book that comes with a friend's stamp of approval.

▶ *Make sure that the book is not too difficult for your child.* See the above section on how to choose a book.

▶ *Read the book and discuss it with your child.* Talking about it will probably make the book and the book report more interesting. You don't have to have a deep literary discussion. Talk about the book the way you would talk about a TV show or a movie—this may show your child that books can be just as interesting.

▶ *If your child likes to draw, encourage her to illustrate her book report.* Showing what she thinks the characters might look like or what happens in the story according to her imagination may make the experience more fun for her.

▶ *Make book reports more special by helping your child make a special cover for the report.* Go to the drug store to pick out a report cover (kids often

get excited over simple clear plastic covers), use the computer and experiment with clip art and borders, or let your child making a drawing to put at the front of the report.

Most importantly, encourage your child to read even when a book report is not due. That way, she won't associate all "free reading" with homework and, when it comes time for a book report, she can choose a favorite from among the books that she has recently read to write the report on.

"Why does my child's teacher assign such strange book reports? Some are in the form of clouds, others are trains— why not just a regular book report?"

Many teachers try to make book reports fun by having children combine the book report with some kind of art project. Books and Internet sites designed for teachers often suggest that teachers make book reports more interesting by having children create book report "projects"—such as building a "book report sandwich," with the bread, lettuce, and meat each containing one part of the report (i.e., the "lettuce layer" might contain the setting, the "meat" the plot).

Although these "projects" may seem like unnecessary work to parents, they do make book reports more fun for kids and they make good classroom displays (so, if the teacher is preparing for Open House, that might explain why she is assigning bizarre projects!). These reports also provide a good format for children if they present the book report orally to the class (it gives the children something to point to while they talk, rather than just reading a sheet of paper). When you help your child with these book reports, remember that the content (and understanding and enjoyment of the book) are the most important parts. Just have fun as you cut out clouds, construct the cars of a train, or build a sandwich—this part of the project simply creates a "more fun" activity for your child.

Science Projects

Science projects are often the low point of parents' years. They usually require parents to put in a great deal of effort, thinking up experiments, building visual displays, and forcing their child to do "some" of the work. At science fairs across the country, parents complain about how much of their children's science projects they had to do. Fortunately, few teachers care how elaborate a science project is. They want children to do science projects in order to learn about the scientific process and experience science "hands-on." In fact, many teachers lament that so many projects look parent-made.

So, remember that your *child's* science project should be hers. Don't do it for her and don't force her to do a project that is more sophisticated than she wants to do. Children have hundreds of questions about the world; let your child investigate a question that interests her. The following information should help you guide your child through the project to ensure that she puts together a project that helps her learn about science and earn a good grade.

"Every year my child has to do a science project and I never know what it is supposed to include—what kinds of projects count as science projects?"

Different teachers have different expectations for science projects. But three key elements will make any science project a success:

◆ An experiment that uses the scientific method (no matter how simple). Bear this is mind as you look through science project books—many of the "experiments" they describe are actually demonstrations that do not use the scientific method.

◆ A well-written report and a neat display that clearly show how the child conducted the experiment, how she recorded her results, and what she learned.

◆ A project that shows an understanding of how the scientific method works and why the experiment yielded the results that the student found (even if the results occurred because something went wrong in the experiment).

Of course, many teachers are just as overwhelmed by science project season as parents are. Projects that don't abide by the guidelines above may get As (for instance, some teachers allow "demonstration projects," which simply show how something works—like a volcano—but do not use the scientific method). However, no teacher can fault a science project that follows the above guidelines so, when in doubt, stick to them.

The Scientific Method

- *Question*—The question your child will answer. Keep it simple. Make sure your child asks a question he can answer. Does mold grow faster on white or brown bread? Does coffee help plants grow faster? Do ants prefer cheese or candy?
- *Hypothesis*—Your child's educated guess about the answer to his question. Your child should know why he made his guess. He can't just say that ants should prefer candy—he needs to say why. Do some research. Look up ants in the encyclopedia. What do they eat in the wild? What nutritional needs do they have? What led your child to make his guess? Push him to explain why he thinks ants will prefer candy to cheese. If he can't, he needs to do more research.
- *Procedure:* Your child must explain, step by step, how he did his experiment.
- *Results:* These are the direct results of the experiment. Your child would report that more ants ate cheese than candy or that more mold grew on white bread than brown bread. The results are the most interesting part of the experiment and the easiest to display. Your child can graph the size of the mold spots on his bread each day. He can take pictures of his ants eating cheese and candy.
- *Conclusion:* This is the answer to the original question. Was your child's hypothesis right? Why or why not? What does this say about mold or about ants? And, if the experiment did not work as it should have, what happened with the experiment (perhaps all of the plants died due to a heat wave or bug attack).

From the book *School Sense: How to Help Your Child Succeed in Elementary School* by Tiffani Chin, Ph.D.
(Santa Monica Press • 800-784-9553). © 2004 by Tiffani Chin.

"I've never done a science project before. What should it look like?"

Science projects usually stand (without support) on a table, display all of the relevant information about the project, and include part of the experiment as a visual display. Before building a science project, make sure you know if your school has minimum or maximum size requirements and make sure to abide by those requirements. (The rules are likely to be strict if your school enters projects in a regional competition. If your school participates in a competition ask your child's teacher for the rules.)

The easiest way to make a display is to buy a pre-made "display board" at an office supply store. Display

Tricks for Making Science Project Displays Neat, Clear, and Interesting

- Your child can *type* information on the computer, print it, and then cut out the words and glue them on the board. Make sure that both he (first) and you (second) proofread the information before he glues it on the board (nothing is more embarrassing than seeing typos on your child's project at Open House).

- Or your child can *write* neatly on paper, cut out each paragraph, and glue those onto the board. If your child writes, have him write in pencil first. Then have him check it. Then you check it. Once you give him the go-ahead, he can copy it in ink.

- If you don't have a computer and your child does not like his writing, he can use a *stencil* for titles and captions. (Find inexpensive stencils at office supply stores.)

- To make information stand out from the poster board, your child can back each piece of information (e.g., title, pictures, graphs, text) on *colored construction paper.* Your child can even try cutting the backing into different shapes.

- If you have a Polaroid or digital camera, it's easy to put *pictures* on the board. If you plan ahead, you can also use a regular 35MM camera or even a disposable camera. Many drug stores have 24-hour processing.

- Your child can use *drawings* to show the results or the process of the experiment. If drawings are neat and accurately done, teachers will appreciate the effort.

From the book *School Sense: How to Help Your Child Succeed in Elementary School* by Tiffani Chin, Ph.D. (Santa Monica Press • 800-784-9553). © 2004 by Tiffani Chin.

boards are made of cardboard and have lines to show where to fold the board. However, you can also make your own display using poster board. For a small display, take a piece of poster board (available at any office supply store, discount store, or large drug store) and divide it into fourths (draw a light line (Figure 1, Line 1) down the middle and then darker lines (Figure 1, Lines 2 and 3) down the middle of each half). Fold the board along lines 2 and 3 (the darker, outer two lines). These two side-pieces will hold the board up as shown in Figure 2. (Fold the board away from the lines to keep the lines on the back-side of the display.)

Figure 1

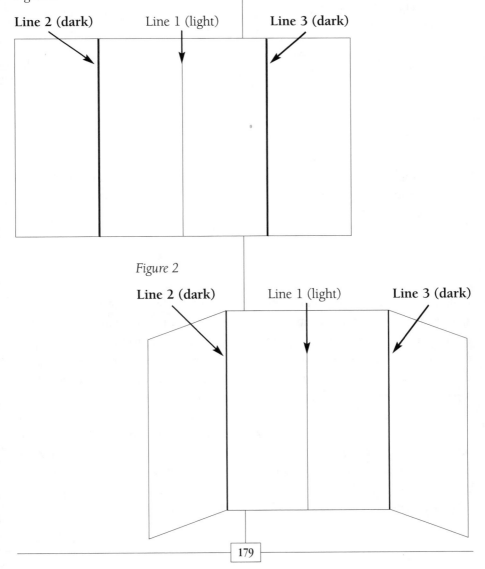

Figure 2

To make a larger display (Figure 3), buy two pieces of poster board. (You can use cardboard, foam-core, or wood instead, but poster board is cheap and easy to cut.) Take the first piece of poster board (poster board #1) and cut it in half. Then tape each half along the sides of the other piece of poster board (poster board #2) to make two "wings" on board #2. Fold the wings forward (away from the tape) at an angle so that the board will stand up.

Figure 3

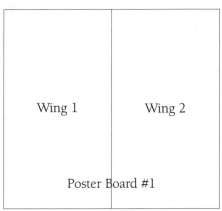

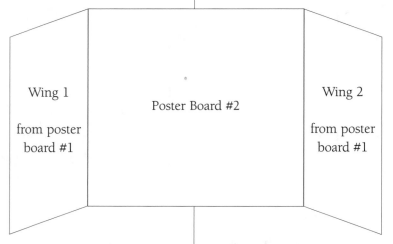

Building a display this way will create a space in front where the 3-D portion of the display (e.g., moldy bread, plants) can stand. On the display board itself, the wings and the main board create separate sections to display different information.

Once your child has built his board and has a sense of its size, he can begin putting together the substantive elements of his display. Every display should include:

▶ *A title.* The title can be the project's question or something catchy. If a catchy title does not explain the project, your child should add a subtitle that does. For instance, your child might title the project below (which investigates how coffee affects plants), "Coffee Kills!" but should add a subtitle explaining that the project investigates the effect of coffee on plants. The full title should look like:

COFFEE KILLS!

How Bean Plants Respond to Coffee

◆ **Each step of the scientific method and how your child implemented each stage.** See the sidebar above for the steps in the scientific method. Each step should be labeled. (If your child does not have to write a report, he should include ALL information in the display. If he does write a report, he can put shorter explanations in the display and go into more detail in the report. The example below assumes that there is a report, so the procedure is not very detailed.)

◆ **A least one visual display of the experiment or the data.** These can include pictures of the child conducting the experiment, drawings of experiment results, or graphs/tables that display the data gathered in the experiment (see Appendix 7 on how to make graphs).

Your child will paste (or write) each of these elements (title, each step of the scientific method, photos, graphs, etc.) onto the display board. He should write or type text neatly. He can back text, photos, and drawings with colored paper. Then—*without using glue*—he should arrange his text and illustrations on the board. Information should be placed in a logical order (i.e., the conclusion does not come first) that makes sense given the size and type of information that he has. Once your child has decided on an arrangement, he can paste elements onto the display board

(using glue sticks, rubber cement, or school glue).

Your child's project should also include:

◆ **A three-dimensional (3-D) example from the experiment.** Some experiments (like those that use plants or bread) easily become visual displays. Other projects, like those that use animals or breakable objects (e.g., thermometers), are harder to display. For hard-to-display experiments, photos or drawings that show the experiment are helpful. For instance, if a child does an experiment to see which colors attract the most heat (by putting different colored cups of water in the sun and tracking their temperatures), he can't bring the thermometer to school. But, to show the experiment, you could take pictures of him checking the temperatures. For the three-dimensional display, he could show the different colored cups, each holding a cardboard "thermometer" showing that cup's final temperature.

In the following example, four plants (two alive, two dead) are displayed in front of the board. The (hypothetical) child who did this project measured the height of the plants each day and made a graph showing plant growth. She also drew the leaves of the plants every week and used those pictures to create a timeline showing how two plants thrived and two plants died. She displayed the graph and pictures on the center pane of the display where there was plenty of room. She also could have used pictures from the Internet to back up her hypothesis about the detrimental effects of caffeine. Another child might have used the center pane to show photographs of how he conducted the experiment. Help your child arrange his information in the way that best shows it off.

Does Coffee Affect Plant Growth?

Question:
Will plants watered with coffee grow more slowly than plants watered with water?

Hypothesis:
I think plants watered with coffee will grow more slowly because caffeine is a diuretic and it will prevent the plant from getting enough water.

Procedure:
I planted 4 bean plants. I let them grow for 1 week. After 1 week, I watered 2 of the plants with ¼ cup of water and the other 2 plants with ¼ cup of water with 2 tbsp. of instant coffee mixed in every day.

Results: For the first week all plants grew at about the same rate. After I started watering two plants with coffee, those two plants stopped growing and started to get brown and die while the other two kept growing (see pictures and graph below).

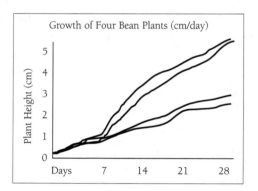

Week 1   Week 2   Week 3   Week 4

Water Leaves

Caffeine Leaves

Growth of Four Bean Plants (cm/day)

Plant Height (cm)

5

4

3

2

1

0

Days   7   14   21   28

Conclusion:
The plants that got watered with coffee stopped growing and eventually died while the other two plants kept growing. Coffee contains caffeine. Caffeine prevents cells from absorbing water and nutrients so the plants that got coffee could not grow and eventually died. Because caffeine has this effect on animal cells as well as plant cells, caffeine is probably bad for growing kids too.

Growing Plants

Dead Plants

REPORT

Does Coffee Affect Plant Growth?

Plant Growth Journal

Some teachers require students to include a report as well as a visual display. Make sure you find out early on if your child must turn in a written report. A written report requirement usually means that your child needs to do more research and supply more background information about his subject. However, if your child is not supposed to do a written report, he will have to make sure to get all of his information on the display board.

"How do you make a science project scientific?"

Almost any question can be answered scientifically. In order to make a project "scientific," your child must:

▶ *Record results consistently.* If something is growing or changing, your child should check it regularly and record changes (e.g., measure, photograph, draw). If your child asks people questions or tests people, she should take down results in a systematic way and make sure to get the same information from all participants (e.g., don't get exact ages for some people and just write "old" for others).

▶ *Have a comparison.* Say, for instance, that your child wants to know if dogs prefer Milk-Bone brand dog biscuits. Your child cannot do a scientific test by simply offering your dog Milk-Bones and seeing if he eats them. Maybe the dog does not like Milk-Bones at all, but was very hungry and willing to eat any-

thing. Maybe the dog just likes all food. A scientific experiment would give the dog a choice of foods. Then your child could see if the dog prefers Milk-Bones compared to other foods. If your child offers the dog Milk-Bones, generic dog biscuits, and lettuce, and the dog always chooses Milk-Bones, then your child can conclude that your dog likes Milk-Bones better than generic biscuits or lettuce.

In many experiments, the comparison group is called the "control group." The control group gets no "treatment"—which means you try to leave that group in its natural state. For instance, if you test the effect of coffee on plants, the comparison group or control group is the set of plants that you treat normally (water them, put them in a sunny spot, even talk to them if you want). Treat the "experimental group" *exactly* the same way you treat the control group (same amount of water, same amount of sunlight, same conversation, etc.) *except* for the one experimental difference—in this case, adding coffee to plants' water.

You can also do an experiment with several experimental groups that get different amounts of treatment (e.g., different amounts of coffee) or different types of treatment (e.g., different forms of caffeine—maybe cola, tea, or coffee). So, in the coffee example, the control group would still get no caffeine (water only). But experimental group #1 might get water with 2 tablespoons of instant coffee while experimental group #2 might get water with 4 tablespoons of instant coffee.

Sometimes you can't have a true control group. For instance, if you want to know if men prefer red cars, you won't find a control group with no gender. But, you can compare men and women to see if men like red cars more than women do.

▶ **Repeat the experiment several times or use several subjects (e.g., people, plants, or dogs).** Your child should repeat her experiment enough times—with enough different research subjects—to know that her results are not due to chance or one subject's strange preference. To use the Milk-Bone example again, your child should offer your dog the Milk-Bone, generic biscuit, lettuce choice many times. Does the dog always choose the Milk-Bone? Or does the dog seem to choose at random? Ideally, your child will also experiment with other dogs. Just because *your* dog prefers Milk-Bones does not mean that all dogs do. However, if she tries the experiment with 10 dogs and they *all* choose Milk-Bones every time, she has much stronger evidence that dogs like Milk-Bones better than generic biscuits or lettuce.

All experiments—even those done by professionals—have some degree of error. Some seeds will not sprout, even in perfect conditions. Some plants are sickly and will never grow very much. Some molds are super

molds that grow tremendously under all conditions. Some dogs love all types of food. In order to prevent these sorts of anomalies from ruining your child's experiment, make sure she uses several seeds, plants, men, women, dogs, ants (or whatever) for her experiment. When presenting results, she can use averages (i.e., the average number of ants that ate each type of food, the average size of the mold spots on different types of bread).

▶ **Have your child research the reasons for her findings.** If your child finds that dogs prefer Milk-Bones, have her compare the ingredients in Milk-Bones with the ingredients in other biscuits, identify unique Milk-Bone ingredients, and then research those ingredients to learn why dogs like them. For instance, do those ingredients resemble food that wolves eat in the wild? Science projects are supposed to help children learn why things work they way they do. Don't skip this crucial step.

"Is it ethical to do experiments on animals or insects?"

The scientific community has firm rules about research with animals (there are fewer rules regarding insects but some people argue that insects have rights too). Obviously, your child's science experiment will not be scrutinized by a research review board. Nonetheless, *never* allow your child to do an experiment that will cause pain or death to an animal or insect. And never allow your child to experiment on pets without the explicit permission of the owner (don't even let your child offer Milk-Bones and lettuce to the neighbor's dog without asking—you never know if that dog is allergic to lettuce).

A good rule of thumb is to never do anything to animals or insects that hurts them or forces them to do something that they wouldn't naturally do. Offering food choices to a dog gives the dog the option to eat what he wants or to eat nothing (obviously, don't offer anything harmful or poisonous). Putting cheese and candy in front of ants gives them the same choice. These experiments would pass even the most stringent research regulations.

"What are the ethical rules for including people in experiments?"

Universities and government research agencies follow rules about research with people. First, you can record any behavior that you see in public. Second, you can't ask people questions or give anyone a test for an experiment unless they give "informed consent." A person gives informed consent if they agree to participate after you explain that you are doing an experiment (say that it is for a school project), they know exactly what they have to do, and they know any "risks" involved in the experiment. For instance, if you give someone a taste test, you must warn him that the food might taste bad. If you want to see how long people can stand on one leg, you must warn them that they might get tired. Professional researchers have people sign "informed consent" forms, but for a child's science project, verbal consent should be enough.

Even after your child gets consent, he should follow basic ethical standards and never do anything that will cause discomfort or pain. It is fine to ask people their opinions. It is also fine to ask them to do taste tests (as long as you don't feed them anything harmful). But don't do experiments that will endanger people's health. Also, never conduct research that might make people feel bad about themselves. For example, don't let your child survey others about which of their classmates are smarter, fatter, or prettier.

Finally, professional researchers often promise to keep results confidential. So, if your child conducts a survey or taste test, he might want to promise to keep everyone's identity confidential (in his report, he can give people pseudonyms).

"I dread science projects because my child and I can never come up with good ideas."

Although many parents dread coming up with science projects, there are millions of experiments that children can do. Many teachers give children examples of typical science projects. There are also many good reference books on just about every science topic. Libraries (including school libraries) often carry these books. Look through them with your child and see if you can find an experiment that she thinks is interesting and you think is doable. Also, look on the Internet for ideas. Or, try quizzing your child on what she wants to know about the world and see if you can figure out your own science question.

When you look at books or on the Internet, many of the suggested projects will be quite complex and children tend to like complicated projects. But, they do not need to do elaborate projects to get good grades. Keep reading for tips on how to simplify projects.

"The science project my child wants to do is going to cost a lot of money for supplies. Do projects have to cost a lot of money? How can I make a project less expensive?"

OR

"My child came home with a list of possible science projects— all of them seem impossible. Can you do a science project without having to be a carpenter or a molecular physicist?"

Although science projects can be complicated and costs can skyrocket (especially if you try to follow the directions in a fancy science project book exactly), science projects do not have to be expensive or impossibly difficult. Many books show elaborate experiments just to justify charging $12 for a science project book! Use the book as a guide but don't be a slave to it. Once your child finds an experiment he's interested in, make sure you both understand what the experiment tests. Then you can adjust it all you like (just make sure to follow instructions above for making the experiment scientific). The following tips should help simplify experiments and reduce costs:

▶ *Focus on the question your child wants to answer rather than the experiment itself.* Most science questions can be answered in many ways. Sometimes books (or even the lists sent home by teachers) show complicated ways to answer easy questions. For example, a book might discuss ways to figure out what kinds of chemicals help plants grow. The experiment in the book might require a chemistry set that includes different chemicals to add to plants' water. However, you could do a similar experiment by trying different types of fertilizers and examining how their ingredients differ. Or you could try giving the plants water mixed with "vitamin-rich" substances you have, such as sports drinks, or crushed-up vitamin-C pills. A science project needs a clear question and an experiment designed to test that question but it does not require parents to spend a lot of money.

▶ **Think about how you can modify the apparati needed to conduct the experiment.** A child once told me that he wanted to do an experiment that tested how friction affected movement. He showed me the experiment in a book. According to the book, he was supposed to build two long boxes, fill one with dirt, and grow grass in the other. Then he was supposed to roll a ball down each box and time how long the ball took to roll down. If the ball rolled faster on grass it meant that *greater* friction led to greater speed. If the ball rolled faster on dirt it meant that *less* friction led to greater speed. It was an interesting experiment but this child's project was due in two days. He didn't have time to build boxes, much less grow grass. But he did have carpet scraps and linoleum at home. He ended up testing the *same* friction question by taking a piece of plywood, putting a strip of carpet on one side and a strip of linoleum on the other, and rolling a ball down each strip (the carpet provided more friction, the linoleum less). Another year, I saw a similar experiment that used different grades of sandpaper instead of carpet and linoleum. Clearly, students do not have to build boxes or grow grass to answer the friction question.

Likewise, your child might be interested in an experiment on magnets but you might be daunted by the fact that the experiment expects you to build an electro-magnet. Before you spend the time making the electro-magnet, see if the same experiment can be done with regular magnets (you can get strong natural magnets at hobby shops and teacher supply stores).

Do you remember using a battery to light a light bulb when you were a kid? Maybe you remember doing an experiment to test which materials (wire, string, cord) conduct electricity the best. Nowadays, experiments like this often call for a special plastic case to hold the battery and a stand to hold the light bulb. However, you can easily forgo the plastic cases and attach the battery, light bulb, and conductors with duct tape (just as you might have done as a child). The finished result won't look as tidy but it will be more of a challenge and a better learning experience for your child.

▶ **Use creative substitutes.** For instance, many experiments require growing plants. What if you and your child have a black thumb? What if you don't have time to wait for seeds to sprout? What if you don't know where to buy bean seeds? You can:

• *Grow plants from seeds you already have.* Most raw beans will sprout if you plant and water them. Moreover, any seeds will work (I saw a child experiment on cilantro plants). Even popcorn will sprout little corn plants. Or, sprout a plant from one you already have. If you put branches from pathos plants or "babies" from spider plants in water, they will sprout roots in a week or two.

- *Buy plants from the store.* You can choose little houseplants from the grocery store or go to the nursery for a cheaper "pony pack" of garden plants. Buying pre-grown plants will save you the time and stress of waiting for seeds to sprout.
- *Use plants you already have.* Use plants that you already have as long as you are prepared to sacrifice some of them in the name of science. To make good comparison groups, the plants should be the same type, size, and age.
- *Designate some patches of your lawn* for the experiment (be prepared for brown spots!). You can mark off the sections that receive different treatments (e.g., coffee, no coffee) with string.

▶ **Be willing to put your foot down.** Many children will want to do fancy experiments. I remember talking to a mother who sighed when she explained that her son insisted on making an electronic bell and that it was going to take her husband all weekend to build it. When they displayed the project and I told her that her son had done a good job, she sighed again—her husband had done most of it. Her son had been involved, but it was far beyond his electrical capabilities. And, although he had learned something from watching his father—and made an electric bell that did work—he missed out on one of the most important aspects of the science fair: learning about the scientific process of discovery by struggling with an experiment.

When families think about science projects, they often have limitations in mind. You might only have a weekend to do the project or you may not have a lot of time to help your child (although you should be available for consultation). Other parents try to stick to a budget. Other children want to do a project that's really original. The following lists of projects will give you some ideas about how to work around your limitations. The lists overlap, so peruse them all. And, remember, these lists are not exhaustive. As you read the ideas, you will probably think of many other projects or ways you can tailor these projects to your needs. The point of these lists is to remind you that you don't have to spend months or thousands of dollars to put together a wonderful science project.

Projects That Can Be Done in a Day

▶ *What colors attract more heat?*
- *What do you need?* Four (or more) clear cups, different colored construction paper, water, a ther-

mometer, and sunlight (you want to make sure that you have a sunny day to do this experiment).

- *What do you do?* Wrap each cup in a different colored construction paper. Fill each cup with the same amount of water. Put the cups in the sun. Measure the temperature of the water in each cup every hour. Record the results and then put results in a table, chart, or graph. The water in some colored cups will heat up faster than the water in other colored cups.

- *What should you research to understand your results?* Look up light and the light spectrum. These resources will tell you which colors absorb more light (and consequently heat) and which colors reflect light (and heat) and why.

- *Other ways to do this project:* 1) Put ice cubes on different colored paper (or in different colored bowls or cups) and see which ones melt faster. 2) If it's a really hot day, you can try to cook eggs on black asphalt and white concrete and see which surface cooks eggs faster.

- *Related projects:* What types of liquids heat up the fastest? Do sunglasses block heat (infrared waves) as well as light? Are shadier areas cooler than brighter areas?

▶ *Do advertisers target different audiences during different types of television shows?*

- *What do you need?* A television, several hours to watch television, and a way to record information about commercials (such as a handwritten chart).

- *What do you do?* Choose several different television shows that seem designed for different audiences (for instance, cartoons vs. prime time dramas, talk shows vs. sports, educational shows vs. movies). Create a hypothesis about what types of audiences different programs target (e.g., adults, kids, men, women) and what types of items will be advertised in commercials shown during those programs (e.g., toys during kid shows, makeup during shows geared toward women). Then watch several shows in each category and record the types of items advertised in the commercials shown during each program. Remember examples from the commercials to put in your report. Make a table showing the types of products advertised during each type of show.

- *What should you research to understand your results?* Look up advertising and marketing practices. Look up polls about what types of programs different types of people report liking. Look up research on gender or age and TV viewing.

- *Other ways to do this project:* 1) Look in the newspaper to see if advertisers target different readers in different sections. 2) Look at magazines targeted to different audiences to see if they advertise different products.

- *Related projects:* Do advertisers match the gender or race of the actors in commercials with the gender or race of the actors in television programs? Do different advertisers run commercials at different times of the day?

Projects That Can Be Done in a Weekend

▶ *Does the shape of ice affect how quickly it melts?*

- *What do you need?* A measuring cup, different-sized containers, spray-on oil, a freezer, a plate or pan, a timer.
- *What do you do?* Pour the same amount of water (say, one cup), into differently shaped containers (for instance, a tall thin cup, a wider cup, a large bowl or pan, several parts of an ice cube tray). (Spray each container with spray-on oil before putting the water in.) Put all of the containers in the freezer overnight (or long enough to make sure all of the water freezes solid). One by one, take each shape out of the freezer and carefully dump the ice onto a plate or pan (the spray-on oil should allow it to come out easily). If your cup of

water made several ice cubes, dump out all of the ice cubes it made. Start the timer. Time exactly how long it takes for each cup of ice to become water again. Record the times. (If you place your ice cubes in the sun, make sure they all get the same amount of sun and that they are all on the same colored plates or pans.)

- *What should you research to understand your results?* Look up the states of water (ice, water, steam) and look up surface area. Think about what causes water to change states (e.g., from ice to water) and think about why surface area might affect how quickly ice melts. Why would pieces of ice with the same mass but different amounts of surface area melt at different rates?
- *Other ways to do this project:* See if shape affects how fast liquids freeze.
- *Related projects:* What types of liquids melt faster? What types of liquids heat or boil faster? What types of liquids (salt water, water, oil) does ice melt faster in?

Inexpensive Projects

▶ *What types of food grow mold the fastest?*

- *What do you need?* Four (or more) pieces of bread (or tortillas or muffins, whatever you have), a variety of "spreads" (e.g., peanut butter, jelly, butter, honey, salsa), and four (or more—one for each piece of bread) plastic baggies.

- *What do you do?* Spread each piece of bread with something different (leave one piece of bread plain—this is your "control" bread). Put each piece of bread in a baggie and leave them out of the refrigerator. Check each piece of bread each day, noting if any mold has grown. Note the color, size, shape, and number of mold spots. Draw each piece of bread every few days. The drawings will make good visual displays. At the end of the project, your child will know if mold grows best on sugar, protein, fat, or vegetable matter.

- *What should you research to understand your results?* Look in the encyclopedia, the Internet, or books for the ideal growing conditions for mold.

- *Other ways to do this project:* See how quickly different drinks (soda vs. diet soda), different fruits, or different breads grow mold.

- *Related projects:* Does refrigeration prevent mold growth? Does freezing prevent mold growth? Do plastic baggies help prevent mold growth? What types of bread grow mold faster? What brands of bread grow mold faster?

▶ *Do men or women (or older people or younger people) have larger lung capacities?*

- *What do you need?* A bag of balloons (all the same size), a flexible tape measure (or a piece of string to measure with), and a group of "research subjects." This project is easiest when you have a ready group of participants (for instance, if you are about to attend a party or you know a lot of people in the neighborhood whom you could ask to participate).

- *What do you do?* Ask people to take the deepest breath they can and then exhale once, emptying their lungs, into a balloon. Record each person's age and gender, measure the distance around the balloon at the widest part, and record the measurement. Ask as many people as you can (20 would be a good number). Write the results in a table and make a graph showing the results.

- *What should you research to understand your results?* Look in encyclopedias, the Internet, or books about lungs, breathing, and lung capacity.

- *Other ways to answer this question:* How long can different types of people can hold their breath?

- *Related questions:* Do men or women run faster? Do boys or girls jump farther? Do young people or old people see better?

Projects That Can Be Done with Minimal Parental Help

▶ **What types of food do ants prefer?**

- *What do you need?* Ants (either captured, or a place in your yard where there are ants), fatty foods (peanut butter or butter), sugary foods (candy or honey).

- *What do you do?* Lay out several different types of food near some ants (not right on them, just nearby). If you have captured the ants release them so that they are in between the two types of food. Note the amount of fat, protein, and carbohydrates in each type of food you put out. Watch the ants and every few minutes record how many ants are in each type of food. You can put these results in tables or graphs.

- *What should you research to understand your results?* Look up ants in the encyclopedia, on the Internet, or in books to learn about their diets.

- *Related projects:* Do ants prefer light or dark? Do ants like water? Try these or other questions with other types of bugs.

▶ **Can microwaves prevent seeds from germinating (sprouting)?**

- *What do you need?* Seeds, paper towels, plastic bags, a microwave oven.

- *What do you do?* Divide seeds into different groups. Set one group aside (these are your control seeds). Microwave the other groups for different amounts of time (e.g., 10 seconds and 30 seconds). Keep the groups separate and labeled. Soak paper towels and fold each group of seeds in its own paper towel. Place each paper towel in a plastic bag and seal (make sure the bags are labeled). Check each group of seeds each day to see if they have germinated and measure how long the sprouts are. Record the size of sprouts in a table or chart and draw pictures periodically. Re-wet the paper towels each day.

- *What should you research to understand your results?* Look up seed germination. Also look up what microwaves are, what they do, and what beneficial or negative effects they may have.

- *Related projects:* Does temperature affect how seeds germinate (put some in the refrigerator, others in the freezer, leave others at room temperature)? Does moisture affect seed germination? Do different types of soil affect how seeds germinate (plant seeds in different soils in clear cups—make sure the seeds are on the edge so you can see them)? Do microwaves affect plant growth?

Projects That Answer Social Science Rather Than Natural Science Questions

▶ **Are people with sports cars (or SUVs, or red cars, etc.) more likely to "roll through" stop signs than people who drive sedans?**

- *What do you need?* An intersection with a stop sign and a way to record who makes complete stops and who "rolls through."
- *What do you do?* Sit on the sidewalk by the stop sign for few hours. Note the type (or color, depending on your hypothesis) of each car that comes past the stop sign. Note whether each car makes a complete stop or a rolling stop. (Ideally, use a piece of paper divided into four parts. If you are testing whether sports car owners are more likely to "roll through" make two columns: one for sports cars, one for other cars. Then divide each column in half. In the top half write "full stop" and in the bottom half write "roll through." When a sports car comes to a complete stop, make a tick mark in the top half of the sports car column. When a sports car rolls through, make a tick mark in the bottom half of the sports car column, etc.). After you finish collecting your data, you can then make a table or chart of your results.

- *What should you research to understand your results?* Look at insurance companies' rationales for why they assign higher insurance rates to people who drive certain types of cars. Look at police statistics on what types of cars get more tickets. Do your results confirm what police statistics and insurance companies think? For more research, look at the sociological or psychological literature on risky behavior, rule breaking, or deviance.
- *Related questions:* Are people who drive different types of cars more likely to park illegally or run through yellow traffic lights? Are men or women (or children or adults) more likely to jaywalk?

▶ **Do young people or older people (or men or women, or heavier people or thinner people, etc.) choose to eat less healthy food?**

- *What do you need?* A good seat in a food court and a way to record the types of people who buy different types of food.
- *What do you do?* Sit in the food court where you can see a vendor selling junk food and a vendor selling healthy food. Record what types of people order from each of the two vendors. Try to observe at least 20 consecutive customers at each vendor and record your findings. Make a chart or table of the results.

- *What should you research to understand your results?* Look in newspapers, magazines, and public opinion polls to see if younger or older people (or men or women, etc.) have healthier priorities or are more likely to diet. Research nutrition and problems or benefits that come from different food choices.
- *Related questions:* Are men or women more likely to go to the mall on the weekends? Are men or women more likely to buy more groceries at the grocery store? Are boys or girls more likely to rent videos from the "Action" section of the video store? Are boys or girls more likely to buy rap CDs?

CHAPTER 5

Enrichment and Remedial Activities You Can Do at Home

O BVIOUSLY, YOUR CHILDREN WILL LEARN A LOT OF THEIR ACADEMIC KNOWLEDGE IN school. But because you, as a parent, know your child best, you will also play a huge role in cultivating your child's academic skills. Parents know what their children enjoy, what they are interested in, and what they need help with. This means that you are well equipped to help your child with academics and enrichment, even if you do not feel like you have exemplary academic or teaching skills. You may be surprised to find that many activities you already do with your child probably help to promote his critical thinking skills. And, with a little adjustment, you can turn many of the activities you do on a regular basis into activities that will improve your child's logical thinking, oral communication skills, literary analysis skills, observation skills, knowledge about science and history, and basic math and reading skills. Moreover, you can work to build your child's excitement about learning everywhere you go: on vacation, while running errands, even while watching TV. As you try out the suggestions in this chapter about how to help your child with academics at home, it may help to think of these three simple guidelines:

Encourage your child to develop his interests and make learning fun.

School is sometimes dull. Homework is often tedious. And no one wants to spend *free* time working on drudgery. So, make learning at home fun and interesting. Describe "academic" activities at home as opportunities for your child to explore his interests rather than as schoolwork. If your child hates math, don't hound him constantly about flashcards. Instead, encourage him to write and produce a play, build a model of the human body, or write a computer program. Take him to the library to get books about his favorite baseball player or spend a day at the local natural history museum looking at dinosaurs—whatever he's interested in! Most of the world's geniuses, entrepreneurs, and visionaries attained greatness because they focused on developing their passions. If your child struggles in school, make sure that the

learning you do at home does not compound his frustration. Instead, focus on activities that build his confidence and expand his talents. When you practice skills that are hard for your child, try to approach them in alternative ways or in the context of fun or practical problems. And, no matter what, never let your child see that your at-home learning activities are a chore for you—he will sense it. Your enthusiasm for learning will be contagious—as will your frustration or exasperation. If you're too tired to help your child put on a puppet show, spend the evening reading together or even watching TV. If you get frustrated while working with flashcards, set them down. You and your child both deserve relaxation time and no one will benefit if your child learns that even "fun academics" are a tedious obligation.

Exploit opportunities for learning in everyday activities (even activities that don't seem intellectual at all).

Academic activities don't have to be tied to books. And you don't have to be sitting upright at a desk to learn. Avid learners know that knowledge is everywhere and school skills come in handy for many everyday activities. Teach your child to analyze literature by discussing movies and television shows (and it doesn't have to be PBS programming—you can discuss *The Simpsons* if that's what your child likes to watch). Reinforce critical thinking skills by debating basketball plays and strategies. Put math skills to work as you figure out how fast you have to drive to get to school on time. The best way to make your child love and value learning is to show her that learning is exciting, often easy, and can be used in dozens of ways in everyday life.

Read, Read, Read.

The idea that free reading is the key to academic success is so overstated that it's almost trite. And yet, skill-appropriate pleasure reading remains one of the best ways for children to improve their vocabularies, reading comprehension, and critical thinking skills. Encourage your child to read—a lot. Do whatever it takes to find books or magazines that he enjoys. Read with him if he wants to read materials that are too difficult for him. Talk with him about books that you read together and cuddle with him as you each read your own books in bed at night or on weekend mornings. Show him that reading can be a window into the world and his own imagination. Once he discovers the pleasures of reading, you will never have to nag him to read. Your efforts to make reading fun now will make the difference between your child disappearing into a sunny corner to read on his own and engaging in a daily battle

over the 20 minutes of required "pleasure" reading your child will likely be assigned to do over the rest of his school career. And remember, reading doesn't have to come from books. Encourage your child to read signs, posters, stickers, and the instructions that come with his new video game—if he reads all the words he comes across in his normal life he will be reading constantly.

This chapter addresses questions that many parents have about what they can do at home in order to help their children do better in school and love learning more. The following sections describe how you can create an educational home environment for your child, help your child to enjoy and benefit from pleasure reading, work with your child on math skills, and create "education" out of fun family games, activities, and outings.

Creating an Academic Home Environment

"I want to create an 'academic' home, where my children can get the background that they need to succeed in school. But, I didn't grow up in an 'academic' home and I'm not sure what to do."

Many people worry that only very smart or very well-educated parents can create enriching home environments for their children. But, in fact, all parents, no matter how much they know, have to work hard to create a stimulating, enriching home. And, much of the advantage that well-educated parents give to their children can be duplicated by any parents who are willing to work at making their home-lives interesting and enriching.

Many of the perks that children of "academic" parents receive are not tricky or hard to copy—they simply result from an education-oriented lifestyle. Here are some things you can do to give your children a "leg up" at school:

▶ **Set an example.** Children look up to their parents and often imitate what their parents do. Let them admire your intelligence, your curiosity, and your quest for information.

• *Read* for fun and relaxation. Make sure that your children see that you enjoy books. Always have magazines and newspapers around and let your children see that you enjoy reading and learning about the world. Bring books to read while you wait for appointments, travel by airplane, or lie around at the pool. Show your child that Game Boy is not the only portable way to pass time.

• *Look up the answers* to questions that you don't know. It's fine not to know the answers to all of the crazy questions that your children ask

you. But don't make up an answer; let your children see you find one. Make sure you have a dictionary and, ideally, some reference books and Internet access at home and make trips to the library in order to answer other questions, even if you have to save them up for the weekend.

• *Enjoy learning* even if it's just learning how to fix the garbage disposal. Ask questions and make sure your children see that you care about the answers.

• *Enjoy school* if you go to school. If you are a student, don't complain about homework and your teachers' demands. Share things that you learn in school with your children. When possible, let your children see you use knowledge that you learn in school. Even if you are out of school, point out when something you learned in school is useful in your adult life.

▶ **Support your child's schoolwork.** Make sure your child understands that school and schoolwork are your family's top priority.

• *Don't set up extracurricular activities* that prevent your child from doing homework. Help your child schedule homework and projects around extracurriculars. And, if something has to give, make sure it's the extracurricular and not the homework.

• *Don't set up social activities* (for yourself or your child) that get in the way of homework. Make sure your child understands that going out to play or going on a play date are contingent on getting homework done. Even if your family visits relatives after school or in the evening, make sure your child takes time out to complete homework.

- *Don't let your child skip school* for fun activities (even birthdays).
- *Make time to help* your child with homework. When you say that you are too busy to help with homework, your child learns that other activities are more important.

▶ **Make reading a big part of your family life.** Think about the time your family spends (hanging around, at dinner, in the car) talking about TV shows or movies—use that time to talk about books (imagine your child telling you about a story he read with the same excitement with which he explains what happens in his favorite cartoon). This is even more fun if you both read some of the same books or articles.

▶ **Take advantage of the similarities between books, movies, and television shows.** Even when you're not talking about books, your discussions can be forums for developing critical thinking skills. Take advantage of every conversation you have with your kids—even if you are discussing a cartoon! Think about the questions you (and your child's teacher) ask about books and stories and ask those same questions

about the movies and shows that you and your children watch. Ask your children to identify the "main ideas" or "plots" from movies. Ask them to figure out the "genre" (common book genres include: science fiction, historical fiction, biographies, adventure, mystery) of their favorite TV show. Ask them to talk about the characters, their emotions, their growth through the story. Ask them to guess why characters act the way they do and what they think might happen next. Children can develop good analytical reasoning skills just thinking about movies and televisions shows. (Remember: Not all conversations have to cover genre or plot—those are just suggestions. Even asking your child what he thinks will happen in the next episode of his favorite show will help him think critically about story lines and plots.)

▶ **Take advantage of the learning opportunities in games and everyday activities.** When you play board games, play by the rules and make sure your child does the necessary counting and math (for example, make him add the rolls of his dice rather than just counting, make sure he counts the money in Monopoly correctly, make him do the thinking in card games like War). When you go shopping, have him count the change or estimate the total amount that you might spend on a shopping trip. Help him write thank you notes for gifts, and cards and letters to relatives. Help him use fractions to figure out how many slices to cut a cake into to make sure that everyone gets a slice.

◗ *Take advantage of downtime.* A lot of learning can be done on the fly. Quiz your child on times tables or spelling words while you're waiting in traffic. Bring flashcards with you to practice while you're waiting for siblings to finish with lessons or sports practice. Have your child tuck a magazine or book in his backpack to read while waiting for doctors' appointments or while waiting in line at the post office.

◗ *Bring new information into the house.* Kids like to learn new things. And, as adults, we learn new and interesting facts every day. Maybe we hear them on the radio or read them in the newspaper. Maybe we hear them from a colleague at work, or even read them on billboards. When you learn an interesting fact or statistic, share it with your children. If you learn the average lifespan of a butterfly, the number of cows in your state, or about a new proposal by your city councilman, share your new knowledge at the dinner table. Make learning part of your family life.

◗ *Have discussions.* Children have opinions on everything—and sometimes they are more astute than adults. Try to have discussions, even friendly arguments, with your children. You can discuss etiquette, politics, cars—anything. Just strike up conversations. Ask them how they like the design of the new SUV you just drove by. Would they design it differently? If you see litter in the street, ask what they might do to encourage people to clean up after themselves. If you see a news story about a court case on TV, ask your child what he thinks the verdict will be. You may be surprised at how much you enjoy hearing your child's insights. And your discussions will help him develop his oral communication and critical thinking skills.

None of this means that you should take all of the fun and relaxation out of your family life. But the more you can bring learning into your everyday life—and capitalize on the learning inherent in the things you already do, the better your child will perform in school.

Pleasure Reading

"My child reads a lot but insists on reading books that are too easy for her. How can I push her to read harder books?"

For your child to improve her reading skills, she should read books that are just a touch above her current reading level. But there are many reasons why she might read books that are too easy for her. She might:

◗ Want to take a break from school books that are too difficult for her.

◗ Want to appease you by reading, but

not want the challenge of reading appropriate books.

♦ Be drawn to picture books and feel like chapter books are too dull.

♦ Not know how to find a good chapter book.

♦ Be intimidated by chapter books.

♦ Want to revisit old favorites or books that bring back good memories.

All in all, it's OK for children to occasionally read books that are too easy. Revisiting an old favorite or relaxing with an easy book won't hurt your child's reading skills. In fact, sometimes reading (or rereading) an easy book will reinforce the idea that reading is fun and relaxing (and just think, even if the book is too easy, it's better than reruns on TV). But, you do want to make sure that your child doesn't *only* read books that are too easy because easy reading will not improve your child's reading skills. If she *only* reads easy books, you need to find out why.

♦ *Ask your child what she likes about the books she's reading and why she chose them.*

• Many kids report preferring easy books precisely because they are easy. If this is the case, tell your child that she can read easy books but that you also want her to try some harder books. Tell her that harder books are often more interesting and exciting and that you think that they will be worth the challenge.

• If your child says that she cannot find harder books that she wants to read, tell her that you will help her find good "hard" books.

• If she says that she thinks that books without pictures are boring (this is a common stumbling block when kids transition from picture books to chapter books), then tell her that you know that books without pictures don't seem as fun, but that they can be even more interesting than picture books because they are designed for older, smarter kids. Tell her that there are also some books "in the middle" that have some pictures.

Of course, just telling your child these things probably won't convince her. The following suggestions will help solidify your case.

♦ *Have your child talk to her friends to see what they are reading.* Recommendations from other kids often go over better than recommendations from adults (and although you might have childhood favorites, chances are kids "nowadays" have different favorites). You might also ask your friends or your child's friends' parents to see what the other children are reading.

♦ *Take her to the library or bookstore yourself.* Work together to find some books that might be interesting. Many children don't know how to pick books without pictures because they often do not know how to get a sense of the plot if they can't look at illustrations. Read the backs together and talk about what you think the book might be about. Think about the types of movies she likes and try to figure out which genre (e.g., mysteries, historical fiction, science fiction, coming-of-age stories about teenage boys and girls, or fairy tales and legends) seems the most interesting to her. Talk to the librarian or store clerk and see if they have suggestions.

▶ **Read the new, harder books WITH your child, especially to start out.** If she's scared, intimidated, or concerned that she won't understand these books, you can help ease her through that. Stories are boring when you don't understand them. But they are often more interesting when you hear them out loud—so read them together. Talk about what's going on in the story. Get excited. Talk to her about what she imagines characters and places in the book look like. Remember, this may be her first foray into reading without illustrations; you may have to help her learn how to turn the words into pictures in her head.

▶ **Don't let her fool you.** If you have your child read for a certain amount of time each day (or weekend, or whatever) make sure that she challenges herself at least some of the time. And make sure that she realizes you *know* when she is not challenging herself. While you can let her read easy books every once in a while, let her know that you know she is doing "light"

reading and that you expect her to push herself more on other days. (It's always a good idea to make sure your child is actually *reading* when she says she is. Many kids learn very quickly that their parents don't check to see if they actually read or understand, so they just pretend to read.)

Ideally, you want your child to learn to love challenging books. Encourage her to read challenging books but remember that reading is supposed to be fun. Push a little if she resists, but go slowly. With some help, most kids will move on to harder books on their own—especially once they find an author or a genre that they like.

"I love that my child reads. But books are so expensive! How can I get cheaper ones?"

New books are very expensive—especially if your child goes through them quickly. There are, however, some good ways to get less expensive books:

▶ **Thrift stores, used book stores, and garage sales.** You have to be lucky. But if you check in on your local thrift stores regularly (including Good Will and Salvation Army as well as smaller, local stores) and peruse yard sales and garage sales you might hit the jackpot and find someone who has just outgrown the level books that your child needs. You may find books for a low as 10 or 25 cents apiece.

● *Library sales.* Most libraries periodically have used book sales to raise money. Ask your librarian or look for signs.

● *Online bookstores.* There are several used booksellers online (including bookfinder.com and alibris.com). Through these booksellers you can often find highly discounted books. Amazon.com also lists used books.

● *E-Bay.* E-Bay sellers sometimes sell "lots" (what they call collections or assortments) of children's books for very reasonable prices. Most show photos or list the titles.

● *Discount stores.* Also check out K-Mart, Target, and discount book stores (sometimes called "remainder stores") for good deals.

general rule, funny books—also look into Roald Dahl's shorter books (which tend to revolve around sort of sick humor)—and "scary" books such as those in R. L. Stine's *Goosebumps* series are often popular. Many boys (and girls!) also like Lemony Snicket's *Series of Unfortunate Events* which is a set of rather sarcastic mystery/adventure books that openly dismiss the notion that children's stories should have happy endings. And, if fiction does not seem to captivate your son, try non-fiction. Many boys who will not read novels will read books about lizards, volcanoes, dinosaurs, sports, or astronomy. And you never know, an interest in fiction may come later.

"My daughter reads but my son cannot seem to find any books that he likes."

Unfortunately, many girls seem to like to read more than boys. This results in more books being written for girls than for boys. Overall (and this, of course, is a generalization) boys seem to prefer books about boys. Science fiction is often a hit, as are fantasy books (the *Harry Potter* craze being a case-in-point). But, for younger boys, these types of books are often too difficult. Although many parents may not be drawn to Dave Pilkey's *Captain Underpants* Series, these easy chapter books with lots of "bathroom" humor tend to be quite popular with young boys. As a

"My kids read a lot of books but I'm concerned that they don't really understand what they are reading."

It's useful for children to read as much as they can. Ideally, they should choose books in which they can read most of the words easily and either know the meaning of most of the words—or can figure out the meaning from the context—but which offer some challenging words every few pages. But many children want to read books that are beyond their ideal reading levels. Children may:

● Want to read the book that all of their friends are reading. During the *Harry Potter* craze many kids insisted on reading the books even though the novels were way above their reading levels.

♦ Simply pick up books that look interesting without realizing that they are too hard.

♦ Be frustrated that books at their level are "too babyish." This is often true for children who read below their grade level. Many older girls (10 and over) want to read about relationships and teenagers. Many older boys (10 and over) want to read thrilling adventure, science fiction, and fantasy books. But students who read at first- or second-grade reading levels often find that books geared toward their reading levels are about puppies, rainbow-colored fish, or "scary" monsters.

♦ Want to show off—for instance, by showing their classmates that they "already" read chapter books.

So, what do you do if your child is reading books that you think are too hard for him to really understand?

♦ *First, see if the books are too hard.* Have your child read a few pages out loud to you. If he doesn't stumble over more than one or two words (and knows the meaning of all but one or two words) on each page, the book is probably at the perfect level for him to read on his own (see tip box for more on assessing your child's reading level). If you still aren't convinced that he understands the books he's reading, read them yourself and then discuss them with him (or, have him try taking

a quiz on the book at www.book adventures.org).

♦ *Try reading the books that he is reading so that you can discuss them with him.* That way you can make sure he understands the book and help him to understand difficult portions by discussing them with him.

♦ *If the books are too hard and he really wants to read them, read them with him.* Take turns reading aloud. That way he can enjoy listening to part of the story and you can help him read parts himself. Reading together gives you some control over his frustration level —nothing turns kids off reading faster than not being able to understand what they're reading. Make sure you read enough to keep the story enjoyable.

♦ *OR—see if there is a "Books on Tape" or "Audiobooks" version of the book that your child wants to read.* He could listen to the tape while following along with the book. Obviously your child should not do all of his reading with an audiotape. But, if he occasionally wants to read along with a book while listening to a taped version, it could be a good way for him to enjoy reading, read the books he wants to, and improve his vocabulary.

♦ *Try to steer your child to books that he can read on his own.* Go to the bookstore or library and have your child try several books. Find the section that contains books at your child's reading level. Help your child learn the distinguishing features of books he can read. Publishers tend to make books for younger children larger, with larger type (they sometimes have pictures too). Many publishers grade their beginner books, sorting them into levels that are written on the cover or the spine of the books. Teach your child what "his" books look like so that when he chooses books in the school library he chooses books at his reading level.

▶ If you simply can't find any books that pique your child's interest *and* that fit his reading level, ask your child's teacher about online and mail order stores that specialize in books for beginner readers on more mature topics. One such company is High Noon Books. (See Appendix 8 for contact information.)

"I know that free reading is very important, but my kids won't read unless they have to for school!"

Some kids love reading, others don't. Although many kids learn to love reading from being read to as a child, even that doesn't work for all children. However, you can do a number of things to try to encourage your child to read. Many of them have to do with the overall environment of your home:

▶ *Always have plenty of reading material (at your child's level) at home.* Make frequent trips to the library or bookstore and make sure that your child always has two or three unread books around. Subscribe to children's magazines (*Highlights* would be great but even *Sports Illustrated for Kids, People for Kids,* or *Vogue Girl* will work). Have children's reference books (almanacs, encyclopedias, reference books, *Eyewitness* books—which cover dozens of topics with text, photos, illustrations, and graphs—are great) that your child can flip through and read snippets from if she's not in the mood for a novel or long story. Subscribe to a newspaper and help your child find portions that she can read (many large newspapers have children's sections).

▶ *Limit TV, video game, and computer time.* You don't have to be a tyrant, but make sure that your kids have some time in which reading might be a good option. Even people who love to read sometimes find it easier to watch TV or play games on the computer. Turn off electronic entertainment for some part of every day.

▶ *Don't let your children have TVs in their rooms.* One of the best times to read is in bed, right before going to sleep. It's a good habit for kids to get into—one that many kids never form because they fall asleep watching TV.

▶ *Make sure you have comfortable places in your house to read.* Have comfortable chairs, couches, bean bags, etc., near good lighting. Try to make some time every day when your home is quiet and your children can read. (For instance, during "TV off" time, turn off *your* television, too, so your

How to Check to See if Your Child Can Read a Book

In order to steer your child toward books at the appropriate reading level, you'll need to know how to check to see if books are too easy or too hard for your child. The best way to check your child's reading level is to have him read a book out loud to you. You want to check three aspects of his reading (which are not always perfectly related):

- *Fluency*—how well (and smoothly) your child can read and pronounce the words in the book.
- *Vocabulary*—whether your child knows the meaning of the words that he is reading.
- *Comprehension*—how well your child understands the ideas conveyed in what he is reading.

There are some quick checks that you can do, right in the bookstore or library, to see if a book is at a good level for your child.

- *Have him read a page of the book out loud to you.*
- *Note the number of words that he stumbles over.* Reading experts suggest that children should have 95 percent accuracy in books that they read on their own—you can divide the number of errors your child makes by the number of words on the page for an exact estimate. If he mistakes over 5 percent (or 1 in 20) of the words, look for an easier book. If you don't have a calculator handy, a good rule of thumb is that students shouldn't stumble over more than one or two words a page in a book that they plan to read on their own. If he's stumbling over three to five words per page (about a word or two per paragraph) he probably needs your help reading the book. If he's stumbling over more than five words on a page (or more than one word every sentence or two) he needs to choose an easier book.
- *Ask him to define some of the more difficult words on the page.* Remember that just because students can read words fluently, doesn't mean that they know the words' meanings. Follow the same guidelines as above—if your child doesn't know the meaning of more than three to five words on a page, he probably needs your help reading the book. If he needs help with more than five words on a page, he should choose an easier book.
- *Ask him to summarize the page for you.* Does he understand what's going on? Locate the most important points on the page—did your child catch

children have peace and quiet.)

▶ *Read.* Parents who read set a good example for children, because children watch what their parents do. If you can only relax in front of the TV, don't be surprised if your children consider reading work. Read, talk about what you read, and be excited about it.

"My child likes to read but loses momentum between books. Is there anything I can do to keep her reading?"

Many kids enjoy reading books they consider "good" but then don't know how to pick their next read. There are several ways to help keep your child reading.

▶ *Sequels.* Try to get your child to read series. That way, she'll want to pick up the next book to "see what happens" to her favorite characters.

▶ *Follow the author.* When your child enjoys a book, check the first and last few pages of the book to see if it lists other books by the same author (sometimes they also list books by other authors with similar subjects). If the book doesn't have a list, look up the

them? If he's following the story, he can probably read the book. If he is not following the basic plotline well, you need to help him with the book. If he's not following at all, he needs to choose an easier book.

Once you identify some books that are at a good level for your child, you can point out the features that distinguish books at that reading level. Have him pay attention to:

- *The section of the library or bookstore where you found the book.* Was it an "easy reader"? A "young adult" book? Help him learn to recognize the section where he can find books at his level.
- *The size of the book.* Typically, books get smaller as they get harder.
- *The size of the print in the book.* Print tends to get smaller as books get more difficult. Teach him to glance inside the book to see if it looks like the books he usually reads.
- *The marked reading level on the book.* Many books report a reading level or grade level somewhere on the cover. Look on the front cover, on the spine, and on the back (right above the bar code). It may have a number, an age, a grade level or a "R.L." which stands for "reading level." Help your child recognize the ages and reading levels that are appropriate for him.

From the book *School Sense: How to Help Your Child Succeed in Elementary School* by Tiffani Chin, Ph.D. (Santa Monica Press • 800-784-9553). © 2004 by Tiffani Chin.

author on the Internet (try a bookseller like amazon.com) or at the library.

▶ *Find a list.* Try to find a booklist that contains several books that your child has liked. Your child's teacher or school librarian might have book lists (these are often sorted by genre and reading level). There are also several books on the market that list children's books on various topics (try Kathleen Odean's *Great Books for Girls* and *Great Books for Boys* or Esme Raji Codell's *How to Get Your Child to Love Reading* which includes dozens of short lists and an appendix that lists award-winning books). The online bookstore amazon.com allows readers to post lists of books that they have liked. See if your child can find a poster who has similar tastes as she does (sometimes the lists are hard to find, but when you look up a book your child liked, a "Listmania" box should show up on the right; click a list, and it should bring you to a window that links to more lists—look for a link that says "Top Listmania Lists"). The California Department of Education has an online book catalog into which you can enter your child's reading level and interests and generate a booklist (http://www.startest.org/my search.html) and Book Adventure.org (http://www.bookadventure.org) will help children build booklists. Using a booklist will not only give you ideas about books your child might like, but children often like "checking off" books that they have read and may be

motivated to read everything on the list. (If your child is interested in a more extensive project, she might consider working with her teacher or school librarian to compile book lists of her own based on other students' recommendations.)

"I take my kids to the library, but we just seem to wander around. How can I find books that they'll like?"

Libraries are amazing places, but they can also be very frustrating. When you take your kids to the library, you'll find several resources to help you guide you to "good books":

▶ *Ask the librarian.* The librarian's job is to help you find books—so don't feel like you're bothering her when you ask for help. And, you might be surprised. Some librarians are great at recommending books (even if you don't know exactly what you want). For instance, if your child likes funny books, tell her that and your child's reading level and she may be able to recommend an author or two.

▶ *Use the computers.* Most libraries use computers (some still have card catalogs) to track their collections. On the computer, your child can look up favorite books to find authors' names. Then, find the authors on the shelves and see if they have any other books that look good.

▶ *Browse the new releases.* Libraries

Hands-On Ways to Expand on Reading

Hands-on activities are a great way to expand on your child's reading—or to encourage a reluctant reader to enjoy stories more. Here are just a few examples of activities your child can do after he finishes a book (or even while he's reading):

- *Draw/illustrate.* Encourage your child to illustrate part of the story or draw characters or settings he has imagined from the story. He can make a comic book version of a book he's enjoyed. He can even try to make a pop-up version.
- *Perform.* Children often like putting on plays or puppet shows that depict stories that they have read.
- *Write the sequel.* Many children like to write but get frustrated when they "can't think of a good idea." Encourage your child to write a sequel to a book he's just finished—or rewrite the book with himself as the main character.
- *Visit a site from the book.* Even if you can't visit the exact site where a book took place, try to find a similar setting. If your child just read a book about children who get lost in the Metropolitan Museum of Art (e.g., *From the Mixed-Up Files of Mrs. Basil E. Frankweiler*), visit your local art museum. If your child read a book about camping, see if you can plan a camping trip (or set up a tent in the backyard).
- *Make a food or craft from the book.* Children often like to try out a scene from a book. This might mean making a food from another culture (or having fun with a take-out menu!) or building paper airplanes just as the characters in the book did.
- *Write a letter.* Your child can write a fan letter to the author (many authors have Web sites and children can e-mail them). He can also write to his friends or cousins and recommend the book he just finished.
- *Chat online.* Many authors now have Web sites where children can chat with other kids who are reading the same books.
- *Earn prizes by acing online quizzes.* A Web site called www.bookadventure.org allows children to take 10-question quizzes on books they have just read and earn points for good scores. They can redeem the points for prizes.

From the book *School Sense: How to Help Your Child Succeed in Elementary School* by Tiffani Chin, Ph.D. (Santa Monica Press • 800-784-9553). © 2004 by Tiffani Chin.

often put new books on special shelves or keep lists of new releases. Chances are, if you look through them, your child might find a book that looks interesting or that one of his classmates is reading and that he would like to try as well.

♦ **Use the Dewey Decimal System to find nonfiction books.** Almost all libraries are organized according to the Dewey Decimal System, which categorizes all nonfiction books by subject and then arranges them in a set order. (Fiction books are usually in a separate section organized by the last name of the author.) Before you go to the library, have your child look over the categories in the Dewey Decimal System (see tip box) to find some subjects he might want to read about. Then, follow the numbers on the bookshelves and you should be able to quickly and easily find the topics he's interested in.

ly want to help her integrate some higher quality material, here are some things you can try:

♦ **Read some of her books.** Try to figure out what she loves about them. You may find that they aren't as bad as you think. Or, you may find that you have just been trying to introduce her to the "wrong" kind of good books. Try to find books in a genre similar to the ones that she likes reading.

♦ **Talk to your child's teacher about what she might recommend.** She might know of some books that are both higher quality than what your child is reading and "cooler" than the books you are suggesting.

♦ **Make a deal with your child.** For every "high quality" book (your choice or teacher's choice) she reads, you'll buy her a new book of her choosing. That way, she'll be reading twice as much and getting some quality reading in, too.

"My kids only read 'trashy' books. Every time I try to give them something more 'high quality,' they say that it's boring."

As a general rule, if your child is reading for fun, be thankful. Even if your child isn't reading the classics, pleasure reading improves reading comprehension and vocabulary. And, if your child enjoys reading, she's creating a lifelong habit that can mature and evolve as she ages. Let her read trash. But if you real-

"I want my child to read but he doesn't seem to have the attention span for books. He never seems to finish them."

Although it is wonderful when children read books from cover to cover, a child does not have to read long novels to improve his reading skills. Many children (and adults) prefer to read magazine articles and short stories that they can finish in a sitting or two. Try to find some short books for your child to read (although, as your child's reading skills

Dewey Decimal System Categories

The Dewey Decimal system contains thousands of entries—and it changes and grows all the time. Here are the general categories and some specific topics within each category that might be interesting for kids.

000 GENERALITIES
- 030 Encyclopedias
- 070 Newspapers, journalism, publishing

100 PHILOSOPHY & PSYCHOLOGY
- 130 Monsters, ghosts, astrology
- 150 Psychology, emotions
- 170 Ethics (ethics in friendships, families, recreation)

200 RELIGION
- 210 Evolution/Creation
- 220 Bible stories
- 270 History of religion, witchcraft
- 290 Mythology, world religions

300 SOCIAL SCIENCES
- 300 Interaction, social groups (gender, race, ethnicity)
- 320 Political science (civil rights, immigration, government)
- 330 Economics (careers, money, work)
- 340 Law (courts, famous trials)
- 350 Military, war, military equipment
- 360 Social problems (drugs, environment, forensics)
- 370 Education, college
- 390 Customs, etiquette, holidays, folklore (scary stories)

400 LANGUAGES
- 410 Sign language
- 420 English language (dictionaries, slang)
- 490 Hieroglyphics

500 NATURAL SCIENCE & MATHEMATICS
- 500 Science experiments, scientists
- 510 Mathematics
- 520 Astronomy (stars, planets, aliens)
- 530 Physics (energy, electricity, magnets, sound, light)
- 540 Chemistry (atoms, chemicals, crystals)
- 550 Earth Science (volcanoes, earthquakes, weather, rocks)
- 560 Paleontology (dinosaurs, fossils, prehistoric animals)
- 570 Life science (biology, microscopes, evolution, genetics)
- 580 Botany (plants, trees, fungi)
- 590 Zoology (animals, sea creatures, insects)

600 APPLIED SCIENCES/TECHNOLOGY
- 600 Inventions, inventors
- 610 Medicine (anatomy, health, disease, nutrition, drugs)
- 620 Engineering (computers, cars, trains, weapons, recycling)
- 630 Agriculture (farming, pets, gardening, endangered animals)
- 640 Home economics (food, cooking, sewing, home remedies)
- 670 Manufacturing (metal, plastics)
- 680 Textiles, upholstery, household appliances
- 690 Buildings (brickwork, construction, carpentry)

700 THE ARTS
- 700 Galleries, museums
- 710 Art appreciation, history of art
- 720 Architecture
- 730 Sculpture, masks
- 740 Drawing, crafts, sewing, making ornaments and costumes
- 750 Painting
- 770 Photography
- 780 Music, songs, instruments
- 790 Recreation and performing arts (dance, games, sports, magic)

800 LITERATURE
- 810 American literature (poetry, plays, fiction, essays, jokes)
- 820 English literature (poetry, plays, fiction, essays, jokes)
- 880 Greek myths
- 890 Literature of other cultures (stories and legends)

900 GEOGRAPHY & HISTORY
- 910 Geography, travel
- 920 Biographies
- 930 History of the ancient world (Greece, China, Egypt)
- 940 History of Europe (medieval history, WWI, WWII)
- 950 History of Asia and Middle East
- 960 History of Africa
- 970 History of North America and Central America
- 980 History of South America
- 990 History of Australia and Pacific Islands

From the book *School Sense: How to Help Your Child Succeed in Elementary School* by Tiffani Chin, Ph.D. (Santa Monica Press • 800-784-9553). © 2004 by Tiffani Chin.

improve, it will get harder to find short books). Look for books that are collections of short stories, fables, myths, or legends. Subscribe to some children's magazines (for instance, *Sports Illustrated for Kids, People for Kids, Time for Kids*). Have your child read articles from the magazines. As your child gets older, he can even start reading articles from the newspaper and from adult magazines (major news articles may be too heavy or complicated but many children enjoy reading the sports section, movie and music reviews, and articles about fashion or local events). To make his reading even more productive, have him share the best article he read with you—or even better, with your family at dinner. That way, he can be proud of what he learned and he can also get practice explaining what he read to other people.

"My child doesn't do very well on the reading comprehension part of standardized tests— what can I do to help?"

The best test preparation that children can do (especially for reading comprehension but also for the vocabulary portions of standardized tests) is to read for fun. Reading is the very best practice for verbal tests, including the SAT. Encourage your child to read as much as possible. Talk with her about what she reads (when you have time, read what she reads so you can have

better discussions). If your child does not read for fun, encourage it. Go to the library or the bookstore together and pick out some books that seem fun and interesting. Ask your child to do a certain amount of reading each day. If your child really resists reading books, magazines and comic books are better than nothing. Try to make sure that "free reading" becomes an important part of your child's daily routine. Your child will reap the results for years—especially when she takes the SAT to get into college.

Many of the suggestions in the answer to the first question of this chapter will also help. For instance, if your child learns to think critically about movies she sees, she will have an easier time thinking critically about passages she reads on standardized tests.

Learning and Practicing Academic Skills at Home

"My child isn't very good at math—for some reason the concepts just don't make sense to her—what can I do to help?"

Many schools are being forced to teach math at an ever-increasing pace. You may notice that your child is doing much harder math than you learned at her age. Unfortunately, this often means that teachers can spend less time teaching children the underlying concepts in math and working with manipulatives (concrete items such as blocks, counting tools, rulers, dice, etc.). Plus, while some children seem to learn math instinctively, others need a lot of hands-on work to really understand it. Fortunately, you can do a lot of manipulative work at home—and it can be fun. You can pull out manipulatives to help your child with a homework assignment or if your child seems confused about a particular concept. But you can also teach math concepts with manipulatives *before* your child learns the concepts in school—perhaps over the summer when she gets bored. If your child learns math concepts with manipulatives, she will have a much easier time when her teacher begins formal textbook lessons.

▶ *Get some manipulatives.* You can use almost anything as a manipulative—especially if you are doing basic math operations. You just need lots of small items you can use to demonstrate addition, subtraction, multiplication, and division (e.g., if I have 4 blocks and I get another 2 blocks, how many total blocks do I have?). If you go to a teacher supply store, you can buy tiny cubes that represent units. But you can also use beans, army people, pennies, or M&Ms.

▶ *Show your child the "real life" side of math.* There are simple ways to demonstrate basic math operations

with manipulatives:

- *Addition.* Try 3 + 4. Give your child 3 beans, have her count them. Explain that adding means to give (or add) a specified amount of beans. In this case, you add 4 beans, so give her 4 more beans. Now have her count how many beans she has total. The answer should be 7. You may have to go over this process many times for it to truly make sense, but working with something physical often helps children understand why math works (and that it is not just a random number game).

- *Subtraction.* Try 15−10. Give your child 15 beans. Tell her that you want her to subtract or take away 10 beans. Have her take away 10 beans from her pile. Let her count how many she has left: 5! Keep working on this with other problems until she can do them on her own.

- *Multiplication.* Show her how multiplication is really just adding groups of beans. So 3 × 6 = is like adding up 3 groups of 6 beans. Let her count out three groups of 6. Then let her add them all up together. She should count to 18. Walk your child through many different multiplication problems until she gets it. When she understands, you can begin helping her to memorize the basic multiplication facts (times tables 1s through 12s) so that she no longer has to count or use her fingers to figure out multiplication problems.

- *Division.* Show your child that division is just the process of breaking a large group of beans (or any other object) into smaller groups. Let's say you have 12÷4. Explain to your child that this problem is asking, "How many groups of 4 beans can you make out of 12 beans?" Lay out 12 beans. See how many groups of 4 beans you can make. You get three groups! That's the answer. What if you have a remainder? Try 13÷4. Again, explain that the question is, "How many groups of 4 beans can you make out of 13 beans?" Explain that "groups of 4" means complete, full groups of 4. Have her divide the 13 beans into groups of 4. She should have 3 groups with 1 left over. Explain that remainder is another word for leftover. Her answer is, "3 remainder 1."

Of course, you can try other examples for all of these types of math problems—basically turn them into word problems. Give your child 20 candies. Tell her that she needs to divide those candies between her and her brother (2 people). Tell her that that division problem would be 20÷2. Ask her how many candies each person gets. When she tells you they each get ten, you get to tell her that she just solved a division

problem. Then try another problem— and have HER tell YOU how the problem would be written.

▶ **You can also use manipulatives to show your child fractions, decimals, and integers.** These are often the most difficult concepts for children to understand abstractly. If your child is having trouble understanding fractions, decimals, or integers, spend some time working on real-life examples.

- *Fractions.* Use pizzas to represent fractions. Make them out of cardboard or paper and divide them into evenly sized "slices." (You can even buy pre-made math pizzas at teacher supply stores.) Have your child show you how to divide the pizza into two equal servings, and show her that she has divided it into two halves. Then have her divide it into four servings and show her that she has made 4 fourths (or quarters). Then have her divide it into sixths and eighths — and so on. Show her how two eighths make up a fourth and how two fourths make up a half and how two halves make a whole. Keep playing with the pie (or other shapes that you cut up) until she starts to understand that a fraction is simply a piece of a whole and that when something is divided into sixths it is in 6 equally sized pieces, and so on.
- *Decimals.* Use money to represent decimals. With a ten dollar bill, ten

singles, ten dimes, and ten pennies, you can show your child how tens can be divided into ten ones (singles), how ones can be divided into ten tenths (dimes), and how tenths can be divided into hundredths (pennies—a whole divided into a hundred equal "slices"). Count out different amounts of money and then write the amount out. Show her that when she counts out a dollar and 13 cents, and writes 1.13— she's representing one whole, 1 tenth, and three hundredths (otherwise known as 1 dollar, 1 dime, and 3 pennies). Then ask her to add 5 tenths (dimes) to her pile and write her new dollar amount: 1.63. (Also show her how she would write the problem—1.13 + .5 = 1.63) As you work with the numbers, switching between using actual money and writing out the numbers, the relationship between decimals and money should become clearer.

- Integers (positive and negative numbers). Use a thermometer (or a drawing of a thermometer) to represent integers. Show your child the 0 on the thermometer. Ask your child, if it is 0 degrees and the temperature goes up 2 degrees, what will the temperature be? If she has trouble answering the question, let her count up the thermometer starting at 0. Then ask her what the temperature will be if the tempera-

ture goes up another 5 degrees (again, let her count if she needs to—but show her how her answer is the same as it would be if she just added 0+2+5). Then ask her what the temperature would be if it went down two degrees. Again, let her count down if she wants to. Keep playing with the numbers, going above and below 0 so that your child can see how numbers become negative when they cross 0.

When you first begin, your child may think that it's impossible to subtract a larger number from a smaller number, since in the early grades, most children are taught that you cannot subtract a larger number from a smaller number. Explain that it is possible—and correct—to do it if you use negative numbers in your answer (and explain how, in the real world, the temperature could be +5 and actually drop 20 degrees (to −15) overnight). (If you don't like the idea of using a thermometer, you can also draw a hole in the ground with a ladder that goes down into the hole and extends above the hole—make ground level = 0.)

Don't expect all of the concepts to make sense to your child immediately. Some concepts are harder than others and some children grasp them more quickly than others. Work a little bit every day (or every day you have time), play-

Materials You Should Have to Encourage Out-of-School Learning

- *Books*—Always have plenty of books on hand that your child can pick up "if he gets bored." Make frequent trips to the library or bookstore and let your child pick out books that interest him.
- *Magazines*—Everyone likes to do "light" reading sometimes. Have magazines around so that your child has ready material if he wants to read for a short period of time.
- *Games with an educational component*—Kids play games when they're bored. Make sure they have some games that will push them to think. Games do not have to be explicitly educational to promote thinking skills. For instance, strategy games (e.g., chess, Connect-4, Battleship) don't make children spell or calculate but do require critical thinking. Have fun playing educational games as a family (e.g., Boggle contests) and your child will be more likely to choose educational games when he plays with friends.
- *Puzzles*—Puzzles of all kinds push children to think. Let your child choose some jigsaw puzzles, crossword puzzle or word search books, and books of "mind benders." Also look for boxes of "quiz cards" and mind bender puzzles (a company called BrainQuest makes question cards on a variety of topics for all grade levels; Mensa makes brainteaser cards). Even kids who balk at the idea of puzzle "workbooks" may enjoy using fun puzzle cards (it's all about presentation).
- *A computer with educational software*—Children love to play on the computer. Make sure that they have educational software to choose from. If the games are fun, they won't mind that they are learning.
- *Research materials/reference materials*—Children have so many questions about the world. Make sure that your child has the materials he needs to search out answers and satisfy his curiosity.
- *Videos or DVDs with educational content*—Most children can spend a great deal of time in front of the television. Take advantage of this by providing educational videos. Again, these do not need to be dull. Many children love Discovery Channel-type videos about animals, space, or volcanoes. Look for videos that address topics that your child is particularly interested in. Also look for videos and movies that depict classic books and stories (e.g., *Anne of Green Gables, Island of the Blue Dolphins, Dracula*)—movies often inspire children to read the book.

ing with the manipulatives and working to get numbers to make sense to your child. In most cases, continued work with manipulatives will eventually "click" and your child will understand how the math works.

"I want my kids to get enrichment at home (especially over the summer) but they hate doing workbooks and playing the educational games I buy for them."

For the most part, kids hate doing workbooks—in or out of school. It's worse over the summer because they don't feel like they should have to do schoolwork at all. As a general rule, don't expect your child to want to do worksheets over the summer. If you feel like he should review a particular subject, you could try to make a game out of it—have him do "Mad minute" math worksheets and give him some kind of prize if he can complete an entire worksheet (100 percent correctly) in a minute (or some other pre-decided time). Or get fun workbooks—like puzzle books or books with logic games. Take your child to the store with you, you might be surprised to find that he will pick out some interesting work that he will actually do (the fact that he picked it out himself will give you more leverage to push him to do it). While you shouldn't expect your child to spend much time doing workbooks over the summer, he can get enrichment in other ways:

▶ *Encourage him to read.* Kids who read for pleasure not only tend to do better in school but on SAT tests. So, take him to the library or the bookstore, help him to pick out books he thinks he will enjoy (see the answers to

- *Journals and notebooks*—Many kids like the idea of keeping a journal or diary or writing their own book. Sometimes special notebooks provide inspiration. Don't invade your child's privacy but offer to proofread her writing or help her with ideas if she wants.
- *Stationery*—Many children enjoy receiving letters (or e-mail) enough to motivate them to write letters. Have your child write to a grandparent or a cousin who lives far away. Or, see if she would be interested in getting a pen pal. Many Internet sites list pen pals. Or, your child's teacher may have a connection for pen pals. Also, fan clubs (for movie stars and music stars) often have pen pal lists. If your child has a favorite band, she might enjoy writing to another child who loves the same band.

From the book *School Sense: How to Help Your Child Succeed in Elementary School* by Tiffani Chin, Ph.D. (Santa Monica Press • 800-784-9553). © 2004 by Tiffani Chin.

questions in the "pleasure reading" section for more details). Encourage him to find a series that he likes so that he will have a whole set of books he wants to read. Try to find a place at home where he can retreat to read—a window seat, a special chair in the yard or on the balcony, a beanbag in a room that is usually quiet during the day.

▶ *Encourage your kids to play games with an educational component.* The best way to do this is to play the games yourself. When parents relax in front of the TV but expect their children to spend their free time playing Scrabble, the children learn that Scrabble isn't fun—it's something that your parents make you do. But if you play educational games like Scrabble or Trivial Pursuit with them (or with your friends), your children will come to think of these games as fun, too. Teach their friends how to play too so that your children will have playing partners.

▶ *Try nontraditional workbooks and educational work.* Very few kids will enjoy (or even agree to) doing pages and pages of math review problems in their free time. But, if you bring home a book of brainteasers, they might be more interested. Many kids get very excited when their teachers pass out puzzles and other critical thinking assignments—and you can get whole books of them at book stores and teacher supply stores.

▶ *Try computer games.* Many kids find almost any activity more fun on the computer. So try setting your child up with some learning games or activities on the computer—you might be surprised to find that he gets into them. Again, look for games and activities (either in a store or online) together so he feels that he has options about what games he plays. And, try to look for games that force your child to think, not just games that have math or reading as a by-product to the actual game.

▶ *Get educational movies and videos. If your child is going to spend time in front of the television, impose some educational content.* Rather than watching *Simpsons* reruns you could get Discovery Channel videos of animals, rocket ships, foreign countries—whatever your kids find interesting. Again, let them pick. Many kids report loving educational videos and report what they learn from them for a long time.

▶ *Start some hobbies.* The kids who get the most out of summer are often not kids who spend a lot of time reviewing math flashcards or going to summer school. The kids who learn the most during the summer learn about topics and activities that they would not experience in school. They go on vacations and they develop new hobbies. Encourage your child to work on a hobby, this could be gardening, training the family dog, collecting stamps, practicing a musical instrument, or learning another language. Encourage him to research his hobby (go to the library and get books on animal training or get cassettes for learning a new language) and encourage him to follow his interests. Kids often learn the most when they choose what to learn.

♦ *Take your kids out* (or sign them up with a summer program that takes them out, or hook up with the parents of some of your kids' friends and take turns taking them out on your days off). Kids learn new things just by experiencing new environments. See the last questions in this chapter for more information on places you can take kids and how to make the experiences educational.

"I want to do things to help my child succeed in school but between my work schedule and my child's activities, we don't have very much time."

There are many activities that parents and kids can fit into busy schedules that can be both fun and academically enriching. Reading the answers to some of the earlier questions will give you some clues, but here are some other suggestions.

♦ *Use car time.* Use car time for conversations. Talk with your child about books or current events. Or use car time to quiz her on spelling words or math facts.

♦ *Use waiting time.* Many families spend a lot of time waiting—waiting for a sibling to finish with soccer practice, waiting at the drive-through, waiting at the pharmacy or doctor's office. Keep some magazines in the car or in your bag. Pull them out while you wait and read and talk together.

♦ *Make shopping a learning experience.* When you are out shopping with your child, get her involved in price comparisons, figuring out sale prices, figuring out tax, using coupons, and counting out money. Many very valuable math skills can be learned simply by going to the mall and the grocery store (e.g., how to add, how to estimate, how to figure out percents, how to add and subtract decimals). Many kids find these exercises a challenge. For an added twist, give her a small amount of money and see if she can figure out what she can afford. If she can, she can spend the money. And, don't forget restaurants. Once your child learns about decimals, she can be in charge of figuring out tips in restaurants. To find 10% of anything (such as your bill total), your child just has to move the decimal once to the left (so 10% of $32.50=$3.25). To find 20%, she doubles that number (teach her to estimate for percentages between 10 and 20).

♦ *Make the most of the time you spend talking with your child.* This doesn't mean you have to talk politics or math or history. Even exchanging jokes and riddles can be fun and use critical thinking. Just be sure to explain jokes and help her understand why punchlines are funny if she doesn't seem to understand.

▶ *Create systems where you and your child do not have to be in the same place at the same time in order to exchange ideas.* For instance, you can use the refrigerator as "learning central" and leave messages for one another. For example, if your children get home from school before you do, you could put a post-it with a new word on it on the fridge every morning. The sibling who uses it in the best sentence at dinner gets a prize—or maybe gets to choose the word for the next day. You could also put a question on the fridge in the morning and give the kids the afternoon to find the answer. (If you don't have time to put these things together in the morning, make five on Sunday night and then have them for the week—or buy a book of questions or vocabulary words that you can pick from.) Or, have your children read the newspaper when they get home. They can each cut out the article that they thought was most interesting and stick it on the fridge. You can skim the articles when you get home (maybe while putting dinner together) and then everyone can talk about the articles at dinner.

▶ *Enlist other adults.* Encourage your child to write letters back and forth with grandparents, e-mail with older cousins, or instant message with college-age friends of the family.

▶ *Read separately but discuss together.*

Maybe your child is a good reader, but you wish that her comprehension was better. If you don't have time to sit and read chapter books out loud with your child, buy (or borrow) two copies of the books that she reads. She can read in her spare time and you can read in your spare time (maybe after she has gone to bed) and then you can discuss when you have a spare moment together.

"I want to do activities that will help my children succeed in school but I don't have time to watch over them all the time. Is there anything they can do on their own?"

There are lots of activities that children can do on their own to help them improve their school performance. Although almost all of these activities require some set-up time, kids can do them while you are busy or out of the house.

▶ *Read.* Get some good books, and they can be set for weeks.

▶ *Puzzles.* Big jigsaws, crosswords, and mind-benders can occupy children for hours and build important critical-thinking skills. (Many adults are surprised to find that "analytic" problems on law school (LSAT) admission exams look just like mind benders they did as kids.) Different kinds of puzzles help children use different parts of the brain. Check your local teacher supply store, bookstore, or the Internet for mind-benders.

◗ *Games.* There are many educational games in stores and on the Internet.

"Is it OK to bribe my kids to do academic activities?"

Yes and no. Everyone likes some extra motivation to do things they don't like—and they sometimes even end up liking the task in the end. So, rewarding your child for learning all of his times tables or finishing a project is OK—as long as you don't reward your child for every academic activity that he does. And, ideally, the reward should be related to the activity. So, when your child finishes a book, a great reward would be a trip to the bookstore and the gift of a new book. If your child wants to do a summertime report on lions because she loves them, a great reward for the completion of the report would be a trip to the local zoo or wild animal park to see the lions. You don't, however, want to undermine your child's personal motivation. Bribing a child too much may make her lax to do academic work that she would ordinarily do unless she gets a reward. So, while it's OK to bribe sometimes, don't overdo the rewards. Remember that your praise and your child's increased success in school should be reward enough. Here are some basic guidelines:

◗ *Reward kids for overcoming challenges.* Sometimes a surprise gift or celebration is better than a bribe, especially when kids want to succeed even without any extra motivation. So, if your child worked really hard on a report and received a good grade, make his favorite dinner or get him a small toy that he has had his eye on. You don't need to tell him you are planning to do this, make it an "icing on the cake" kind of reward for getting a good grade.

◗ *Institute a system that encourages children to do academic work that they enjoy without bribing them to do it.* If your child loves to read, don't bribe her to read. She's doing it on her own. But do encourage her reading— either by buying her new books or taking her regularly to the library. If your child loves MathBlaster computer games, when she masters one, get her the next level.

◗ *Try to make your rewards reinforce the learning process.* Don't reward doing an extra credit project with un-limited mindless time in front of the TV. This makes the report a chore and mindlessness the reward. Instead, if your child found that the almanac at school was the coolest reference source he had ever used, reward him with his own copy.

◗ *Save bribes for activities that your child particularly hates.* Don't make your child feel that she should be bribed to do all academic work. Academics are her job—it won't all be fun but most of it should be tolerable. So, save bribes for tasks that are particularly distasteful to your child—such as the book report that she has to finish on a book that she absolutely hates (and yes, although I believe that all children can enjoy reading—not all children enjoy all books).

"Am I a horrible parent if I don't make my kids look up every word that they don't know in the dictionary?"

No. In fact, one of the best ways to make reading boring is to force kids to look up every word they don't know. Every child should know how to use a dictionary and should be encouraged to use one. But no one likes looking up words. If you want to encourage your child to read and to learn new vocabulary, make it easy. Help her out with words that she doesn't know. Give her good definitions, good examples, even act words out for her. Don't be afraid to look words up together if you're not sure of the exact definition (or how to explain a word—people often know words but still cannot define them), but don't force her to spend hours slaving over the dictionary.

A good rule of thumb is to tell children the meanings of words you do know and look up words you aren't sure of together. That way, she learns how to look words up and learns the value of the dictionary without learning to hate it. Once she becomes comfortable with the dictionary, feel free to occasionally say, "Look it up!" Do it when you're busy or when your child is just wasting time anyway. But if she's in the middle of a good book or a homework assignment and you know the meaning of a word—feel free to tell her. She'll appreciate it.

"I know that I am supposed to do educational activities with my kids, but we're usually so tired that we have our 'family time' by watching TV together."

Then make the most of your TV time! Although it's great when families play Trivial Pursuit together and discuss politics after dinner, many families don't have the time or energy to do this on a regular basis. But that doesn't mean that downtime has to be non-academic or non-intellectual. Talk about what you see on TV. On commercial breaks ask your children to predict what they think will happen next in the program that you are watching (this is an important skill in analyzing literature) or ask them how they think different characters are feeling at different points in the story line (another reading comprehension skill). You can also talk about words, phrases, or allusions from the dialogue that they might not have understood. Watching television and movies (especially animated movies) with children is always interesting for adults because the adults realize just how much goes over the children's heads. Talk with your children about some of these references and what they mean.

You can even talk about commercials. Make a game of discussing with your children what aspects of each commercial they think the advertising executives are using to convince people to buy their products (attractive models, the image of being rich or powerful, the adorable look of a puppy). See if your kids can figure out who the target audience is (e.g., men, women, adults, children, people of different religions or ethnic groups) for different ads. Ask your children how they would design the ads to make them better. You could have a great time picking apart commercials and developing your children's critical thinking skills (and perhaps even priming them for jobs in public relations).

Educational Materials

"Where can I get 'enrichment' materials to use with my kids?"

There are many places to get academic materials. The most basic supplies (magnetic letters, flashcards, chalkboards) can often be found in discount stores (such as Target and Walmart) and well-stocked drug stores. Many bookstores also stock workbooks, books of puzzles and mind benders, vocabulary books, and test preparation books. If there is a teacher supply store near your house, they stock all kinds of books, workbooks, flashcards, manipulatives, learning games, and other materials. If you can't find a good supply store near your home, ask your child's teacher where she gets her teaching supplies (teachers almost always have a source for things like posters, awards, and bulletin board decorations—if they order through the mail ask if they have an extra catalog; if they order on the Internet, ask for the Web site).

And, of course, you can order just about anything on the Internet. Start with searches on amazon.com (which stocks just about everything nowadays) but if you are looking for something in particular, do a Web search (use a search engine like google.com) or check out the sites in Appendix 8.

Also, don't forget your local library for books, videos, and books on tape. And, most toy stores have lots of games and toys that can be educational. Any game that involves counting will build younger children's math skills (including very simple games such as the card game War). Working with money (e.g., in games like Monopoly and Life) is also good for math skills. And, don't forget games that involve strategy (e.g., Battleship, Connect-4, or Mancala) or those that improve memory (such as Memory). Many games do not explicitly involve academic practice but are great for developing critical thinking skills (try Checkers and Clue for some classics). Many kids enjoy jigsaw puzzles, which are good for concentration and critical thinking—and there are fantastic 3-D puzzles made of foam on the market now that build into castles, pyramids, and other historical buildings.

Specialty stores are great places to find a lot of games, puzzles, videos, and books. The Discovery Channel Store, for instance, carries wonderful animal videos and books as well as puzzle books, boxes of mind bender books, and games. Look in your local phone book to see if you have a puzzle store nearby—you'll be amazed at all of the different types of puzzles available for children.

Most electronics and computer stores carry children's software, much of which is educational. If you are unclear how to choose among different educational products, ask your friends what software their children enjoy. Your child may have even tried out some games that he likes at a friend's house. Or, if you want to make sure that the games you are buying are truly educational, ask your child's teacher if she has any recommendations. After watching children try many different games in the classroom and in the school computer lab, many teachers have a sense of which games really push kids to think and which are mostly "fluff." If your child's teacher does not have any rec-

ommendations, ask your school's computer expert. And, if that fails, many Web sites post reviews of children's games and software. For instance, Superkids.com (http://www.superkids.com) reviews children's software much the same way a magazine would, rating and commenting on the "fun" of the games as well as the educational value and how easy they are to use (most reviews also list the skills that children can learn and improve with each game). PC magazine (http://www.pcmag.com) also reviews children's software. Or, if you would prefer to learn the opinions of other parents, check out http://www.eopinions.com (look under computers and then search for educational software). On the "eopinions" Web site you can look up reviews of different programs (many programs have dozens of reviews written by parents). Also try amazon.com's online store (http://www.amazon.com)—they have parent reviews for most of their educational software.

"Do I have to buy fancy teaching supplies to provide my child with enrichment?"

No. In fact, you can help a child almost exclusively with materials that you have at home. But do remember that kids love new things and are often more interested in using them, so sometimes even inexpensive learning toys are a good investment.

Educational Outings

"My kids get bored with reading and playing computer games at home. What else can we do that is educational?"

Even though reading for fun is crucial to academic development, there is more to life than books. Make sure you and your kids get out of the house and explore . . . everything. One great idea for parents who are at a loss for what to do on weekends and during the summer, is to get a guide book (a Fodors or Frommers, even an "Access" book) for your area (check out the "Travel" or "Local Interest" section of your local bookstore; you will probably find a wide variety of guide books). Many stores carry travel books specifically designed for families with kids. Think about all the cool things you see when you visit a new city—you have probably never seen the equivalent "sights" in your own town.

So, take a handful of Saturdays or some days over the summer and do "the tourist thing" in your own area. For instance, in Los Angeles, you might take your kids to see the Watts Tower or the Queen Mary. In Boston, you might visit Paul Revere's house or the site of the Boston Tea Party. In Washington, D.C., take the White House Tour. In New York City, go to the top of the Empire State Building and take the Ellis Island tour. And, although these are highlights, don't forget the lesser-known sites in your area. Sometimes small monuments and museums are the most interesting (for instance, check out the small-but-fascinating Tenement Museum in New York City). Let your child look through the guide book himself and see what he would like to do. Check off sights and activities as you do them and see if you can work your way through the entire book (the great thing is that many tourist sites are actually pretty cheap).

What if there isn't a tour book for your area? (Or, if you want to a get a jumpstart but don't have time to get the book...) Here are some ideas for day trips you can use to enrich your children's experiences and springboard into challenging conversations and long-term interests.

▶ *Go to the zoo, wild animal park, marine park, or aquarium.* Even the petting zoo at the local county fair or pumpkin patch will do. Kids love to talk about animals. And animals often inspire great questions. While you look at the animals, take the time to read the signs that give information about the animals and their habitats. Talk about which animals are carnivores and herbivores. Talk about why some animals seem to be awake during the day while others are sleepy (otherwise known as diurnal versus nocturnal animals). (See the next question for more on things to do at the zoo.)

▶ *Check out the local architecture.*

Many towns have architecture from many different eras and styles. Some cities have famous buildings and sky-scrapers. You can drive (or walk) around and check out buildings for free. And, if you do some reading before hand, you can play a game to see who can pick out the most distinctive features of different buildings and guess what style they represent. Many tour books include "walking tours" of cities' architectural landmarks. Look through the "local interest" section of your local bookstore or public library for a book on your community's architectural styles.

♦ *Explore your local museums.* Many kids love dinosaurs and love to draw and paint. So, what could be better than taking them to a natural history museum or an art museum? Natural history museums are a great place for your kids to show off how much they know about dinosaurs—and then learn some more. They will also see models of other prehistoric animals such as woolly mammoths and saber-tooth tigers. If you read up on some of these creatures before you go, you will have even more fun seeing the skeletons you have read about. Art museums can also be very fun, even if they are a little more intimidating. There are dozens of art books for children (many are quite fun, including cartoons and funny facts about artists) which you can use as "preparation materials" to get your child excited and interested in art before you go. And don't forget science

and technology museums—which can be wonderful for budding astronauts and engineers—and children's museums. Children's museums usually have lots of hands-on activities for children of all ages. For instance, The Exploratorium in San Francisco has mazes for children to crawl through and a "touch dome" where children can use senses other than sight to explore their surroundings.

♦ *Go to the county fair—and don't just hang out at the carnival.* County fairs are some of the most interesting places in the world—but many families spend all their time on rides and playing games. Take some time (or make a second visit) and check out the other features. Most fairs have large livestock sections (where local farmers display pigs, goats, cows, and horses) for kids to look at. Often the animals are raised by *other kids* in 4-H clubs, and many will even answer your kids' questions about how they raise the animals. Many fairs also have special exhibits such as an area with all baby animals (including chicken eggs incubating and hatching). Some have egg-laying contests and you can watch hens lay eggs. You can even watch some of the events as animals get judged. And, there's more than just animals. Many fairs have displays of fruits and vegetables, handicrafts, art, and more. Art displays are particularly fun, because local children often enter their work. Your child might even be inspired to enter a work of art next year.

● *Keep your eyes out for murals and other public art.* Many communities have murals, public sculptures, and statues, even artful fountains in public spaces. Some are new; others are quite old and well preserved. Go and see them with your kids. You can talk about the art, why the artist chose that design, what people see in it when they go by. And, if you are unlucky enough to live in an area where murals get defaced, you might even talk about graffiti and how it affects the urban landscape (and then you can talk about the difference between muralists painting on walls and graffiti taggers painting on walls).

● *Go for a hike.* If you live in a place where you can get out of town, go on a day hike. You can learn about local trails from your tourist center or welcoming center or at the local bookstore (again, look in the local-interest section). Try to pick a trail that has something fun at the end (waterfalls are always nice; vistas are nice but a little less thrilling to kids). Wear good shoes, bring a picnic (or water and snacks), and go for a walk. If you live in the city, being out in nature, seeing the trees and animals, will be a whole new experience for your child. If you can't get out of town easily, go to the nearest big park and try to do a little nature walk— check out the trees, the squirrels, even the fountains. You might even talk about what your child would include if he were designing his own park. And, if

there are no good parks in your area, do an urban walk. Check out the local stores, restaurants, billboards. Try to talk about better ways to organize a city or how your child would arrange the streets and buildings.

● *Visit local ethnic enclaves.* Many towns and cities have areas where new immigrants live and operate stores and restaurants. Chinatowns are probably the most well-known ethnic enclaves (and seeing ducks roasting in the windows, live frogs for sale, and bins and bins full of spices will have your children asking questions for days), but keep your eyes open for other ethnic neighborhoods as well. For instance, Los Angeles has Mexican, Japanese, Central American, Indian, and Vietnamese enclaves (just to name a few). Go and walk around, eat in a new restaurant. Let your kids pick out some souvenirs. Try to learn the proper names for the foods you eat and the toys that they buy.

● *Keep your eye out for special events.* Many cities and towns have special children's exhibits at museums and libraries. Many libraries and book stores have story reading hours and puppet shows—even book signings. If you see that a good children's author will be signing books in your neighborhood, read some of the author's books with your child, think of a good question she might ask the author, and go to meet him and get the book signed.

If you have time for more than a

day trip, think about:

▶ *Vacations.* Even weekend trips expose children to a world of new sights, sounds, and ideas. And, when you get to your destination, make sure you explore interesting new places, including sites of interest, museums, zoos, even different restaurants.

▶ *Camping.* On top of seeing new places, camping exposes today's modern kids to a whole new way of living. What do you do when there is no TV? How do you cook without a stove? How do you bathe without running water? If you're up for it, camping trips are inexpensive ways to open up a new world for your children.

And, believe it or not, all of these fun outings can be very educational. Just keep up the conversation, encourage your kids to ask questions, propose theories, and make comments and comparisons about their new experiences. And, try to build on these questions and insights when you get home (for example, look for books about the new animal you saw, study a trail map) and you will have created a truly enriching experience *without* getting bored.

"My kids love the zoo, but is going to the zoo really educational?"

Of course the zoo is educational—and, like most things, the more you work to make it educational, the more educa-

tional it becomes. First of all, just seeing new animals, thinking about where and how they live, is stimulating for young children. When children see animals and their "natural" habitats in the zoo, they see animals that they will later hear about and read about—a trip to the zoo will stock your child's imagination with memories of real-life animals. (Once, while working with a fourth-grade reading group, we read about African animals. One of the animals was an antelope. I paused the group to ask them if they knew what an antelope was. One of the girls raised her hand and said, "A melon that you eat with sugar!") Just seeing a real live antelope (and all of the other animals in the zoo) will help your child understand what she reads for the rest of her life.

But, of course, you can also make your child's educational experience at the zoo even more powerful. Read the signs in front of the animals with your child. (If your children are very young, just skim the signs and tell your children the most interesting facts.) Encourage your child to pick a favorite animal and learn the most about that one. And then cultivate that interest—stop by the gift shop and pick up a book about that animal or get one from the library the next day. Also look for videos about that animal and check your local toy store for models or puzzles. Look up that animal in the encyclopedia at home, or even on the Internet. Turn your trip to the zoo into a learning experience and a casual research project. And, pick a new interesting animal each time (if your child is very attached to her first favorite, say a bear, suggest that that be her favorite mammal and that this time she should pick a favorite reptile—or bird or amphibian—or go for even smaller categories, such as canines or simians (monkeys), so she can keep learning about different types of animals). If you need a refresher course on animals, do a little reading before you go to the zoo. But remember, no parent is expected to know everything—especially about exotic animals—so if your child asks a question that you don't know, tell her you don't know the answer, but she can help you look it up when you get home—and make sure you do it. This will not only answer your child's question but teach her how to satisfy her own curiosity.

"I know I should take my kids to art museums, but I don't know anything about art, and I get bored in museums. So, how can I keep my kids interested?"

Unless you grew up going to art museums or majored in art, chances are you don't know much about art. You may not even like it very much. Strangely enough, that doesn't mean that you have to stay out of art museums. In fact, it may mean that you and your kids can have even more fun in museums than more "art-educated" parents

have with their kids. Rather than you dragging your kids around the museum lecturing at them, you can learn together. How? The secret is to go straight to the gift shop and buy a book (just get the paperback book that covers the museum's "highlights"). Grab a museum map (usually free at the information desk) and you will be all set to go through the museum. With the book and the map you will be able to take yourselves on a self-tour where you can move at your own pace (rather than the pace of a tour guide) and see what you want to see. (This also means that if you find you really hate a particular artist, you can skip him—even if he is really famous.) You can also play fun games with art using just a tidbit of knowledge (for instance, in high school, I learned that seventeenth-century Dutch still lifes always had bugs in them. I have since gone through many hallways of Dutch art trying to prove this theory wrong). See if you and your children can discover some games of your own. For instance, see who can find an example of pointillism (paintings made entirely of tiny dots—Seurat's work is a classic example).

Before you start walking, sit down with your child and look at the map. Show him what types of art are in different parts of the museum. Ask him what he would like to see—and go with his choice. Open your book to the proper section (most museum books are divided into sections that correspond with the museum layout) and match the art on the walls around you with the art in the book. When you find some that match, read out the interesting parts of the descriptions. For instance, the description might say that the artist painted a particular picture during an especially sad time in his life. Ask your child if the painting looks sad to him. Why or why not? (Sometimes this is obvious. For instance, in Picasso's sad period—known as his "Blue Period"—he used mostly blue paint.) Ask your children what they think of the art, the colors, or the representations. If they decide that they hate the art, ask them why. Encourage them to be polite and speak quietly but let them express their feelings and explain what they like and don't like—even if they just like a painting because their favorite colors are in it.

When you get home, you can do some art projects of your own. Your kids may want to copy a picture they saw. Or, if you saw some modern art (such as a canvas painted blue or a Jackson Pollock-style splatter painting) your child may want to see if he can do something even better. Let him try. Imitating someone else's style is one of the best ways to learn the traits of an artist.

"How do I make vacations educational? Do we have to go someplace historic like Washington, D.C. or the state capital?"

Historic sites are rich with educational stimulation. But so are other vacations. When you go on vacation (even if you just go to a nearby city to visit some relatives) get a guide book and follow the same suggestions listed above for exploring your hometown. Seeing new sites is always stimulating for children and will always incite new interests and curiosities (even if they only ask why your town is so much better, cleaner, brighter, or flatter than the town you are visiting). Here are some other tips:

▶ *Visit historical sites.* When you get there, pick up the free literature, and consider either buying a book or taking a tour. There is no point in going to historical sites if you don't learn the history behind them. Why is the site historically important? What can you learn from it? (Perhaps when you get home you and your children can do some research on the grander historical significance of the places you visit—if you visit Paul Revere's house, study the Revolutionary War when you get home; if you visit Pueblo ruins in Arizona, learn the history of the tribe.)

▶ *Visit scientific sites.* Children often love science more than they love history. Visit volcanoes in Hawaii. Visit canyons (e.g., The Grand Canyon, Bryce Canyon) in the Southwest. Visit shuttle launching sites at Cape Canaveral in Florida. Make sure you learn about the science behind the sites while you are there (e.g., How did the volcanoes form? How did the canyons form?

How were the shuttles built?). Pick up postcards and you can put together a scrapbook or photo album when you get home.

▶ **Learn the local culture.** Many communities and regions have their own folktales, legends, even ghost stories. Look for local books (either children's books for your child to read or adult books for you to read to your child). You might find them in book stores, tourist sites, or even in discount stores (such as Wal-Mart). If you go to a country or region with a different language, pick up some easy books on learning the language (your kids will probably enjoy learning to count and say basic words in Spanish or Hawaiian!).

▶ **Pay attention to the local wildlife.** Look for different types of animals, birds, fish. In some locations you can even make a game of identifying new types of bugs and seashells. If you go somewhere famous for snorkeling or bird watching, you can probably find cheap books or guides to help you and your child identify different fish and birds (for instance, in Hawaii you can buy laminated sheets of paper that show and name all the different local fish you will see while snorkeling). Also look for different types of flowers and trees that you might not have at home. Your child might want to try drawing some of the new things he sees in order to look them up at home.

▶ **Pay attention to the urban landscape.** Although urban vacations usually don't provide too much new wildlife to look at, encourage your child to make observations about the cityscape. Does she see the same types of grocery stores and gas stations? Does this city offer the same types of restaurants as your hometown? Are the streets, sidewalks, and traffic signals the same? Do people dress differently or talk differently? Do they move faster or slower than they do in your hometown? Many children are fascinated by how much things that they consider constant (such as the name of the local supermarkets) change from one town to another.

▶ **Get maps.** Whenever you go somewhere new, get your child a map. Let her figure out where you are and show her the routes you take as you walk and drive around. Let her try to navigate your group to the sites you are visiting. You'll be amazed at how much more interested your child will be in the process of traveling when she understands where she is going and how she is getting there. (Plus, she will develop important map-reading skills. Show her how to use the legend and the scale to read the details in the map.)

"My kids get so excited when we go on our outings. How do I maintain that enthusiasm when we get back home?"

Don't forget to build on the new things that you learn on your outings. Use your new experiences as a springboard for discussions, "studies," and activities for your kids.

▶ **Reading.** Get books about the things (animals, artists, historical sites) that you see. Either fiction or non-fiction will do. But encourage your child to learn as much as she wants to know about a subject.

▶ **Art.** Whether you go to an art museum, visit murals, or go on an architecture walk, when you get home, read together about the paintings and artists that your children really liked (or really hated) and the styles that those paintings represent. See if your kids can imitate those styles—or create improved versions.

▶ **Research projects.** No matter what specific subject captivated your child, you can always learn more. Get on the Internet, go to the library, and then help your child write a little report or make a little scrapbook about a subject that she found interesting.

▶ **Imagination projects.** Discuss how your child might improve or build upon something that you saw on your outing. How could an animal's zoo habitat be improved? Maybe your child felt the tiger didn't have a good cage. How would she redesign it? Maybe she felt the layout of the museum was confusing; how would she fix it?

▶ **Hands-on projects.** Don't limit yourself to research projects. You and your child can also build models (of animal skeletons, trains, airplanes, ships, etc.), design your own buildings, make pot-

tery (like the pottery you might have seen at a Native American exhibit), try your hand at photography, or paint your own mural (if you are willing to sacrifice a wall in the name of art). If your child loved reading maps on vacation, help her try to make a map of your neighborhood (or even your house). Just be creative and encourage your child to think of activities she would like to do in order to further her interest.

▶ **Watch videos.** See if your local library or Discovery Channel Store has videos on an animal, dinosaur, or artist your child really liked. Although reading is wonderful, it doesn't always convey the excitement that a video can, and kids can learn a great deal from videos and movies. Make sure to talk with your kids about what they see in the video.

▶ **Choose new outings.** Build on your child's newfound interests with related outings. If your child fell in love with Picasso, find some other museums that host his paintings. If she is very interested in penguins, see if any of the local zoos or marine parks have different species of penguins and keep your eyes out for special penguin exhibits (and, if you go on vacation to a new town, be sure to check out the penguins in its zoo as well). Keep your eyes out for movies on the subjects your child likes (IMAX movies often feature animals and geography). You might even build your next family vacation around a specific interest developed on an outing.

For instance, if your child decides she wants to know everything about prehistoric animals and why they became extinct, you might plan to visit Los Angeles, so she could go to the La Brea Tar Pits and learn more about the animals that got trapped there.

Children love to learn about things they enjoy. Build on your child's interests. Encourage her talents. Feed her curiosity. If you work to make learning fun, you will find that she will naturally gravitate toward learning more and more as she gets older.

CHAPTER 6

Special Programs and Resources

VERY CHAPTER IN THIS BOOK NOTES THE FACT THAT SOME CHILDREN STRUGGLE IN school more than others. Some children do homework without any help. Others require constant monitoring. Some children sail through classes. Others struggle to keep up with their peers. Many of these differences can be handled through frequent communication between parents and teachers, strong and consistent help with homework, and a family commitment to providing enrichment outside of the school day. However, some children have additional educational needs. Although these needs can be daunting—especially to parents who have never dealt with learning disabilities or gifted education—there is a wide range of resources available for children with special needs. Although parents of learning disabled or gifted children must be vigilant in getting the appropriate help and resources for their children, that help is often readily available and children with special needs are legally entitled to receive a great deal of help from the public school system. If you think your child has special needs or if your child's school approaches you about testing your child, bear the following three principles in mind:

Work with your school to gain the resources your child needs.

Children with special needs are legally entitled to specialized programs and instruction and most schools regularly provide special services. Your child's school likely has special classes, teachers, and programs already in place that your child could benefit from. Don't hesitate to ask for testing or for special resources, if you feel your child needs them. The federal government guarantees all children a "free and appropriate public education" (also called FAPE) and provides funds for schools to use for special education and gifted programs.

Seek information from multiple sources.

Diagnoses can be difficult. Results are subjective. Although schools are obligated to perform testing (at their expense) sometimes they're slow in evaluating children—and unfortunately, their assessments are not always the best. When you're getting a diagnosis, talk to everyone who knows your child well (including former teachers, your family doctor, relatives, friends) as well as other professionals. Get second and third opinions. Don't be afraid to get your child reassessed if, after getting a diagnosis and an education plan, you don't see progress.

Take control of your child's education.

Although federal law stipulates that schools provide testing and "educationally appropriate" educational interventions, sometimes these services will be too little, too late, or of poor quality. As your child's primary advocate, you need to make sure that your child receives services in a timely manner (with learning disabilities, early detection is crucial), that your child receives all of the services he needs, and that you hold the school accountable for showing that your child is making progress. Obviously, all of the principles for school-parent communication from Chapter 2 still apply—always be respectful and considerate, but fight for your child. Be willing to seek help outside the public school system. Although federal law requires schools to provide services to children with special needs, school psychologists and special education teachers are often overwhelmed. Many deal with very large caseloads. Others do not have the specific training that will best help your child. Be willing to invest in outside educational programs and professionals.

"My child's school just contacted me about testing my child for a special program—should I be worried?"

Before you start to worry, find out everything you can about the program. Schools generally initiate testing because they feel that they can give your child more help if he qualifies for a special program. Special programs address a wide range of needs, which can include a child's academic advancement, learning difficulties, emotional problems, behavioral problems, physical problems, or even speech impediments. When a teacher recommends testing, it does not necessarily mean that there is something wrong with your child. If a teacher recommends testing your child for a gifted and talented (sometimes called GATE) program, she probably suspects that your child is particularly advanced, perceptive, or intelligent.

Even if your child's teacher is recommending testing for some kind of difficulty or disability, you shouldn't interpret this to mean that there is something wrong with your child. Your child's teacher may simply have noticed that a few of his behaviors (e.g., the way he sounds out words, the way he writes) indicate that he might benefit from some kind of early intervention. And, many problems are not permanent. For instance, some teachers recommend children for speech therapy or occupational therapy when they notice that a child has a minor problem (e.g., a slight lisp, a clumsy gait). Many small problems are easily cured with specialized help that can be provided at school.

Obviously, other problems are more serious and more difficult to overcome. But even serious problems (including most learning disabilities) are easiest to overcome when children are young. A teacher's recommendation to a special program may be a great way for your child to get extra help at school.

"The school wants to put my child in a special program—should I agree?"

Understand the program fully before you agree to enroll your child. Many special programs, such as gifted programs or Individualized Education Plans (IEPs), provide extra resources for your child. When children are placed in these programs correctly, the children often get extra resources that are specifically targeted to their needs. However, some placements might label or stigmatize your child and others can be made incorrectly. Sometimes teachers and administrators mistake *behavior* problems for academic problems or learning disabilities. Some schools have been accused of disproportionately assigning students of color, boys, and students who "act up" to special education. You must make sure your child is being placed in a program appropriate to her needs.

Most teachers recommend children for special programs with the best intentions. However, make sure to get

Special Programs Terminology

The special education system is both medical and legal—so the terminology can get dense. As a rule, never hesitate to ask a teacher or administrator what they mean when they use a special term or acronym. School personnel use special education jargon unconsciously but will be happy to explain the meanings of the terms they use. You may hear the following terms:

- *Accommodations:* Changes made to tests and curricula to make them a better match for your child's needs and abilities. For instance, a child with a learning disability might get extra time to take tests.
- *Due process:* The hearing or mediation process that determines services when parents and school districts cannot agree on how to best meet a special education child's needs.
- *Free and Appropriate Public Education (FAPE):* What every child (even a child with special needs) is entitled to according to federal law.
- *Gifted Education, Gifted and Talented, or GATE:* An enrichment program for children who are academically accelerated. Children usually gain admission through IQ tests, achievement tests, and teacher recommendations.
- *Individualized Education Plan (IEP):* The education plan developed and agreed to by teachers, psychologists, school administrators, and parents for a child who qualifies for special education services. The IEP is a roadmap that details curriculum, modifications, and goals for the specified child.
- *Individuals with Disabilities Education Act (IDEA):* This updated (1997) law was designed to improve education for children with disabilities. The law added more stringent requirements for IEPs and for progress reports made to parents.
- *Least-Restrictive Environment (LRE):* Schools must provide services to children with disabilities in the least-restrictive environment possible. This means that, if possible, children should be placed in regular classrooms, not special education classrooms. Many schools use pull-out programs to augment LRE placements in regular classrooms.
- *Mainstreaming:* The practice of including special needs children in regular (or mainstream) classes for all or most of the school day.
- *Modification:* Like accommodations, modifications are made to curriculum and tests to make them more suitable to a special education child's needs.

all the information you can about the specific program your child is a candidate for, such as:

◗ How does my child qualify for the program?

◗ What benefits will my child gain from this special program?

◗ Are there any drawbacks from my child's enrollment in this program?

◗ If my child qualifies for the program, does any notation or label go into my child's file?

◗ If so, how will this notation or label influence my child's placement at other schools or in future classrooms?

◗ What do I and my child have to do in order to participate in this program?

◗ Will my child's participation in this program take time away from her usual academic program?

Ask administrators, your child's teacher, your child's former teachers (especially if there is one you particularly trust) and other parents about the program. See what they think about the program and whether they would recommend that your child participate. Learn as much as you can. You may find the program seems like a perfect fit for your child. Be especially diligent in learning about the program and making sure that it is a good fit for your child if:

1. *You do not agree with the school's diagnosis of your child OR you do not see your child exhibiting the behaviors that the school cites as the reasons for the recommendation.* For instance, a teacher might tell you that your child is extremely argumentative

---

For example, a child with autism might get modified homework assignments that are shorter (or require less reading) than the rest of the class.

● *Pull-out programs/pull-out classes:* Students who participate in pull-out classes attend a regular classroom for most of the school day, but are "pulled-out" for a prescribed (according to their IEPs) portion of each school day to receive specialized instruction in a resource or special education class.

● *Resource classes:* The name commonly given to pull-out programs for students with IEPs.

● *Special Day Classes (SDC):* Classrooms in which all students qualify for special education or gifted education and remain in the same specialized class all day. SDCs for special education are typically smaller than regular classrooms.

and distracted and she suspects she has Attention Deficit Disorder (ADD). If you find that your child is easy to get along with, compliant, and focused at home, you need to investigate. You might start with asking if you could observe in your child's class for a day or two. Your child may be having problems that are specific to her school, classroom, or classmates. Or, she may just be clashing with her teacher. You should look into all of these possibilities (especially before engaging in any kind of medical intervention such as having your child take Ritalin, a drug commonly prescribed for children with ADD). On the other hand, watching your child interact in the classroom may allow you to see a new (and perhaps troubling) side to your child. Although the revelation may be unpleasant, it will help you and your child's teacher work together if you both recognize your child's problems. (See below for what you can do if you really disagree with the recommendation.)

2. *If your child is very upset about the recommendation.* Many small children take special programs in stride. Throughout the school day, many children go in and out of their classrooms to attend resource classes, get special therapy, or go to enrichment classes. These comings and goings are taken for granted and often barely noticed. However, if your child is upset about having to take part in a particular program, she may be reacting to negative rumors about the program (I worked at a school where the children believed that all "resource kids" had to repeat their grade level) or to conflicts she has with other children in the program. Although you may decide that your child should participate in the program regardless, you should talk with your child and the teacher to see how you can remedy your child's (and other children's) misconceptions about the school's special programs.

"I observed my child at school and he seemed fine to me. The teacher said he was just being good because I was there. How do I learn how my child actually behaves in class?"

Sometimes children do adopt their "best behavior" when their parents observe in class (although, remember that most children cannot turn learning disabilities on and off on demand). So, if you like and trust your child's teacher, try to put some faith into what she's telling you. Also talk to your child's past teachers, who may be able to shed some light on the situation. You might also try volunteering in your child's class on a regular basis. Your child probably can't keep up an act forever. Also, talk to other adults who spend time with your child at school. Talk to teacher's aides, P.E. coaches, music teachers, and even other parents who volunteer in the class. Ask people to be honest with you about your child's behavior—and try to be open to what they have to say. You might also try talking to people who work with your child outside of school including sports coaches, Boy Scout troop leaders, even baby-sitters. If you talk to enough people and observe your child in the classroom several times, you should be able to get a good sense of whether or not his teacher is giving you an accurate picture of his behavior.

Gifted and Talented (or GATE) Education

"I think that my child should be in the 'gifted' program. How can I ask to have him tested?"

Different schools have different policies for testing children for gifted programs. You need to check with your school and district for their particular policies but some of the ways in which students are identified for gifted testing are:

▶ Teacher recommendations.

▶ Standardized test scores above a certain threshold (usually between the 75th and 98th percentiles).

▶ Parent recommendation.

▶ Student self-recommendation.

Although most schools test students for entrance into gifted programs, they have different policies about when to test. Some schools test children in kindergarten or first grade. Others prefer to wait until third grade (or, rarely, later). Schools and school districts also offer various types of gifted designations. Although the "gifted" designation has historically been assigned to children who score over a certain cutoff on IQ (Intelligence Quotient) tests, many schools now offer gifted designations in reading/language arts and math, depending on students' scores on standardized tests and other criteria. Federal and state policies almost uniformly insist on the identification of gifted students through multiple measures.

"My child is being tested for the gifted program at school. What kind of test will they give her?"

Different states, districts, and schools use different criteria and administer different tests for gifted education qualification. Many schools administer IQ (and other aptitude) tests such as:

▶ The Wechsler Intelligence Scale for Children (WISC) (individual)

▶ The Stanford-Binet Intelligence Test (SB) (individual)

▶ Otis-Lennon School Abilities Test (OLSAT) (group)

▶ The Ravens Progressive Matrices (group)

Others use more content oriented tests such as the:

▶ The Woodcock-Johnson III (individual)

▶ The Cognitive Abilities Test (CogAT) (group)

Pay attention to different testing methods. As indicated above, some tests are offered individually; others are administered in a group setting. Many teachers worry that a group setting may not be the best way to assess shy or self-conscious students. The National Association for Gifted Children reports that group tests can underestimate children's scores and recommends requesting individual tests.[8] Some schools administer group tests as an initial screen and then follow up with individual tests.

To save money, some districts simply use test scores from annual standardized tests (such as the CAT/6 or the Stanford-9) to qualify children for gifted programs. Many districts have pre-established cutoffs for qualification based on these nationally normed tests. For instance, children who score above the 90th or 95th percentile on national achievement tests may automatically qualify for the gifted program. Check with your child's school about its policies.

"Is it a good thing for my child to be labeled as gifted?"

For the most part, children benefit from gifted designations. Some schools accept only gifted students. Others have enrichment programs for gifted students. Students with gifted designations often get automatically tracked into honors programs in middle school (which generally lead to honors and Advanced Placement (AP) tracks in high school). Students with gifted and highly gifted designations also qualify for gifted and highly gifted magnet schools in districts with magnet programs.

"I don't agree with the school's test results. Can I have my child tested privately?"

Most schools will allow you to have your child tested privately and will recognize the results from private tests (although, you should make sure that the person testing your child has the necessary qualifications for his evaluation to be accepted by the school). Almost all schools require you to pay for your own private assessment.

"The school is resisting my requests for a GATE test. Are there any reasons not to have my child tested for the gifted program?"

For the most part, children benefit from the GATE or gifted label (as long as parents don't allow the label to go to the

---

8 Callahan, Carolyn and Howard Eichner. "IQ Tests and Your Child." Undated. The National Association for Gifted Children. 16 April 2004. <http://www.NAGC.org/Publications/Parenting/ig.html>

children's heads). The only reason I would caution against having a promising child tested for a gifted program is if the child is old enough to understand the meaning of the test (remember, children think of the gifted test as something that tests "how smart you are"). If your child attends a school where children are tested early and she was not recommended for testing at the same time as her peers, you have to ask yourself if your child is likely to qualify. If she is not, it might be embarrassing for her to take the test and not pass.

First-graders rarely understand why they are taking an IQ test. But, fourth-graders are old enough to understand what it means if they do not score high enough to be called "gifted." Think hard before you submit an older child (older than first or second grade) to gifted testing (unless all of the children at your school get tested at an older age). No matter how old your child is, never let her see that you care whether or not she passes the test. And *never* convey to her that this test (or any test) accurately reflects her intelligence (whether she passes or not). No tests are perfectly reliable—even fancy IQ tests given by schools or psychologists. Finally, don't expect less from your child if she does not qualify as "gifted." If she got straight-As before she took the test, she should continue to. If she seemed sharp and witty to you before, she still should. Many children who didn't qualify for gifted programs are

successful students and adults—never make your child feel like a failure for not qualifying.

If the school is resisting your request for testing, have a candid talk with your child's teacher and try to find out why. There are several reasons why the school might be resisting you:

► **The school may think your child is unlikely to pass the test.** If this is the case, ask why, specifically. Sit down together and look at your child's most recent achievement test scores. This is the time to think very critically about whether or not your child is likely to pass the gifted test. If she is not likely to pass, why put her through the stress of taking the test (and bearing the burden of your expectations)? If the school is concerned that your child will not qualify, it's worth your time to think realistically about her odds and reevaluate your desire to push for testing.

► **The school may have a particular time at which it tests students for the gifted program.** If your school has a particular grade or time of year when it does testing, it might be easier to wait than to push for testing now. Only continue to push if you have a really compelling reason to want testing now (perhaps a unique program that would be a great fit for your child if she passes the test)—and be prepared to have your child tested privately. Public schools do not have the resources to cater to every family's particular scheduling needs.

► **The school wants to save money or**

does not have a gifted program. The school may have to contract out for testing. It may want to wait until several kids need to be tested—or it may want to skip testing all together. If this seems to be the only stumbling block, either continue to push for testing, have your child tested yourself, or see if the school has alternate means to qualify children into the gifted program (e.g., annual standardized test scores). However, if your child's school does not have a gifted program, it may not offer gifted testing at all. Federal law does not require schools to screen for gifted students although the federal government does provide statewide grants to fund gifted education. (Over 30 states have mandatory gifted testing and services; other states only offer discretionary funds to districts that choose to apply. Check your state's department of education Web site for more information on your state's policies on gifted education.) If your school does not have a gifted program but your child scores sufficiently high on achievement tests, you may choose to have him tested privately, especially if you plan to move to another district that does have a gifted program.

"My child attends private school. Can she participate in the public school district's screening for gifted students?"

Many districts allow private school students who live within their district boundaries to participate in gifted screenings. Call your local district office to learn your local district's policies. Also, check with your private school—it may offer testing to students.

"My child qualified for the gifted program at her school. What happens now?"

Gifted programs vary considerably from state to state, district to district, and school to school. Some districts give gifted students IEPs to monitor their work and their progress, but most don't. Most districts and schools rely on one or two of the following gifted programs:

▶ *Special day classes* in which all of the gifted students in a grade (or sometimes a few grades) are taught together, in one classroom. If your school does not have special day classes and you think your gifted child would benefit from one, contact your district office. Another local school might have a special day class that your child could transfer into (many schools allow within-district transfers so that children can join special day classes).

▶ *Cluster classes* in which groups of gifted students are clustered together in one (or a few) classes. These classrooms also include non-gifted students but bring together enough gifted students so that they can work together on activities specifically geared toward gifted students.

▶ *Pull-out classes* in which gifted students are pulled out of their regular classes for portions of each day (or some days) to do accelerated activities.

▶ *After-school or summer programs* in which gifted students participate in accelerated or enrichment activities outside of regular school hours.

Districts and schools generally have a great deal of flexibility in determining how they use their gifted education funds (e.g., for assessment, a special teacher, special programs, special field trips, etc.) so if you are unhappy with your school's gifted program, you can ask around to see if other local schools have better programs (or get involved in governance at your school to influence the way it uses its gifted funding—see Chapter 2 for more on getting involved at school).

"My child is highly gifted and his school does not offer a special class for gifted children. Do I need to find a new school?"

Not necessarily. Many gifted and highly gifted children get good educations in regular school programs. But, if your gifted child is enrolled in a regular classroom, make sure that:

▶ *The teacher gives him advanced and challenging work when he completes regular assignments.* Your child should not be sitting around bored if he finishes his work more quickly than other students. Make sure his time is filled (or nearly filled) with work that is challenging and enriching for him. Also make sure that the teacher grades and monitors his "extra" work to make sure that he is learning and benefiting from this material.

▶ *You provide challenge and enrichment outside of school.* You can provide this enrichment at home (see Chapter 5 for ideas) or you can enroll your child in special after-school and summer programs for gifted children. Several national summer programs cater specifically to gifted children. The best-known of these programs is run by The Center for Talented Youth (CTY) which is based at Johns Hopkins University and offers programs for children (second grade and up) in the Washington, D.C., Baltimore, and Los Angeles areas (http://www.jhu.edu/gifted/). Most areas also have regional programs for gifted children (see Appendix 8 for links to more Web sites).

For many children, being in a regular classroom with enrichment is enough. However, if your child is bored (as always, talk to the teacher to make sure he is doing the work assigned and challenging himself appropriately before you believe his claims of boredom) and acting up because he's not being challenged, it may be time to look for a school that has a rigorous gifted program. If you have the resources—or might qualify for financial aid or a scholarship—look into private schools as well (read Chapter 1 for more information on choosing schools).

If a new school is not an option, try to collaborate with your child's school and teacher to come up with new ways to challenge your child. (See Chapter 2 for suggestions.)

"My child is highly gifted. Should I push to have her skip a grade?"

I don't recommend that children skip grades—but many experts on gifted education do. The most important factor to bear in mind when considering "a skip" is to consider the whole child—remember that your child has academic, social, physical, and emotional needs. Even if a higher grade is a better fit academically, will she fit in socially and physically with older peers? How mature is your child? How will she handle the switch (and the probable loss of her former peer group) emotionally? For some children, skips are easy. Some children make new friends quickly and fit in easily with new peers. For other children (especially children who are already somewhat awkward), the transition is difficult and may even impede their academic progress. If you are considering skipping your child, ask yourself the following questions:

▶ *Will the curriculum she receives be more challenging than what she receives now?* For some gifted children, regular fourth- and fifth-grade curricula are different but equally unchallenging.

▶ *Will the curriculum she receives in her new grade be more challenging than the curriculum she might receive in a gifted program or at a gifted school?* Gifted programs have special curricula and activities geared toward accelerated children. That sort of program may be a better fit for your child than simply moving her to the next grade.

▶ *How does your child deal with change?* Skipping a grade involves a great deal of change, from losing a peer group (which she may have been with since kindergarten) and moving into a new peer group (which may view her somewhat suspiciously) to losing her identity (becoming a "super-smart fifth grader" rather than a "regular fourth grader"). If your child takes change in stride, the move may be fine. If she has trouble fitting in or dealing with disruption, the change may be very hard on her.

▶ *Does your child want to skip?* Children who are forced to skip sometimes undermine the purpose by deciding not to try when they arrive in their new classrooms. Talk with your child about all of the pros and cons of skipping a grade. Talk about her friends, the academic challenge, even talk about the fact that she will get her driver's license a year later than the rest of her classmates. Don't forget little things, like the school's fourth-grade trip to Astronaut Camp (or whatever big events students at her school participate in) that she will miss if she skips fourth grade. Discuss all the aspects of the skip and make the decision together.

Obviously, skipping has some advantages. Children who skip finish high school, college, and often graduate school a year early—getting a jumpstart on their careers. But before you jump into a skip (it can be very flattering if the school offers to skip your child, but that's not a great reason to do it!), consider all the factors and make a decision that is a good fit for your child.

Learning Difficulties and Other Disabilities

The information in this section comes largely from federal law (especially the 1997 IDEA) and provides a cursory description of how to deal with learning difficulties, disabilities, and special education. I've tried to wade through the legal terminology and present the facts most relevant to parents whose children have learning difficulties. If you want more complete, detailed information, start with the federal laws and the helpful "Question and Answer"

pages on the U.S. Department of Education's Web site (www.ed.gov). You may also want to consult books that deal with your child's specific learning difficulty. Appendix 8 includes references to books that I have found helpful as well as references to additional Web sites.

"What exactly is a learning disability?"

Learning disabilities are disorders that interfere with people's ability to learn (including the ability to read, write, spell, listen, think, or do mathematical calculations) but do not stem from sight, hearing, motor, mental retardation, or emotional problems.

According to federal law, children can be diagnosed as having specific learning disabilities if they: 1) achieve below grade level when provided with grade level instruction; and 2) have a "severe discrepancy" between academic achievement and intellectual ability in one of the following areas: oral expression, listening comprehension, written expression, basic reading skill, reading comprehension, mathematics calculation, or mathematics reasoning. That discrepancy must be determined by professional evaluators and the evaluation can include achievement testing, IQ testing, qualitative assessments, and even anecdotes from teachers and parents. In some schools, "discrepancy" is interpreted as performing a year or two below grade level, but definitions vary across states and districts.

"How do I know if my child has a learning disability?"

It's often hard to diagnose learning disabilities—although there are a number of widely recognized warning signs (see tip box) that can help you decide if you should have your child tested for a learning disability. Your child's teacher may also recommend that your child be tested. If you request an evaluation and the school agrees that your child might have a learning disability, the school district must provide a complete evaluation of your child within a timely manner. (There are no federal guidelines on how long schools can wait before granting a request for evaluation. Many states, however, do have guidelines. For instance, California requires the school to develop an assessment plan—which notes how the child will be assessed—within 15 days of a parent's request. Check with your state's department of education to see if any guidelines exist in your area.)

An excellent book from NOLO Press (*The Complete IEP Guide,* by Lawrence Siegel) walks parents through the special education laws step by step and provides form letters that you can use to request testing. You can also read tips about writing letters to schools (as well as sample letters) from the National Dissemination Center for Children with Disabilities Web site (http://www.nichcy.org). (See Appendix 8 for more information.) Finally, if you want results faster or don't feel confident in the school district's ability to properly evaluate your child, you can also consult with private educational evaluators. If you obtain a private evaluation, the school is required to include it in its official evaluation of the child. Because learning disabilities are complex and often hard to diagnose (especially in very young children), you may want to consider hiring a private evaluator for a second opinion as well.

"Can children get special academic help in school for all disabilities or only for specific learning disabilities?"

Federal laws states that students with the following disabilities qualify for special education services if the disability affects their educational progress:

- Deaf-blindness
- Deafness
- Hearing impairment
- Mental retardation
- Multiple disabilities
- Orthopedic impairment
- Other health impairment (i.e., having limited strength, vitality, or alertness that affects a child's educational performance)
- Serious emotional disturbance
- Specific learning disability
- Speech or language impairment

▶ Traumatic brain injury

▶ Visual impairment, including blindness

A child must, however, meet two requirements in order to qualify for special education:

1. Have one of the above disabilities; and

2. The disability must affect her educational performance

Signs That Your Child Might Have a Learning Disability

The National Dissemination Center for Children with Disabilities[9] lists the following problems as possible signs that your elementary school child might have a learning disability (children with learning disabilities will probably exhibit *several* of the following problems):

- Trouble learning the alphabet, rhyming words, or connecting letters to their corresponding sounds.
- Mistakes when reading aloud, frequent repetitions and pauses.
- Lack of reading comprehension.
- Trouble with spelling.
- Very messy handwriting, awkward pencil grip.
- Difficulty expressing ideas in writing.
- Late language acquisition, limited vocabulary.
- Trouble remembering the sounds letters make or hearing slight differences between words.
- Difficulty understanding jokes, comic strips, and sarcasm.
- Trouble following directions.
- Mispronunciation of words or use of a wrong word that sounds similar.
- Trouble organizing what he or she wants to say or unable to think of the word he or she needs for writing or conversation.
- Failure to follow the social rules of conversation, such as taking turns, or standing too close to the listener.
- Confusing math symbols, misreading numbers.
- Inability to retell a story in order (what happened first, second, third).
- Uncertainty about where to begin a task or how to go on from there.

[9] National Dissemination Center for Children with Learning Disabilities. "NICHCY Disability Face Sheet No. 7: Learning Disabilties." October, 2003. NICHCY. 16 April 2004. <http://www.nichcy.org/pubs/factsh/fs7.pdf>

Federal law does not specify what "affect the child's educational performance" means. The courts have upheld several definitions including low grades and behavior problems that have worsened consistently over a period of time. Schools usually make the determination about whether your child's disability "affects" her educational performance. If you disagree with the school's decision, read answers below about how to challenge school decisions.

"Do Attention Deficit Disorder or Attention Deficit Hyperactivity Disorder count as learning disabilities?"

Attention Deficit Disorder (ADD) and Attention Deficit Hyperactivity Disorder (ADHD) are not specifically considered learning disabilities but federal law considers them "other health impairments" (OHIs) which means they are considered to be disabilities. Like other students with disabilities, students who are diagnosed as having ADD or ADHD and who are academically behind qualify for special education services and IEPs.

"The school wants to have my child tested for a learning disability. Should I consent?"

This should be an easy question—and in good schools, where you trust the teachers and administrators, it is. If you feel the teachers and administrators are genuinely trying to find a solution to your child's learning difficulties, go ahead with the testing as soon as possible. If your child has a learning disability, it's better to know about it now so you can work with your child in special ways to overcome or circumvent the learning disability. Knowing why your child is struggling with some or all schoolwork also helps avoid some of the frustration that can come with trying to help a child who has a learning disability. It may also save your child from deciding that she hates school because it's so difficult for her. In most schools, children with diagnosed learning disabilities qualify for extra help at school (such as one-on-one or small group teaching) and these resources can help your child succeed in school despite the learning disability. Almost all learning disabilities are more easily overcome when diagnosed early.

Nevertheless, there are a few reasons to be wary when the school wants to have your child tested for a disability. Not all schools and school districts are well-equipped to handle learning disabilities. In some cases, students with learning disabilities are automatically shunted into special education classrooms where the teaching may be aimed well below your child's academic level. In other cases, a learning disability designation may prevent a child from getting into non-remedial classes in middle school and high school. Moreover, some schools (not many—but enough for parents to be wary) test children for learning disabilities when students have *behavior* problems rather than *learning* problems. They do this precisely because they would like the children to be pulled out of regular classrooms where they cause problems for the teachers.

Thus, if your child's teacher recommends testing your child for a learning disability ask *a lot* of questions. Chances are, the teacher is looking for a way to give your child the best possible education. And, in many cases, parents *are* relieved if a teacher thinks their child should be tested— often these parents were already worried about their child's progress. But, even if you are relieved, make sure to ask a lot of questions. And, if you are *surprised* that your child's teacher thinks your child might have a disability (and you have not noticed any problems)—be especially wary. Make sure to ask the following questions:

◗ Why does the teacher think your child might have a learning disability?

◗ How is testing done and who does it?

◗ What can you do if you disagree with the evaluation results?

◗ Can you get a second opinion on the testing? What can you do if the school's evaluation and your second opinion don't agree?

◗ What happens if your child tests positive for a learning disability? Does your child get special services? Does she get

placed in a special classroom?

◗ If your child will receive special services, ask exactly what those services will be.

◗ If your child will be placed in a special classroom, ask about the classroom. Who teaches that class? What other children are enrolled in that class (find out their ages, grades, academic achievement levels)? What skills and academic content are taught in that class? How does your child graduate from that class? What benefits does your child get from that class? If your child has a learning disability, do you *have to* place her in the special class?

◗ How does the school try to conform to "least restrictive environment" (LRE) regulations? How can your child be served in her regular classroom?

◗ Is there a way to "graduate" from special education? Do the special services help the child overcome or circumvent the disability?

◗ Will the learning disability designation affect the child's course placement in middle school or high school?

If, after hearing the answers to the above questions, you are still suspicious of, or uncertain about, the school's desire to test your child, talk to more people:

◗ *If your child will receive special services, ask to speak to the teacher who provides the special services* (at many schools this teacher will take part in the conference with us as you decide whether or not to have the child tested). Again, ask specific questions about the curriculum this teacher provides, the methods she uses, and why her methods are better for your child than those provided in the regular classroom. Ask if you can sit in on one of her sessions with children who are about the same age as your child.

♦ *If the child will go to a special classroom, ask to talk with that teacher and observe in that classroom.* If, in your estimation, your child does not have a severe learning problem (for instance, if she is not struggling in all subjects or only seems to struggle a little), I would be leery of any school that automatically places all children with learning disabilities in a special day class.

♦ *Finally, call the middle school and high school and speak to counselors there.* Ask how they place students who have diagnosed learning disabilities.

If, after finding the answers to all of these questions, it seems as though the school wants to test your child so she will qualify for special services that seem, to you, to be good, then allow the testing. The testing will give you and her teachers more insight about how to best teach and make learning fun for your child. And, the federal government provides special funding to schools to help children with special needs and learning disabilities, which means your child will probably benefit from smaller classes and more learning resources if she does qualify for special

education services.

If, however, you do not feel that your child has difficulties learning AND either:

♦ The school seems to want to label your child as a problem and move her to a different class; or

♦ The middle school and/or high school have strict guidelines about putting children with disabilities in remedial classes, then hold off on having the school test your child. Monitor her progress (and ask her teachers to keep you informed) until you feel certain that your child really is struggling and could benefit from extra help. If you have your own suspicions that your child might have a learning disability, have your child tested privately. That way you can know the results and find academic help accordingly but, then you can make the decision about whether or not you want the disability on your child's permanent school records.

Again, remember that in most cases, if your child has a learning disability, it's better for her teachers to know about it. Then they can adjust their teaching styles to fit your child's abilities and they can temper their frustration if they have trouble getting through to your child. Some parents whose children genuinely struggle refuse to accept that their child has a learning disability—which punishes the child by depriving her of the special resources for which she qualifies.

The only time you might want to try to keep a disability out of your child's records would be if, at your school or in your school district, it seems as if having the label "learning disability" will disadvantage your child more than it will help her.

"I think my child has a learning disability. He goes to a private school. Do I have to pay for private testing?"

Under federal law, the school district in which you reside has to evaluate your child for disabilities if the district agrees that your child might qualify for special education. Put in a request at your local district and, by law, they must respond in a timely manner.

"My child has a learning disability and he goes to a private school. The public school provided free testing—will they provide free special education instruction as well?"

Public school districts are required to devote some of their special education funds toward providing services to students who do not attend public schools. However, the district gets to determine how the funds will be spent (e.g., what services will be provided and where). The public school district is not obligated to serve every private school student it tests, nor every type of disability that private school students within its jurisdiction have been diagnosed with. Call your local district to see what services it provides and if any of them would be useful for your child. If not, you will need to either work with your private school or find special education services in the private market (perhaps through a special tutor or educational consultant). Obviously, if you decide to enroll your special-education-qualifying child in a public school, he will receive special education instruction there.

"What's the difference between resource and special education?"

OR

"What's the difference between a pull-out program and a special day program?"

Schools are required to provide special education in the "least restrictive environment" (LRE) possible. That means, whenever possible, students who qualify for special education services should be in a regular classroom receiving regular instruction. However, in order to appropriately serve children's special needs, they often need special instruction, which is provided by a special education teacher. Sometimes children attend "pull-out classes" (which are often called resource). In these cases, children leave their regular classrooms for some portion of the school day and go to work with a special education teacher (often on materials that parallel the materials being taught in the regular classroom but with more intense instruction and with a smaller student-teacher ratio).

Other times, the IEP team determines that a student would benefit more from special education all day. They provide this through "special day" classes in which all of the children attend the same special education classroom for the entire school day (these students usually attend recess and lunch—and sometimes P.E.—with the rest of students). Because of their unique populations, special day classes often move at a slower pace than regular classes.

Children are often assigned to special day classes for several reasons:

1. They do not benefit at all from regular instruction. When students are so far behind or have such severe disabilities that they cannot follow instruction as it is presented in the regular classroom, schools often move them to a special day class. Likewise, students who seem more demoralized by their failures in the regular class than they are buoyed by being surrounded by mainstream peers may be moved to a special day class.

2. They require more special help than a regular teacher could possibly provide. The threshold of what a regu-

lar teacher is expected to provide varies from school to school. Most schools do what they can to mainstream students—especially students who can (at least to some extent) keep up academically with their peers in a regular classroom. Many schools give students one-on-one aides to help them with day-to-day activities (and take the burden off teachers). However, if a student requires constant attention or significant physical care, the school may opt to house the student in a special day class where there are more adults and fewer students.

3. They dramatically disrupt learning in a regular classroom. Some children get so bored and frustrated in a regular classroom in which they do not understand the material that they lash out and create problems in the classroom. This disruptive behavior, combined with the fact that the child is not benefiting from the regular classroom, may make the child a good candidate for a special day classroom.

"Should I allow the school to place my child in a special day classroom?"

It depends on your child. Some children benefit from special day classrooms while others get held back. If your child is struggling tremendously and feeling frustrated in a regular classroom, and having extra help or a one-on-one aide doesn't help, a special day classroom may be a good placement. However, if your child's academic status and intellectual abilities are similar to those of the students in the regular classroom, it might be to her benefit to find a way to keep her in a regular classroom. Otherwise, she will probably fall behind academically in a special day class because these classes usually offer a more slowly paced academic curriculum. Perhaps a one-on-one aide could help her overcome her disabilities and succeed in a regular class. When trying to make this decision, ask to observe in your child's regular class and in the special day class she would go to. Seeing the students and teachers interact, as well as the level of the curriculum in both classes, will help you make a good decision.

"I think my child might have a learning disability (or some other disability that makes it hard for him to learn) but his teacher says that he'll outgrow it. Should I push for testing or should I wait?"

Ask to have your child tested. Learning disabilities are most easily tackled when children are young. And, when children get help earlier, you spare them the feelings of failure that many learning-disabled children experience when they cannot keep up with their peers. If the school absolutely refuses to evaluate your child (and you strongly suspect that he has some kind of disability) you can have him evaluated privately or initiate due process in order to force the school to evaluate him (a due process mediator will hear from you and the school and decide if your child should be evaluated). (Read the answers to the next two questions to learn how to initiate due process.)

"My child's school evaluated my child for a learning disability but decided that she does not have one and does not qualify for special education services. I disagree. What can I do?"

You have two options. You can request that the school pay for an independent evaluation, or you can pay for an independent evaluation yourself (the district must tell you what an independent evaluation must include). The district is required to pay for the independent evaluation if you can prove that the prior evaluation was not done properly or was, for some reason, insufficient. If you have your child evaluated privately (whether you or the school pays) the school must incorporate the results of the private evaluation in its official assessment of your child. If the district challenges your request, you may have to go through a due process hearing to prove your case. A due process arbitrator will resolve your dispute with the school. If you officially request a due process hearing, the district hearing officer has 45 days to rule.

In a due process hearing, parents and schools present a case (parents argue why they need services that are not being provided while schools show what they have done and argue why those steps were appropriate) and an arbitrator makes a ruling (just a like a judge). The process is often long and emotionally taxing (and there is no guarantee that you will win) but it can be useful in gaining extra (or more appropriate) services for your child. (If you and the school disagree about your child's special education designation or program, you can also consider due process mediation which is less formal and sometimes less adversarial than an official due process hearing.)

If you decide to hire a special education attorney for either a due process hearing or mediation (which some parents do), the process can also get expensive. However, if you hire an attorney and win your due process hearing, the school district must reimburse your legal fees. You can also considering hiring a special education advocate—they also specialize in due process hearings but usually cost less than lawyers. (Attorneys and advocates who specialize in special education may be hard to find. School districts are required to keep lists of attorneys and advocates to recommend to parents. You should also try asking other parents and other attorneys for references.)

When you request additional (or different) services, remember that the school's greatest priority is your child's *academic* progress. Thus, you have the strongest case when your child's educational program is not *academically* appropriate. So, although children with special needs often struggle with emotional and social problems, the ones that will be most convincing to a due process mediator are those regarding your child's academic progress. For example, if your child is in a classroom where the students are learning material that he has already mastered, you will have a strong case for arguing for a new classroom (or, perhaps, a new school).

If your child struggles in school because of a disability but does not quite qualify under IDEA, you can investigate the possibility of receiving services under Section 504 of the Rehabilitative Act of 1973. Section 504 is a civil rights act that protects students whose disability "substantially limits one or more major life activities," which include seeing, hearing, speaking, and learning. Students served under 504 plans (these plans are called 504 Accommodation Plans or Individualized Accommodation Plans (IAPs) rather than IEPs) have less severe disabilities than those served under IDEA or have disabilities that don't quite fit under the IDEA "educational performance" qualifications. Section 504 guarantees that, as a public institution, the public school must not discriminate against a disabled child—and that it must provide reasonable accommodations to ensure that the child receives a free and appropriate public education despite his disability. Accommodations made through Section 504 can include modified curricula, assignments, and tests, and an array of other modifications (including seemingly simple prescriptions such as requiring teachers to seat your child in the front row of the classroom). See Appendix 8 for some Web sites that can help you navigate the legal issues involved in special education.

"My child has a learning disability (or some other kind of disability that impedes his learning process). How will we decide how best to help him to succeed in school?"

There is a formal process for determining how to best serve children with disabilities. That process is called an IEP. An IEP is an "Individualized Education Plan" designed specifically for the child. The IEP should include an evaluation of your child, set goals for your child, and outline the academic program your child will follow. Once it has been determined that your child needs special education services, the school district has 30 days to hold a meeting and write an IEP for your child.

"Who determines my child's IEP?"

Children who qualify for special education services have an IEP team. By law the team must include the child's parents (or guardians), regular classroom teacher, special education teacher, a school administrator, and someone who can interpret the tests and evaluations taken by the child. Your child might also be included in the meeting. This team is supposed to meet to create, evaluate, and reevaluate the child's IEP on a regular (usually annual) basis.

Both of a child's parents can attend the IEP meeting and they can bring other "helpers" or consultants if they wish. For instance, parents may bring an advocate (if they suspect they may encounter problems). If you have a private educational psychologist, you can ask that person to attend the conference. Or, if you tend to be shy and your child has another relative who is more assertive, you can ask him or her to come with you to the conference. Or, if you get frazzled easily, you can bring someone to be a "note-taker." The idea is that the IEP team includes a group of people who care about the child and can work to put together an education plan. Don't create a three-ring circus, but make sure that you include everyone who can make an important contribution. (Just as a benchmark, many IEP meetings include just parents and school staff.)

Finally, if English is not your

first language, you have the right (according to federal law) to a translator. Make sure you let the school know beforehand if you need them to provide a translator for you.

"What is my role in my child's IEP meeting?"

When you arrive at your child's IEP meeting, be prepared. Read through the next few questions and some of the information on the Internet (see Appendix 8 for Web sites) about what to expect from an IEP meeting. But remember, you are not expected to be an education expert or a teacher when you attend your child's IEP meeting. You are expected to be a parent. As a parent, you have several roles:

▶ *Provide information about your child that school personnel don't know.* Your child's teachers only know one side of your child. Allow them to see the other side (which may be the compassionate side, the scared side, the curious side). The IEP is supposed to help guide your child's education for the next year—make sure that you (as a group) come up with a plan that fits your child's needs and personality. Remember, you are the person who knows your child the best.

▶ *Advocate for your child.* The school, hopefully, wants what's best for your child. But it also has constraints: limited funds, limited staff, and limited time to spend on your child. However, your

child is entitled to a free and appropriate public education (FAPE)—which means that the school needs to provide anything within reason to improve your child's education (bearing in mind, of course, that the FAPE the school must provide does not have to be the best that money can buy). If you think your child will benefit from extra services, ask for them. If you think your child needs a one-on-one aide, ask for one. If you think your child needs services that are not available within the school, ask for permission to search for them in the private sector (and have the school reimburse you). If you think that the resource or special day placement the school recommends is inappropriate, say so. Remember all the guidelines from Chapter 2 (about parent-teacher communication). Be respectful and considerate. But also remember that if the school will not provide an appropriate education for your child, you do have recourse. You can go through due process and fight for the services your child is entitled to.

▶ *Keep everyone's eye on your child as a human being.* The new IDEA has imposed a number of new requirements on schools in terms of assessment and reporting (in compliance with the national "No Child Left Behind" legislation). Your child's IEP will not only have to detail the accommodations that will be made for him in the classroom, but any accommodations that he will get for assessments and accountability reporting. Don't let the teachers and administrators get bogged down in these details and forget that they are supposed to be finding a way to educate your child. You want your child to get a good education that will help him to be a successful and productive adult. Don't let the IEP team lose sight of that goal.

"What should my child's IEP include?"

Ideally, your child's IEP should include everything you need to put together a complete and functional education plan. But, for starters, by law, it must include:

1. *Your child's current levels of educational performance.* These can include grades, test scores, and evaluations of how well your child has mastered particular grade-level skills.

2. *Measureable annual goals and short-term objectives.* Like above, these can include grades, test scores, and the improvement or mastery of particular skills.

3. *The specific special education, related services, and supplementary aids and services to be provided to or for your child, including program modifications or supports for school staff.* This will detail all of the special help your child will receive; how his assignments, tests, quizzes, and curricula will be modified, and how the school will support your child's teachers so they

can best help your child (e.g., by providing teacher's aides).

4. *An explanation of the extent (if any) to which your child will not participate with nondisabled children.* For instance, as a group, you may agree to exclude your child from certain activities (such as P.E. or certain fieldtrips).

5. *Any modifications your child will need when taking state or district-wide assessments.* For instance, your child may get unlimited time to take the tests or someone may read the test questions out loud to your child.

6. *The dates when services will begin and end, the amount of services, as well as how often and where they will take place,* including whether your child will receive pull-out or special day services.

7. *How you will be informed of your child's progress.* These can include formal report cards and more frequent reports.[10]

For you, as a parent, the most important parts of this document are parts 1, 2, 4, and 7. Here's some more information about each of them:

◗ *Present levels of educational performance.* You want to make sure that these accurately reflect your child's current performance. The success of the IEP will be judged based on progress,

---

[10] U.S. Congress. "Individuals with Disabilities Education Act Amendments of 1997" Washington D.C.: U.S. Congress, 1997. World Wide Web. 16 April 2004. <http://www.ideapractices.org/law/law/index.php>

so you want the starting points to be accurate. (This becomes particularly important if you feel that your child does not make progress and requires even more services later on. In order to prove that your child needs more services, you will need to show that he did not make progress. That will be hard if the starting levels are wrong.)

▶ *Goals.* Make the goals as specific as possible. You want everyone (including yourself, the teachers, and your child) to know exactly what you are aiming for. What skills should your child develop and improve? Exactly how much will these skills improve? How will you measure that improvement? So, for instance, don't simply say "improve writing skills." Instead, specify that your child should be able to "write a coherent three-paragraph essay on a specified topic." With specific goals, it will be much easier to assess whether or not your child has attained those goals.

▶ *Supplementary services and aids.* You want to know exactly what the school is going to provide for your child. What extra classes will he get? How often will they meet? How much time per day? Does he get teacher's aide time? How much? Who will the aide be? Get the school's promises in writing. The IEP is a legally enforceable contract. You may have trouble getting the school to follow through on anything promised "off the record."

▶ *Progress reports.* You should, obviously, still receive your child's report card. But, make sure you know what other reports you should expect from the school. Also come up with a plan for when you will reevaluate the IEP and assess whether the current program is working for your child. Remember, the school is required, by law, to provide you with regular progress reports.

And, if you are going to an IEP conference, do some additional research. It's a complicated process and, because they usually only happen once a year, you want to make sure you get the best IEP that you can. There are many excellent government publications that provide more information about IEPs. Check Appendix 8 for more information.

"What do I do if the school is not providing appropriate services for my child?"

According to IDEA, all children must receive a free, appropriate public education. So, if you do not feel that your child is receiving an appropriate education (and remember, "appropriate" does not always mean the very best), you can request additional services. The school district is required to provide a free and appropriate education, even if the only way your child can get an appropriate education is at a private school (in those cases, the school district pays the tuition). (Obviously, school districts consider private placement a last resort after it has been determined that no placement in the public system will suffice.) So, if you believe that your child requires additional or different services than he currently receives, write a letter to the school (you can bring up your requests with teachers or at IEP meetings but make sure that all formal requests are made in writing).

As with any other problem, you should be professional and considerate when telling teachers and school administrators that the services they are providing to your child seem inadequate. First, make an appointment to talk with your child's teacher (and special education teacher if appropriate). Follow the guidelines outlined in Chapter 2 about talking with teachers. Have some positive remarks. Have specific examples of the problems that you sense. Suggest possible solutions. But, if talking to teachers and making a formal request for different services do not yield results, consider initiating due process (see above).

"I am working with the school to provide a good education for my child (who has a learning disability). But what else can I do to help?"

Educators and psychologists have come up with hundreds of techniques to help children overcome (and work around) most learning disabilities. They have not, however, come up with one surefire cure for most learning disabilities. Although there are dozens of techniques and strategies that you can adopt and teach your child (to improve her reading and math skills, her organizational skills, her attention span, or whatever she struggles with), you will likely have to go through a "hit-or-miss" process to find the techniques that work for you and your child. Here are a few resources:

▶ *Talk to whoever diagnosed your child.* Whether your child's learning disability was diagnosed by the school psychologist or a private therapist, make an appointment and talk with her about strategies you can try at home (or hire someone to try). She will likely have a number of suggestions, ranging from tutors who specialize in reading problems to behavior management tips you can implement at home.

▶ *Read.* There are scores of books on the market that deal with nearly every learning disability imaginable in the education section of your largest local bookstore or library. Unfortunately, although most books claim that they have "the answer," their answers are often very different (sometimes downright contradictory). While some authors recommend skill-based tutoring for dyslexia, others recommend visualization techniques. While some experts advocate carrot-and-stick (e.g., rewards and punishments) approaches for ADD/ADHD children, others abhor them. Read everything you can about your child's disability and try the techniques that seem like they might work for *your* child. If the first strategy you try doesn't work, try another. Although most techniques probably don't work for every child—every technique probably works for some children. And, if your child has trouble reading, I would recommend *Parenting a Struggling Reader* by Susan Hall and Louisa Moats (see Appendix 8). The book is clear, easy to read, and provides a wealth of information on strategies you can try at home, how to find a tutor, and how to find an educational therapist.

While you're sorting through strategies to try at home, don't be afraid to get professional help. Many educational psychologists and educational therapists are trained to treat children with learning disabilities. They may be able to help your child in ways you cannot (and, like teaching strategies, don't be afraid to try several psychologists or therapists if the first one you try doesn't seem to be able to help your child). If you can, get help sooner rather than later. Most learning disabilities are most easily overcome when children are diagnosed and treated early.

Overall, the most important factor to bear in mind when dealing with a learning disabled child is to not let the disability overwhelm you or your child. Work with your child to help her overcome her disability, but also focus on her talents. Help her develop her strengths and encourage her to be proud of her accomplishments.

Other School Resources

"I heard that some of my child's classmates get special instruction (for instance, in speech or occupational therapy) and I think that my child would benefit from that kind of special help. Can I go in and ask for it?"

Most large school districts have a number of programs through which children can receive auxiliary help in speech, fine motor skills, or gross motor skills. However, children are usually not screened for these programs when they enter school. Rather, the system relies on teachers to recommend children for special services (for instance, a teacher realizes that a child has a lisp and recommends him for speech therapy or she recognizes that a child seems behind in his motor skills and recommends occupational therapy or physical therapy).

Obviously, this system means that many children get identified for help, but others slip through the cracks. If you feel that your child has a special need, be sure to bring this up with your child's teacher, either during a special appointment or your first conference. You child's teacher may not have noticed the problem (possibly because your child is quiet and doesn't stand out) or she may be reluctant to approach parents about the type of

Keeping Good Records

Because special education negotiations are a kind of legal process, it's essential that you keep good records of all of your communications with your child's school, your child's evaluations, samples of your child's work, and any other relevant information. When you are seeking placement, additional services, or due process, you will find that good, well-organized records are essential. You should make sure to keep copies of:

- *All correspondence to and from the school and school personnel.* This includes all letters you send requesting testing, evaluation, IEP meetings, or additional services. Make all requests in writing. If you make a request verbally, follow up with a written letter restating your request and confirming the school's response.
- *Test results and evaluations.* Don't rely on the school to keep your child's records in order. Keep copies for yourself.
- *Reports and report cards.* You may have to show that your child is not making adequate progress. Keep all report cards so that you can document your child's progress (at least as it was presented to you by the school).
- *Samples of your child's schoolwork.* Your child's schoolwork (including tests) provides another benchmark of your child's progress (one that can be more easily evaluated by an outsider than grades). Keep copies of work—particularly any work that seems to indicate that your child is not progressing as she should be.
- *A journal or diary.* A log of your child's activities, difficulties, and accomplishments will help you to document her progress. Note changes in behavior and academic performance as well as changes in your routines at home (especially changes in medication or discipline systems you are using with your child). Also note comments that teachers and school staff make about your child. Finally, keep detailed notes on your child's IEP meetings. You can use your notes to make sure the school's official IEP is consistent with what you agreed to in the meeting.
- *Official records.* You have the right to receive a copy (for free) of your child's evaluation and IEP. You also have the right to review your child's school file and make corrections if you find errors. Keep copies of any official documents that you receive.

problem your child has. Other teachers simply may not like to recommend children for help. In any case, mention the problem to the teacher and see if your child can be signed up for extra help. The teacher may explain why your child is *not* qualified. You may debate this with the teacher but if you find yourselves at an impasse, simply tell the teacher that you respect her opinion but you would like to have an additional opinion and that you are going to talk with the principal. Follow through by explaining to the principal that you are concerned your child may need extra help and ask if there is an evaluation that can be done.

If your child does qualify for special services, keep a few things in mind:

◆ *Children do not always like being pulled out for services.* Some find it embarrassing. So, be sure to explain to your child why he is receiving these services, and how he can explain it to his friends.

◆ *State-funded services are often minimal* (maybe half an hour a week). Talk to the teacher and the service provider at your school to see if your child might benefit from additional services outside of school. Many problems (such as speech impediments) can be fairly easily cured, but the process is easier when the therapy is intensive.

Although some children receive these supplemental services (officially called "related services") through IDEA, some districts argue that they only need to provide *educational* services under IDEA. If your district gives you that argument, investigate services that should be provided to your child under the Rehabilitative Act of 1973 (specifically Section 504) which may be useful in pushing the district to provide your child with extra services. Read answers above regarding Section 504 and see Appendix 8 for some Web sites that can help you navigate the legal issues involved in special education.

Choosing After-School and Summer Programs

I F YOU'RE LIKE MANY PARENTS, YOU NOT ONLY WANT TO MAXIMIZE YOUR CHILD'S SCHOOL experiences, but you want to make sure that she makes the most of her out-of-school time as well. And, if you're a working parent, after-school programs and summer programs may also constitute a major form of childcare for your family. This appendix provides some quick tips for choosing the best after-school and summer programs for your child.

Look for a good match.

Just like schools, not all after-school and summer programs are ideal for every child. When choosing a program, try to find one that fits with your family's needs and schedules as well as your child's needs and interests. While good programs can be expensive, the most expensive program may not be the best program for your child. For instance, what local parents consider "the best" local program may emphasize sports or music and your child may need more academic support. Or, the most expensive local program may provide one-on-one tutoring, which your child may not need.

Be willing to "mix and match" programs.

Very few after-school or summer programs provide children with "everything." When looking for after-school and summer programs for your child, investigate the possibility of having your child take part in several. Obviously, not all communities have several programs to choose from and cost and transportation can be an issue, but, providing your child with variety will expose him to other children and more experiences, and will likely help to stave off boredom. (Even the best after-school programs get boring after a while.)

Be creative and ask for help if you need it.

Organizing after-school and summer activities can be extremely difficult, especially for working parents and parents on tight budgets. But, you might be surprised to find that, with a little assertiveness and some creativity, you can get your child into a great program (or several great programs). For instance, if you find a program you like but think it's too expensive, don't be afraid to ask about discounts, sliding scales (where families pay according to income), or scholarships. You might even ask if it's possible for your child to attend the program a few days a week to cut down on cost. If transportation is an issue, talk to other parents—the program might even help put you in contact with other parents. You are probably not the only parent trying to figure out how to arrange pick-up and drop-off to different programs and you might be able to set up a carpool. In addition, some programs have vans that pick students up, extended hours for parents who begin work early or stay late, and affiliations with other programs that might be able to provide additional before- or after-care. Never hesitate to ask.

After-School Programs

"How can I find a good after-school program?"

There are several ways to get information about after-school programs. Your first stop should be the school's main office. They probably have literature on after-school programs that operate on campus and may even have information about other local programs. If the programs at your child's school do not seem appropriate, try:

♦ *Asking your child's teacher.* Teachers often know what programs their students are involved in and your child's teacher may be able to suggest programs that other students "like him" have enjoyed or benefited from.

♦ *Asking other parents.* Parents are your best source of information for out-of-school activities. Not only can parents tell you what programs exist, but if you talk to enough parents (to get a well-rounded set of opinions) you will probably learn the inside scoop on which programs are good, the best ways to get discounts, and any other parents who are looking for carpools.

"What should I look for in a good after-school program?"

After-school programs vary tremendously—as do parents' and students' needs. At the most basic level, after-school programs should:

♦ *Be safe.* Visit the program. Look around the facilities. The area should be safe (preferably in an enclosed area, such as a school yard) and personnel should be available to watch over and help children. Program staff should know any other adults who are in the facility or interacting with children.

♦ *Be accessible.* Your child should be able to get from school to the program. Many after-school programs are on school campuses, so your child may be able to walk out of his classroom after the last bell and find himself at his after-school program. Other programs provide buses, vans, or designated "walkers" to get students to after-school programs.

♦ *Provide adequate supervision.* It's hard to define "adequate" but you should know it when you see it. When you visit the program, make sure children are occupied and that the staff-to-student ratio is high enough so that when children get in trouble or squabble with each other, someone is available to get kids back on track.

♦ *Provide activities.* The types of activities that after-school programs offer vary a lot. But, ideally, children should not seem idle. They should be engaged in some sort of activity. Activities do not have to be formally organized—children do enjoy talking with friends and playing casual games—but children should not be just wandering around aimlessly.

Beyond the basics, assess after-school programs based on the specific needs of you and your child. Does the program fit your schedule? Can you afford the program? Are there other children your child's age? Do any of your child's friends attend? Do program participants engage in your child's favorite activities (whether she loves basketball or art)? Unlike summer programs, most after-school programs are not particularly specialized, so you probably can't be be too picky about the specific activities. However, if your child needs homework help from her after-school program, you should make sure to assess the quality of that help (see the next question).

"My child needs help with homework after school. How can I find the best academic program for him?"

"Homework help" is offered in most after-school programs. Although some help is better than no help at all, the quality of homework help can vary drastically from program to program. When you investigate a program make sure to ask:

◆ *How long is homework time?* Some programs have tutors to help with homework throughout the afternoon. Others set aside specific hours for homework help. Think about how long it typically takes your child to finish his homework and make sure the program will provide enough home-

work time for him to finish.

◆ *Are children required to work on homework at the program?* Some programs require all students to sit inside, working on homework or reading, for a designated amount of time each day. If your child tends to "forget" to do his homework and needs structure, this may be a good program for him. If your child often has little or no homework, he may find this rule frustrating. Moreover, if the program has a "forced homework" policy, sit in and watch a homework session. Are children paying attention or do a lot of children seem to not have homework and instead spend their time bothering other students?

◆ *What is the staff-to-student ratio during "homework help"?* Although many programs offer "homework help" this can mean anything from intense individual tutoring to having children do homework in a classroom where one or two adults supervise 20-30 students. If your child just needs a quiet place to work, this may be fine. If he tends to need a lot of help, he may require a lower student-to-staff ratio.

◆ *What are the qualifications of the staff members who help children with homework?* Some after-school programs hire teachers to help with homework. Many hire "teacher's assistants" (sometimes called paraprofessionals) from the local schools. Some hire local high school or college students. Ask about the homework helpers. How much education do most of them have? Although teachers should have the skills necessary to help students with homework, don't make the same assumption about teacher's assistants. Although some teacher's assistants are smart and college-educated (many are training to be teachers), others are not particularly well-educated and may struggle to help your child with basic elementary school concepts (the same, of course, goes for high school and college students and other recreational staff members). And, if a program hires teachers and teachers' aides who teach during the regular school day, make sure that they aren't too exhausted from their "real jobs" to keep teaching and explaining with enthusiasm after school. Ask about staff members' qualifications and observe some homework sessions if you can. It can also be very useful to ask children who are enrolled in the program how well the staff helps them with homework. They will be better able than anyone else to tell you how helpful staff members are with homework questions.

▶ **Where do children do their homework?** Most after-school programs set aside a classroom, library, or other room for "homework help." Make sure that the environment in which they do homework is conducive to your child's learning style. So, for instance, if your child needs silence, and the room is chaotic, you may need to investigate another program. Also make sure that

your child will have access to the resources she needs to complete her homework. So, for instance, if she often has to type stories or reports, make sure there is a computer available. If she needs to do a lot of research, make sure that she has access to a library or at least some decent reference books.

▶ **Are resources available for children who need more intensive academic help?** If your child needs more than just "homework help," local after-school programs may be able to help you find a tutor (they may even have tutors who volunteer with them or work for them). If the program at your child's school does not have connections with tutors, you might want to ask if they are amenable to having a tutor that you find (and hire yourself) work with your child at the program.

If your child needs really intensive academic help, a general after-school program is probably not your best option. You need to locate a tutor or a learning center that specializes in academics (see Chapter 3 for more on finding a tutor).

"Many of my child's friends go to after-school programs. My child usually just comes home. Is he missing out? Should I enroll him in a program?"

Most parents enroll their kids in after-school programs because they need childcare. If you do not need daycare for your child, there are only a few situations in which you should consider enrolling him in an after-school program:

▶ *Many of his classmates, who also do not need childcare, are enrolled in the program.* High enrollment of students who do not need childcare might indicate that your local after-school program is exemplary (since most parents do not choose to spend money on after-school programs when they do not need day care). It's probably worth checking the program out.

▶ *You can't motivate your child to socialize with other children or be active at home.* Some children are too drawn to the TV and video games when they're home. If this is the case with your child, enrolling him in an after-school program may be an easy way to put him in contact with other children and push him to engage in more active entertainment.

▶ *Whoever cares for your child after school cannot transport your child to extracurricular activities.* If, because of other responsibilities, disability, or any other reason, the person who cares for your child after school cannot transport him to other activities (or if your child stays by himself and is not allowed to go out on his own), an after-school program might be an easy way to get him involved in some extracurricular activities. Although most after-school programs do not offer the "best"

lessons, classes, or sports programs in the community, many have art classes, sports teams, and other organized activities that children enjoy. If this is the only way your child can participate in such activities, and they are available at your local after-school program, you should consider enrolling your child in the program at least a few days a week.

▶ *Whoever cares for your child cannot help him with homework.* Some children are old enough to take care of themselves but need help with homework. Some caregivers don't have the time or the academic or English-language skills to help children with homework. In these cases, an after-school program with a strong homework component would be a good option for a child who often needs help with homework assignments.

However, if you (or someone else) is available to care for your child after school and can provide transportation to other activities, there are many ways you can keep your child busy and social, and help him discover and develop his talents and interests.

▶ *Investigate local sports teams (either community or club-based), lessons (through private teachers, schools, or recreation centers), and clubs (such as Boy Scouts or Girl Scouts or youth groups) for your child.* Many children enjoy participating in extracurricular activities and individual activities (rather than comprehensive after-school programs). Allow your child to choose which activities he would like to try out and when he would like to participate (most teams, clubs, and lessons meet once or twice a week, not every day as after-school programs do).

▶ *Arrange play dates with your child's classmates.* Don't forget the classmates who attend after-school programs. Although many children love their after-school program, most would also be thrilled to "have a break" and go home with a friend after school.

Summer Programs

"How can I find the best summer program for my child?"

Unlike after-school programs, summer programs often get quite specialized and can provide anything from general recreation to a focus on aerospace engineering or modern dance. When you evaluate a summer program, start with the essentials listed above (for after-school programs) to determine whether a summer program is safe, supervised, and at least minimally active.

Then, you have to ask yourself and your child what you are looking for in a summer camp or program. Ask yourself:

▶ *Do I need day care for my child?* If you need childcare over the summer, "general" day camps are often a great way to make sure that your child is occupied. If daycare is a primary objective, make sure to check out summer program hours—many end in the late afternoon. And, remember, even if your need for daycare all summer long means that you need to choose a relatively inexpensive day camp, you might also consider investing in one or two weeks of a more specialized camp to give your child some variety.

▶ *Do I need help giving my child fun summer experiences?* Many "general" day camps provide fun. Popular camps take a lot of day trips—to the beach, parks, miniature golf, IMAX movies, and amusement parks. For parents who have busy schedules or limited transportation, these general camps can be a great way to keep your child active and give her a "fun" summer.

▶ *Do I need help exposing my child to other children during the summer?* General day camps are also great for providing children with playmates. If you do not live near many of your child's friends or don't have the time or transportation to arrange play dates, a general day camp may be a good solution.

▶ *Does my child need academic help or enrichment?* If your child needs academic help or you want to provide her with special enrichment instruction, you probably aren't looking for a general day camp, because general day camps usually provide, at best, minimal academic instruction. Instead, look into summer schools. Your child's school may offer remedial or enrichment classes. Also look for summer programs at local community colleges and universities. Local museums and science centers often offer academic programs as well, as do some local corporations (especially those in the technology fields). Ask your child's teacher and other parents if they can recommend academic summer programs.

♦ *Do I want my child to gain or improve any particular skills, "talents," or knowledge this summer?* Many parents use summer as a time to provide instruction in non-academic subjects. You might consider religious school, sports camp, or an art or music program. Churches, colleges and universities, art museums, music studios, and concert venues would be good starting places for gathering information about these types of programs. If your child already attends religious school or takes sports or art lessons, talk to her instructors to see if they can recommend good summer programs that focus on these topics (see the next question for how to evaluate specialized programs).

Ask your child:

♦ *What would she like to do for the summer?* Large communities have summer camps designed for just about any type of child. If you make a list of the things that your child would like to do and learn over the summer, you can figure out which experiences your fam-

ily can provide (through vacations, daytrips, etc.) and which ones you would like her to get through a camp or summer program. Discussing the range of activities and experiences your child would like to have over the summer will also help you decide if she should spend all summer in one program or attend several different programs over the course of the summer.

♦ *What, if any, camps will her friends attend?* Many children want to attend the camps their friends are going to. And many children attend the same camp year after year. If your child's friends are going to a particular camp, it's worth investigating. Talk to your child's friends' parents to see why they like that program.

♦ *Are there any particular skills or talents that she would like to explore, learn, or develop?* Your child might surprise you. She may have a secret desire to learn to play guitar or take up volleyball. Summer programs are great opportunities to try out new skills and see how she likes them.

"What should I look for in a high-quality, specialized summer program?"

Although summer programs vary dramatically in content, there are several hallmarks of a high-quality, specialized summer program, no matter what the specialization:

♦ *Highly qualified staff.* Of course,

qualifications will vary depending on the camp's focus. Summer schools and academic camps should be staffed by people who are qualified to be teachers (they don't have to be credentialed teachers but they should have college-level specialization in the subjects they are teaching to your children). Specialized sports camps should be staffed by athletes—preferably athletes who competed at the college, professional, or at least elite high school levels. Art and music camps should be staffed by professionals from the art or music worlds who have impressive artistic talents of their own. Beware of specialized camps and programs that hire unspecialized staff. Although your child might have fun at a summer camp in which sports instructors are local high school students, she is unlikely to gain specialized sports skills from such a camp.

▶ *Structured, active programs and agendas.* A high-quality summer program should be able to tell you what your child will be doing each day of the program. Each day should include several well-supervised (or coached) activities in which children learn, develop, or practice skills. An art camp might include morning sessions where students learn about color and composition, afternoon sessions where they try new techniques, and time where they paint (or sculpt or draw) under the supervision of more experienced artists who can help them improve their techniques. A science camp might involve lessons or lectures in which students learn scientific concepts, periods of directed experiments or hands-on demonstrations, and then periods in which children work in supervised groups designing, executing, and documenting their own experiments and inventions. High-quality, specialized programs will not involve a lot of "free time" or time when children get to choose their own activities. Don't pay a lot of money for a camp that gives your child hours to "paint whatever she wants" or play pick-up basketball without coaching.

▶ *Specific goals.* A high-quality summer camp or program should be able to tell you explicitly what skills and talents your child will develop in the program. The camp's literature should tell you the camp's goals and any program director you talk to should be able to elaborate on them.

Of course, children do not need to spend their entire summers in high-quality, specialized camps. Most children enjoy having some time to hang out with their friends and engage in leisurely recreation. Some summer programs provide exactly those kinds of experiences (for instance, taking campers to local parks, pools, and amusement parks). But, if you are considering paying a lot of money for a high-quality, specialized day camp or summer program, it should meet the above criteria.

"I would love for my child to go to a summer day camp, but they all seem to end at 3 or 4 o'clock and I don't know how I am going to get out of work early enough to pick him up. Is there anything I can do?"

Summer day camps and programs are notorious for ending before most parents' workdays are finished, which can wreak havoc on parents' schedules. There are three common solutions to this problem:

▶ *Ask the summer program if they have "extended care."* Most programs will keep children for a few hours after (or before) the program officially starts —for a fee. Many programs allow parents to pay for extended care only a few days a week if they don't need the extra hours every day. Although "extended care" will increase your summer camp costs, it may allow your child to experience camp. A decent number of children usually stay during extended care (most children just hang out or play sports), so your child won't be alone.

▶ *Talk to other parents.* Many parents organize after-program play dates and carpools to help accommodate everyone's schedule. Organizing with four other parents might mean that you only have to take off work early one day a week to pick the children up. And, if leaving work early is impossible, ask around anyway. Some parents have flexible schedules over the summer and wouldn't mind having an extra child

around the house (to play with their own child) a few afternoons a week.

▶ *Coordinate camps with some of your child's friends.* Many working parents arrange ahead of time to sign their children up at the same camps as their close friends. They then arrange for their child to go home with his friends in the afternoons (after the camp ends). Although it would be nice to reciprocate this kind of favor somehow (perhaps hosting your child's friend on the weekends, or driving the early morning shift), you might be surprised at how helpful other parents can be.

"The summer program I would like my child to attend has scholarships available but you have to apply for them.
Are there any secrets to writing good admissions essays or letters of recommendation?"

See the tips at the end of Chapter 1 (on how to apply to private schools) for guidelines that are appropriate for all admissions and scholarship applications.

Looking Ahead... What to Do Before Your Child Starts School

A LTHOUGH WE OFTEN THINK OF THE FIRST DAY OF KINDERGARTEN AS THE MILESTONE at which kids "start school," children start learning long before they set foot in elementary school. Every time you talk to and play with your child (from birth to school age) you expand his mind, his thinking skills, and his knowledge. In the process, you teach him that thinking, reading, and learning are fun (which will make school seem much more fun). Here are a few tips on how to talk and play with your baby and preschool child to help him learn and think.

"What's the best way to prepare my young child to succeed in school?"

The best ways to build your child's mind and prepare him for school can be incorporated into the daily activities that you probably already do together:

▶ *Talk, talk, talk.* Never underestimate the impact you can have on your baby or young child just by talking to him. Even when children are not old enough to understand what you're saying, they will respond to your voice. By talking to them, you introduce them to vocabulary, grammar, and ideas. And, your child will probably begin to understand you long before he can tell you how much he understands. So, have conversations with him, even if they are somewhat one-sided. Talking with your child will boost his verbal reasoning and vocabulary.

▶ *Read, read, read.* When you read with young children, they not only gain exposure to written words and phonics, but they learn that books are fun. Have lots of children's books around the house so that you can expose your child to a wide variety of stories and vocabulary words (remember, you can always borrow books from your local library to keep an ever-changing array of books around the house). Even if your child is not old enough to read—or old enough to understand the books you read with him—use reading as play time and together time. Cuddle your child when you read together and he'll associate reading with good times spent being close with Mom or Dad. And, if you read enough, you'll be surprised at how quickly he'll catch on about letters, words, and reading in general. It's never too early to read to your child. Start reading with your newborn and make bedtime stories and other "book time" part of your daily routine.

▶ *Integrate learning into your everyday life.* It's never too early to teach your children how fun it is to learn new things. Point out new things (for a small child, this could be a bulldozer, a new dog that moved in down the street, a new kind of flower that just bloomed, or a new character on his favorite cartoon). Ask him questions and let him try to answer you. Ask him for his opinions. Push him to formulate opinions. When he asks you questions, let him see you seek out the answers (by asking others, looking in books, searching on the Internet). In the process, you'll teach him how he can seek out answers on his own.

▶ *Think of "educational materials" as toys.* All parents know that little children's taste in toys can be very unpredictable. Many kids like the boxes that toys come in as much as they like the toys themselves. So, don't shun educational toys. You might find that your toddler loves playing with plastic letters as much as he loves playing with toy cars. You might find that playing a game in which you count blocks is just as fun (or more fun) than watching TV.

You might find that he loves learning to write letters in crayon or on a magnetic slate (the most popular brand name is a "MagnaDoodle"). Buy educational toys and encourage your kids to play with them.

▶ *Have lots of educational materials around the house.* Keep lots of books on your bookshelves (including sturdy books that your children can look at). Keep magnet letters on the refrigerator (or somewhere where your children can access them easily). When you integrate learning into the normal things you do (such as playing games with letters while you make lunch) your child will develop academic skills naturally and easily.

▶ *Help your child experience a variety of places and activities.* Like adults, children love going new places. Fortunately, unlike adults, they can get excited over fairly small changes. Going to a new park—maybe one that has a great slide or a particularly good jungle gym —creates a whole new set of experiences for a child. Vacations, day trips, and even trips to the mall open up new realms of people to talk to, things to point out, and experiences to discuss and remember.

▶ *Enjoy learning yourself.* Children tend to emulate their parents. If they see you reading the newspaper, reading in your spare time, discussing current events with your friends, looking up answers to questions in books and on the Internet, and seeking out learning experiences, they will see that learning is something fun, mature, and "adult-like," and they will want to learn too.

"I know I'm supposed to talk to my child, but she's so little and she doesn't talk back and I don't know what to say."

For some people, babbling endlessly is easy. For others, it's a real chore. If you have trouble talking with your child, try the following techniques:

▶ *Tell stories.* Babies and toddlers pay more attention to the sound of your voice than to the content of what you're saying. Tell them stories. You can make stories up or recite stories that you've read. You can even tell your child stories from the office (she's the ideal audience for all the stories that your friends are tired of hearing). It doesn't matter what you tell her as long as you talk. (Feel free to get creative—your child will respond even more if you get dramatic and use funny voices.)

▶ *Tell facts.* If you can't think of good stories, then talk to your young child about something you know. You might talk to her about how a computer works or about how to make great cornbread stuffing. I once held a colicky baby for an hour while his mom was at the doctor. I told him all about how bills become laws and how the U.S. government works (we were inspired by the City Hall building across the street). He had no idea what I was saying, but he didn't cry.

♦ **Teach.** Remember, babies don't know anything. So, teach them. Point out colors. Point out numbers. Point out different types of cars or different types of dogs. Show your child the airplane that is flying across the sky and the different types of vegetables on her plate. Talk to her about the ant that is crawling across the ground. Count the number of flowers blooming in your garden and read restaurant menus. Chances are, if you talk to your child about letters, numbers, and colors from the time she is born, she'll know them long before preschool (where she's supposed to learn them).

♦ **Sing.** You talk to your child because you want her to hear words and interact with you, so songs work, too!

Also, your baby may not exactly talk back to you, but she will probably react to you (with baby noises, gestures, or smiles). Watch her and listen to her and, every chance you get, respond to her noises and gestures.

"I try to read with my child, but he always grabs the pages and turns them before I'm done reading. How can I get him to cooperate?"

You probably can't get him to cooperate, but that doesn't matter. Read with him anyway. Most toddlers will not let you read them an entire book. They will try to turn the pages faster than you can read. They will skip pages. They will refuse to move from a page that you find boring. It's OK! Don't worry about it. If you want to know how stories really go, read the books on your own while your child naps. Then, when you read *with* your child, let *him* set the pace. You can either read the snippets of words that you can catch on each page before he turns them, or make up a plausible story based on the illustrations. Or, if he's engaged, use the book as a teaching tool. Have him point to different parts of the illustrations (e.g., "Where's the cat?" "Which little boy looks happy?" "Show me the green hat.") and ask him questions (e.g., "What do you think the dolphin is going to do next?").

As your child gets older, he will sit through stories better. But even three- and four-year-olds often don't have the attention span to last through an entire story. Don't let it frustrate you. Remember, your reading time together is supposed to convey the impression that reading is fun—not something that frustrates you or your child. Also, try reading during quiet times, like right before nap time or bed time. When your child's mellower, he might be more willing to go at a slower pace.

And, don't forget to give your child books to play with on his own (at his own pace). Make sure you have plenty of sturdy board books or cloth books that your child can look at whenever he wants to "read." If you want, leave the paper books (that most kids love to tear) out of his reach until he's old enough not to ruin them.

"We have lots of books, but what are some other good educational toys?"

You can use almost any toy as a learning tool for your child. Barbies become characters in imaginative stories. Grocery store play sets can lead to math lessons (counting merchandise, adding, etc.). But some especially good toys to have are:

▶ *Puzzles.* There are all kinds of puzzles ranging from soft foam ones for babies, to wooden ones for toddlers, to more complex "jigsaw" puzzles for older kids. Puzzles force kids to think and manipulate pieces (good for hand-eye coordination). Many puzzles for little kids also teach some kind of content (e.g., the pieces are letters, numbers, different shapes, different animals, or different types of transportation).

▶ *Building toys.* We all know about blocks and Legos. These are actually great learning tools. What better way for children to learn about basic physics, engineering, and architecture (although they will have no idea they are learning all this) than by figuring out how to make walls and buildings that don't fall down? You can also use blocks for counting and sorting games. You can use a good set of blocks to teach your child numbers, colors, and shapes.

▶ *No-mess writing tools.* It's often dangerous to give little children pens and crayons without close supervision. But, children as young as 2 years old can begin to learn how to write letters (and draw pictures, of course). So, invest in a gadget that allows your child to "write" without using an ink pen. I already mentioned MagnaDoodles above. There are also other kinds of "wipe-off" slates that don't make messes. Check your local toy stores.

▶ *Basic science toys.* These don't have to be fancy. But, at your local teaching supply store, you will probably find all kinds of items that will entertain your child. Even very little kids can have fun with magnets (e.g., What do they stick to? What does it feel like when they repel each other? Can they move paper clips through tables or chairs?) or with binoculars (see what your child can tell you about the airplanes passing by in the sky).

"It seems like my child is too young to go anyplace 'educational' like a museum. How can I expose him to new environments?"

Because little kids have seen so little, every new place is a learning experience. Anytime you go out and point out new things (e.g., new buildings, new bugs, new plants) or try out new activities (e.g., swimming, climbing a tree) your child gets a new experience. Although not everywhere is "kid-friendly" there are plenty of places to take small children where they can explore new things and activities. Try:

♦ **Parks and beaches.** From crashing waves and seashells to squirrels and swing sets, parks and beaches offer a wide array of sights and experiences.

♦ **Farms, petting zoos, county fairs, and pumpkin patches.** Little children are fascinated by living things—both plants and animals. If you're lucky enough to live by a farm, you can go by frequently and watch how crops and animals grow. If you live in a more urban area, try petting zoos and simulated farms (check out your local pumpkin patch at Halloween). Never underestimate how interesting a goat, chicken, or humongous pumpkin can be to a two-year-old.

♦ **The zoo.** Zoos are notoriously kid-friendly and offer any family a million things to look at and talk about.

♦ **College campuses.** These are often great picnic places. Find some green space, or a fountain, and people-watch with your preschooler.

♦ **Pet stores.** Even your local pet store can be a fun learning experience for a young child. Look for puppies, kittens, hamsters, and all different kinds of fish.

Obviously, those are only a few ideas. Even the mall and the grocery store can be stimulating outings for kids (frankly, any place where there are lots of bright colored objects to look at can be fun). In the end, you just want to make sure that your young child gets out and experiences a wide variety of places and activities.

"What should I look for in a daycare or preschool?"

Obviously, when you're looking for a daycare or preschool, you will have some minimal qualifications in mind: it should be safe and clean and you should trust the adults who will be in charge of your child's well-being. But, beyond the basics, there is one simple guideline that you should follow: *you want to find a daycare or preschool that will be the best substitute for the care that you provide in your home (or, in some cases, the best improvement over what you can provide in your home).*

Just as parents should talk with their children, read with their children, and play with their children, staff members at your child's daycare or preschool should do the same. Just as you should have books and educational toys around your home, you should see these same items (and more of them) in a good daycare or preschool. Just as the play activities you do with your child should incorporate both learning and fun, so should the activities at the daycare or preschool. You don't want to choose a preschool that is going to make your child do work-sheets all day (she'll just learn to hate schoolwork) but you don't want her to sit mindlessly in front of the television all day either. Ideally, you might find a preschool that will allow your child to experience new activities and set-tings—perhaps through fieldtrips.

Many parents enroll their children in preschool so that they can have more contact with other children. That's a great idea. Children should be encouraged to develop "people skills" early. But, again, look for a setting in which children are social but also learn-ing while they play. Learning doesn't always involve books or numbers, but children should be encouraged to be curious, ask questions, seek out an-swers and solutions to their questions and problems, use their imaginations, and be active.

As a general rule, when choosing a preschool, you can follow the steps outlined in Chapter 1 for choosing a school. Check out local preschools' backgrounds, talk to other parents, do drive-bys, and talk to principals (or directors) and teachers. Finally, take the time to observe in any daycare or pre-school that you're considering. Try to determine if it can offer all or most of the activities listed above in a caring way that you think your child would enjoy.

Looking Ahead. . .
How to Prepare Your Child for Middle School

T HE LEAP FROM ELEMENTARY SCHOOL TO MIDDLE SCHOOL OFTEN SEEMS HUGE TO BOTH children and parents. Surprisingly, in the end, most children make the transition much more smoothly than they anticipate. However, there's actually a great deal of planning to do before children leave elementary school. Below are some of the most common questions that parents have about middle school.

"What's the best way to choose a middle school?"

When you choose a middle school for your child you can follow the same general strategies outlined in Chapter 1 for choosing an elementary school. The main exception is that, for middle school, because there are so many more teachers (and your children will have four to eight teachers every year), classroom visits are less likely to give you an idea of the classes that your child will take. The good thing about selecting a middle school is that by the time your child is ready to go to middle school, you will probably be in contact with many more parents than you were when your child started kindergarten. So, talk to a lot of parents, especially those with children already in middle school. What do they like about their children's middle schools? What do they dislike (or wish they could change)? Some good questions to ask other parents are:

◆ Does your child feel safe at his middle school?

◆ Does your child like the teachers?

◆ Do you feel the schoolwork appropriately challenges your child? (Make sure you talk to parents whose children have similar academic skills as your child.)

◆ How much homework does your child get? Does it seem like good homework or mostly busywork?

◆ Are the counselors and administrators responsive if you have a problem?

◆ And, if your child is interested in developing his art or music skills, ask what electives are available and how strong the art or music programs are at each middle school.

Middle school counselors are also good people to talk to when looking for information about middle schools. Since children have so many teachers at middle schools, they often get assigned to a counselor who is quite involved in their scheduling and any problems they might have at school (either academic or disciplinary). Talk to some counselors to try to find a school whose philosophies and academic programs are a good match for your child.

"Our local middle school is not very good. Can we go to a different one?"

Again, look at the information in Chapter 1 to help you learn about school choice options in your district. Your district may allow inter-district or intra-district open enrollment in junior high schools and middle schools that are not overcrowded. You may be able to apply to magnet schools or charter schools. Or, you may be able to get a permit to attend a school that you prefer. Call your district office to gather information about your middle school choices. Get this information as soon as you can so that you will have enough time to prepare for or comply with your particular district's requirements and rules.

"How can I calm my child's anxieties about middle school?"

Many children feel scared and anxious about going to middle school. Some are simply worried about leaving the school that they have attended for the past six or seven years. Other kids are concerned about getting lost going from class to class. Other kids hear rumors that they are going to be called "scrubs" and that the other kids are going to do mean things to them (beat them up, put their heads in toilets, and all sorts of other horrible things). Most children get over these fears shortly after arriving at middle school. They quickly realize that they have plenty of time to get from class to class and that most older kids are too busy to even notice them. But there are several things that you can do to calm your child's fears:

▶ **Visit** *the middle school your child will attend.* You and your child probably won't be able to visit during the school day, but drop by right after school gets out. Most school campuses are open when school first lets out so you will be able to walk around the campus freely. Your child will be able to see that the kids there are very similar to him—just a little taller. He will also see that they are not ruthlessly pursing younger kids but talking with their friends and minding their own business. (Obviously, if older students are harassing younger students, you might want to consider choosing another middle school!)

▶ *Get and study a map of the middle*

school. Drop by the main office and they should be able to give you a photocopy of the middle school map. Sit down with your child and study the map. Learn where the P.E. field is, where the cafeteria is, where the library is, where the restrooms are. When you get your child's schedule, try to map out his classes so he knows where he will have to go. Just knowing the lay of the land will give him some confidence.

▶ *Try to find some middle school students for him to talk to.* Almost all students are scared just before they go to middle school and almost all students find that their fears are greatly relieved once they get there. Some older students should be able to set your child's mind at ease.

"Are there any new organizational skills my child should have for middle school?"

Your child doesn't need *new* organizational skills as much as she needs to perfect the organizational skills that she already has. If your child has a good system for writing down her homework, making sure she brings home the supplies that she needs to do her homework, and budgeting her time for long-term assignments (including studying for tests), she should be in good shape for middle school. If, however, your child's organizations skills in elementary school are shaky or done "on the fly" (in other words, she relies on her memory to figure out what homework she has and tends to do projects at the last minute) then she needs to start working on her organizational skills as soon as possible. Because middle school students have to keep track of assignments for six to eight classes, they can't rely on their memories. So, before your child finishes elementary school, make sure she:

▶ *Consistently uses some kind of assignment book or planner to write down her work.* If she's not using one, have her start as soon as possible.

▶ *Can set incremental deadlines for long-term projects and stick to them.* When your child finds out that she has a report due in two weeks, she should be able to lay out a plan detailing how much progress she is going to make between now and the due date. And, she should be able to stick to the plan (so, if all of her research is supposed to be done by the end of the first weekend, she should hold herself to that commitment). Although she may be able to pull off last minute assignments in elementary school, it will get harder and harder as she moves through middle school and high school and she should start building good habits as soon as possible.

▶ *Can keep a neat backpack.* In middle school, teachers expect students to be able to keep their materials neat and orderly. They need to be able to get their hands on their math notebook and their math homework at a moment's notice. Make sure that your child keeps papers put away in their proper places in her notebooks and doesn't have loose papers floating around in her backpack.

"Are there any skills, such as note-taking, that my child should know before going to middle school?"

Aside from organizational skills, your child's middle school teachers will teach him the skills he needs for middle school. Although some middle school teachers lecture and expect students to take notes, most will teach children how to take notes by giving them summaries and outlines to work with. If your child finds outlines useful for taking notes when he reads and for doing research for projects, by all means, teach him to make them, but knowing how to make outlines is not a prerequisite for middle school.

"How can I make sure that my child will be in classes that are challenging enough in middle school?"

OR

"How can I make sure that my child will not be in classes that are too hard in middle school?"

Unlike elementary schools, most middle schools have official, academically stratified "tracks" (although they may not call them tracks). The most common tracks are "honors," "regular," and "remedial," although larger schools sometimes have more and smaller schools sometimes have fewer—or none at all. (Schools with special magnet or gifted programs may have additional tracks that serve students in specific magnet or gifted programs—admission into these tracks is usually determined through an application process and you should consult with the school if you think your child belongs in one of these tracks.) Middle schools typically determine children's track placement based on four criteria:

▶ *Special designations.* If your child qualifies for a GATE or gifted program at her elementary school, she probably will be automatically placed in the honors track in middle school. If your child receives special education or resource in elementary school she may be placed in remedial classes in middle school.

▶ *Elementary school grades.* Most middle schools will not assign children to an honors or high track unless they maintain good grades in elementary school.

▶ *Test scores.* Some middle schools look at students' standardized test scores at the end of elementary school to determine track placement. Many schools have a cutoff above which they assign students to honors. Test scores are usually most important for high-achieving students who are not official-

ly in a gifted program.

▶ *Teacher recommendations.* Middle schools vary in how much weight they give to elementary school teacher recommendations. But, it's definitely worth talking to your child's fifth- or sixth-grade teacher, *at the beginning of the year,* to see if she will have input into your child's middle school placement.

If you want input into your child's placement, you should follow several steps:

▶ *Call the middle school to find out what its policies are.* Talk to a counselor. He may be unwilling to commit to how they plan to place your child (especially without all of the relevant information—such as fifth- or sixth-grade grades). But he should be able to give you some basic guidelines.

▶ *Talk to your child's elementary school teacher.* If you have a strong opinion about what kinds of classes your child should be in (perhaps you think she is ready for honors even if she is not in a gifted program in elementary school, or perhaps you want to make sure that she has the comfort of some resource classes at least for the first year or two of middle school), discuss them with your child's teacher. See what she thinks. She may agree with you and advocate for that placement. Or, she may disagree, and you should listen to what she has to say. She may know more about your child's school performance than you do.

▶ *Stay in touch with your child's middle school counselor as the first day of school approaches.* Call the school to confirm your child's placement. Stay in touch with the counselor if the placement does not work out. Many children change classes in the first few weeks of school. So, your child's initial placement is probably not set in stone. Talk with your child frequently about her classes and keep a close eye on her work and how hard she's working. And, if need be, go to the counselor and request a change.

If your child is borderline, always advocate for the harder, more challenging placement (at least for an initial trial run). You can always adjust and move your child down if the classes are too difficult (make sure your child realizes that everyone expects the classes to be challenging and that it will not be shameful if she decides to move down later). She may find that the classes are not as hard as she expected them to be. You may also find that your child is able to rise to the challenge of a harder class. As a general rule, it will be harder to get your child moved up later than it will be to get her moved down—so start with the higher placement.

"My child is very strong in math (or language arts) and not very strong in language arts (or math). Do we have to enroll him in all honors classes or can he take just honors math (or language arts)?"

Unlike most high schools, many middle schools consider honors tracks to be "all or nothing." So, children either attend all honors classes or none at all. However, each school has different policies and, if you make a good case, the school may be able to accommodate your child. Make an appointment to talk to a counselor or assistant principal at your child's prospective middle school. Before you go, read the sections in Chapter 2 about requesting teachers to see how you can best frame your request for a particular accommodation from your middle school.

If the middle school will not accommodate your request for your child to attend some honors and some regular classes, you still have a few possible courses of action:

▶ *Enroll your child in all honors classes* (hopefully, your child's grades in his weaker subject are strong enough to support this strategy). You may be surprised to find that, although your child has to work a little harder in his weak subject, he can succeed in an honors class. If the placement does not work, you can always go and talk to the counselor again and see if you can work out a compromise now that your child has proven that he has very different levels of skills in math and language arts.

▶ *Get a tutor or some enrichment help* over the summer. If you help your child bone up on his weak subject, he may be better prepared for the honors class in the fall. Keep the tutor on stand-by for the school year in case your child needs some extra help with homework.

Again, as a general rule, when in doubt go for the more challenging placement at first and then adjust later.

"Everyone says that the middle school my child will be attending next year is very hard. What can we do over the summer to make sure that my child is academically prepared to start next year?"

If your child is behind academically, it would be a great idea to hire a tutor for the summer to help her improve—and maintain—her skills. Talk to her elementary school teachers to see what she struggles with most. Talk to a counselor at the middle school to see what skills they want children to have when they start school. If your child's tests from the past school year are accessible, these would be a great reference for a tutor to use with your child.

   If your child is not behind academically and you just want to give her a head start, you have a few options:

▶ *Ask the middle school if the children do a lot of book reports—and for a list of acceptable books if they have one.* Your child can get a head start reading over the summer and then take notes on her favorite books to use for book reports over the school year.

▶ *Ask the middle school what math textbooks it uses.* See if you can buy, borrow, or photocopy one. The first few chapters of most math books contain a quick review of materials that children should already know. Make sure that your child knows how to do this work. If she is clueless about most of it, work with her (or hire a tutor) to prepare for this work. (Don't force her to learn the whole book—that's what the school year is for! But, if she's strong on the review material, it should ease her transition into the harder work of middle school.)

▶ *Finally, make sure your child reads, writes, and thinks over the summer* (you can probably get her excited by going shopping for puzzles, mind teasers, and lots of books). And, if she tends to forget her math, ask her elementary school teachers for a some worksheets that she can do over the summer to practice her skills. The most important thing is to keep your child's mind active over the summer so that she does not have a rude awakening when she begins middle school.

"They don't let the students at my child's middle school use lockers and everyone says that their backpacks get outrageously heavy. Is there anything I can do to help my child with the burden of carrying so many books around?"

Although most of us probably remember that learning how to use a locker (and a combination lock) was a central part of going to middle school, many middle schools no longer use lockers. Some are simply too overcrowded and don't have enough lockers to serve their students. Other schools (usually those in urban areas) cite safety concerns at the primary reason that their students do not use lockers. Although ridiculously heavy backpacks are becoming the norm, here are a few strategies for easing your child's backpack burden.

❧ *See if it's possible to get a home set of books.* Some schools have extra books. Others can at least point you in the direction of how to acquire your own set of books. The bonus with this technique is that you don't have to worry about your child forgetting to bring his books home for homework.

❧ *Consider getting your child a backpack with wheels.* However, before you do, drive by the school to see how many children use these types of bags. At many schools, they are considered "nerdy" and the kids who use them get picked on. Most children would prefer to have a sore back than to get teased (or have their backpack constantly kicked by other students).

❧ *Invest in a good, supportive backpack for your child.* Check out sporting goods stores for backpacks that are used for hiking and backpacking. Some of these backpacks offer much better support than typical school backpacks and will help distribute the weight of your child's books so that they do not injure his back.

❧ *Help your child develop a good organizational system so that he doesn't carry unnecessary materials around.* Set up a filing system at home so that when your child finishes a unit at school, he can file his materials at home rather than continuing to carry them around in his binder. Set up a system so that he knows which books he needs each day (especially if his school uses a rotating or block schedule in which every class does not meet every day).

"How can I help my child choose good electives in middle school?"

The electives that your child chooses in middle school will probably not have a huge impact on her future life. But, it's still a good idea to help her make good choices. Contact the middle school relatively early in the school year before your child goes to middle school (after winter break should be early enough) and ask them about the procedure for having children choose electives and when those choices are made. Many schools have children choose electives in school or on a visit to the middle school during their last year in elementary school. Others send letters or notices home to parents. Either way, know when to look for a sign-up sheet.

Also ask if you can have a list of the electives offered, so you can discuss them with your child. This will give you some lead time to discuss the pros and cons of different options. What should you consider?

▶ *A musical instrument.* For many children, middle school is their first real chance to play a musical instrument in a group setting (band or orchestra). The quality of music programs varies tremendously from school to school (I have seen some truly amazing middle school music teachers), but if your child takes music she will probably at least learn how to read music, along with the basics of an instrument. Many children try an instrument, never practice, and give it up in a year (in other words, just because your child takes orchestra does not mean you should necessarily run out and buy her a cello right away). But, for other children, the instrument they learn to play in middle school becomes a life-long passion. If your child starts in sixth or seventh grade, by the time she goes to high school, where she may have to compete for a spot in the band or orchestra, she will have a head start.

▶ *Foreign languages.* Many middle schools offer foreign languages and allow students who take them to apply their classes (or some portion of their classes) to the foreign language requirement at the high school level. Getting a head start with foreign languages during middle school may gain your child an extra elective in high school—or an extra AP class if she chooses to take, for instance, AP Spanish in her senior year of high school. Since children also learn new languages better at younger ages, getting a head start in middle school could also improve how well she speaks her new language by the time she finishes her high school classes.

▶ *Art, cooking, woodshop, home economics, etc.* Many middle schools still offer the traditional electives most of us are familiar with. Although these electives do not give students a "head start" on any potential high school activity, they do serve as a nice break during the day and your child can learn some important skills.

▶ *Being a teacher's assistant.* Many schools allow students to work in the office, the library, or as a teacher's aide as their electives. Although there are probably skills to be learned from all of these jobs (e.g., how to answer phones, shelve books, and grade papers), I would not recommend this elective to most parents. Most children use these electives as free time and most middle schools offer at least some better electives where children can learn a new skill of some kind.

So, when your child brings home her list of possible electives, go over them together and discuss what you think your child would like to do. In the end, her elective will probably not make or break her middle school career, but do make sure you at least get to talk about her options rather than just signing off on whatever she puts. Many students simply choose the electives their friends sign up for even if they don't interest them at all.

Looking Ahead... What to Do NOW to Prepare Your Child for College

EACH LEVEL OF SCHOOL TRAINS STU- dents for the next. Children learn letters and numbers in preschool to prepare them for the reading and math they'll learn in elementary school. These basic skills translate into critical essays, science labs, and calculus in middle school and high school. And, all those high school skills prepare students to study a field of their choice in college. Thus, *everything* you do to help your child succeed in school and enjoy learning *now* will help her prepare for college—and your immediate focus should be on what your child is doing now. However, you can also use the following tips to help your child plan for and work towards college.

"I know that it's important to start early—what can I do with my child now to help her get into a good college?"

It's true. Although your child won't apply to colleges until her senior year in high school, you will be building up to that moment (in some ways, at least) from the moment she's born. The best way to think about how to prepare your child for applying to college is to think about what she'll have to submit to colleges when she applies and what she can do now to make sure her application will be as strong as it can be:

▶ *Grade point average (GPA).* Most colleges look at grades from tenth, eleventh, and twelfth grade. Thus, some kids, as late as middle school, claim their grades don't matter—but they do. Your child needs to know how much work it takes to get good grades and know how to maintain that effort throughout high school. The best way to learn those skills is to get high grades throughout elementary and middle school. At many top colleges, almost all of the applicants have GPAs over 4.0 (this is with weighted grades —so these students do not all have straight As but they likely come close). If your child strives to keep her grades up all through school, she will not have to drastically change her efforts in tenth grade, when the grades start to "count."

▶ *Standardized test scores.* Many colleges have recently questioned their reliance on SATs for college admissions decisions. Some have stopped requiring the test all together. Others are placing more weight on other tests such as the ACT or the SAT IIs (which are subject-specific standardized tests). Regardless, your child will likely have to have good scores on some kind of standardized test in order to get into a good college. How can you make sure that her test scores are high?

• *Make sure she READS.* The best way to boost verbal scores on standardized tests is by reading—a lot. Reading helps children improve their vocabularies and their reading comprehension skills. It is the single best life-habit for raising test scores. But, it only works if your child starts reading long before the test date (ideally, from early elementary school on).

- *Make sure she has good test-taking skills.* Monitor your child's test scores—both the scores she gets on classroom tests and those she gets on standardized achievement tests (the national percentiles that she gets on the standardized achievement tests will probably be similar to the ones she will get on the SATs if she does not dramatically change her school performance in the meantime). If your child shows any sign of test-taking anxiety, try to deal with it immediately. Work with your child on pacing herself and on relaxing during tests. If your child shows any signs of having poor test-taking skills, get a test-taking book and work with her or enroll her in a test preparation class. These skills are important—and if she learns them early, she will master them by the time she needs them for the SAT. (For more information, see the question on test anxiety in Chapter 3.)

▶ *A record of having taken challenging classes (including honors and AP classes).* This is another way in which your child's elementary school grades matter. Most applicants to selective colleges take many honors and AP classes (and earn weighted grades in those classes). The easiest way to get into those honors and AP classes is to be tracked into them from middle school honors classes. And, most middle school students get tracked into honors classes from having high test scores, good grades, and good teacher recommendations from elementary school. Students who do poorly in elementary school will struggle to get into challenging classes later in their school careers, which can hurt their college applications.

▶ *Extracurricular activities and accomplishments.* Many college applicants try to pad their applications to look "well-rounded." But, if your child begins exploring lots of interests at a young age, she won't have to pad her application. By the time she reaches high school she will already have found interests and talents that she loves and has pursued for many years. All she will have to do for her college application is describe the sports teams, music lessons, or community service that she already does and genuinely cares about (and remember, colleges prefer students to have genuine interests—they can usually tell when people conjure activities up specifically for the application). So, let your child try out different activities. If she expresses an interest in something (e.g., art, music, karate, basketball), let her try it. Always do what you can to nurture your child's talents and interests.

▶ *A personal essay.* There's not much that your child can do during elementary school that will impact her personal essay. But, she should always work on her writing skills. Keep an eye on your child's papers, reports, and essays. Hopefully, her teachers will grade her written work and give her comments and suggestions on how to improve it. Writing is one of the most important skills that your child should develop in school, so make sure that someone is monitoring her writing and helping her improve. If her teachers neglect this task, you should take it on yourself, enlist the help of a friend or relative with good writing skills, or hire a writing tutor.

▶ *Letters of recommendation.* Again, there's little that your child can do now to influence her letters of recommendation. But, teachers write the best recommendations for students they know well. Encourage your child to participate in class discussions and raise her hand in class (not enough to be annoying, but if she has something interesting to contribute, she should not shy away from adding it). If your child becomes comfortable participating in class and talking with her teachers in elementary school, these skills will carry over to high school.

"Are there particular skills my child should develop in preparation for going to college?"

Most of the skills that your child will need in college, he will learn in middle school and high school. But there are a few good habits he can work on as early as first grade that will help him become a more successful college student:

▶ *Good organizational skills.* College (especially the first year) can be very hectic for students. Many are away from home for the first time—experiencing all the freedom that comes with being on their own. Having strong organizational skills (e.g., having a good filing system for old notes, being able to keep track of assignments and projects) to fall back on will be invaluable. If those skills are ingrained from elementary school, they will be unforgettable by college.

▶ *Good time management skills, especially for long-term projects.* Students who try to get by on cramming will have an increasingly hard time in college, where exams typically all happen in the same week and professors don't care that students have other tests on the day that they give their exam. If your child can manage his long-term projects and reports (e.g., breaking work down into manageable bites and sticking to a schedule) from elementary school on, he will find it easier to manage his time in college.

▶ *Strong reading skills.* The amount of reading that college students get saddled with can be overwhelming. But, if your child does a lot of free reading in elementary school, he'll be better prepared to tackle evenings of philosophy and genetics from dense (and often poorly written) college textbooks.

"I've tried to tell my child that she has to get good grades to go to college, but the whole idea seems too abstract to her. How can I get her excited enough to work harder in school?"

For some children, the idea of college is simply too far in the future to motivate their work now. But, to the extent that you can, make college a concrete idea for your child.

▶ *Visit college campuses.* Visit colleges in your hometown and when you're on vacation. Watching so many cool, young adults hanging around college campuses is often very exciting for kids. So are the coffee shops, old buildings, and bustling student unions on many campuses. Go when school is in session and tell your child that one day, she could be one of the students she sees on campus. You might even get a college pennant, flag, or mascot doll so that your child can have a memento (and a concrete reminder) of her day at college.

▶ *Get into college sports.* Not all colleges have good sports teams. But if your local university has sports teams, follow them. Take your child to games. Get into the team spirit and your child will probably get much more excited about attending college. (Going to games is especially fun if you can watch a sport that your child plays and might like to play at the college level.)

▶ *Try to connect your child with some college friends.* Maybe your friends or relatives have children in college. Or maybe you know some college students through a church, temple, or community organization. See if one of them might be interested in being a pen pal, e-mail pal, or even an instant message buddy with your child. Having a college student to talk with will make the college experience more tangible and may inspire your child to work hard now to become a college student in the future.

"Should I encourage my kids to look forward to college even if I'm not sure that I'll be able to afford to send them to college?"

Absolutely. All parents of elementary school students should assume that their children will attend (and finish) college (and maybe even go to graduate school). Growing up, your child should take it for granted that college is something that people do when they graduate from high school. If you're worried about the cost, remember that although many colleges have very high tuitions, others don't. Many state schools are quite affordable. And many colleges (especially the most expensive and elite schools, like Harvard and Princeton) offer great financial aid packages to disadvantaged and underrepresented (either in terms of race/ethnicity or social class) students. In addition, many grants and scholarships are available to students who have strong grades and test scores. And, almost all students can qualify for some kind of financial aid (which can come in the form of grants, loans, or work-study funds—which students earn as they work their way through college). Obviously, if you start saving now, you will be better prepared to help your child pay for college when she finishes high school. But no matter what your financial situation is, all parents should encourage their kids to plan on (and work toward) going to a college or university.

Interpreting Standardized Test Scores

U.S. STUDENTS TAKE MANY TESTS OVER THE COURSE OF THEIR ACADEMIC CAREERS, from regular spelling and math tests, to annual achievement tests, to SATs (for college admission), LSATs (for law school admission), and MCATs (for medical school admission). Although the regular tests that your child takes in the classroom will be graded by his teacher according to her standards (and if her standards don't make sense to you, you should ask her about them), the other tests are "standardized," which means that they are written, graded, and scored according to state or national standards.

"What exactly is a standardized test?"

"Standardized tests" have several common features. The first, and most important, is that:

▶ *They are standardized,* which means that every student who takes the test takes the same test, has the same amount of time, and gets the same directions—which makes all students' scores comparable.

In addition, standardized tests are usually:

▶ *Multiple-choice tests.* This means that every test question comes with four or five possible answer choices for your child to choose among. (Tests are increasingly adding fill-in-the-blank and essay questions, but most standardized tests still contain mostly multiple-choice questions.)

▶ *Tests that require students to fill in answers on a "bubble sheet" or "Scantron,"* which are forms with little circles or squares corresponding to each answer choice. Your child will mark her answers by filling in the appropriate circle or square with a No. 2 pencil. These answer sheets will be read and graded by a machine. (Because of the way these answer sheets look, kids often call these tests "bubble tests.")

"Are all standardized tests the same?"

There are two main types of standard-ized tests:

▶ *Norm-referenced tests* are designed to compare test-takers to other test-takers of the same age or grade. Norm-referenced tests are usually normed nationally so that when students take the test they will be compared to other U.S. students who took the same test. Students' results on nationally normed tests will show how they rank compared to other students nationally. Normed tests are scaled so that students' test scores are distributed over a normal curve. As the picture in the "Normal Curve" sidebar shows, in a normal curve, most students score in the middle and increasingly fewer students score at higher and lower points. Using this curve, the companies that grade your child's standardized tests can tell if your child is average or above or below average in different subject areas. (Tests usually report your child's rank in the percentiles or stanines (shown under the normal curve)—see the sidebar for more information on what these numbers mean.)

▶ *Criterion-referenced tests* are designed to show how well test-takers have mastered a particular curriculum. Although some criterion-referenced tests reflect national standards, they more commonly reflect state curriculum standards. These types of tests typically tell you whether your child is "proficient" in various academic subjects.

Some states administer tests that have a norm-referenced section as well as a criterion-referenced section. Thus, your child's test report may show how she ranks nationally on the norm-referenced portion, as well as her proficiency levels on the criterion-referenced portion.

"What do the results on my child's standardized test mean?"

Results from standardized tests come in several different forms. Both norm-referenced tests and criterion-referenced tests will probably show you several different types of scores, including some (but maybe not all) of the following.

▶ **Raw scores.** These show you the number of questions that your child got right. These are easy to interpret. The more questions your child got right, the better she did on the test and the more of the material she probably knows.

- Instead of showing a raw score, some tests show the **number of questions** on each topic and the **percent correct** that your child received. You can interpret these percentages the same way you would interpret the percentages that your child gets on regular school tests. If she gets a 90% it means she got 90% (most!) of the questions right.
- Sometimes raw scores are given for overall subject areas (such as math or reading). Other times they are given for specific skills (such as

decimals or punctuation). If your child's report shows how many questions your child missed on individual skills, you can use those scores to figure out where she could use extra practice.

▶ **Scale scores.** Test companies translate raw scores into standardized scale scores that allow them to compare scores from one year to the next and from one version of the test to another. For instance, the SAT uses a 200-800 scale. No matter how many questions are on the SAT in a particular year, every student's verbal (or math) score will be between 200 and 800. When people talk about scale scores on a particular test a lot (like the SAT), you may learn what a "good score" is but, as a general rule, scale scores are hard to interpret.

Because scale scores are hard to interpret, they are usually translated into scores that are easier to understand. On **norm-referenced tests,** scale scores are translated into:

▶ **National percentiles or national percentile rank scores.** These scores tell you where your child ranks in relation to other students in her grade. If your child is at the 59th percentile in reading, it means that she scored better than (or as well as) 59 percent of the other students in her grade, nationally. If she scores at the 99th percentile, she is scoring above almost all other students in her grade in the country.

▶ **Local percentiles or local percentile**

ranks work just like national percentiles but compare your child to other students in a more local area (e.g., her school or school district).

♦ *Percentile ranges* account for the fact that all tests have some error built into them. The range shows you the range of scores your child would probably get if she took the same test (or different versions of the same test) several different times on several different days. (Scores will vary because some children perform better in the morning, some children perform worse on Mondays, or some children get lucky and know specific items on one particular version of a test.)

♦ *Stanines.* Stanines are similar to national percentile ranks, but they break students into nine standard categories. Stanines range from 1-9, with 5 being the average score. Stanines are distributed over a normal curve so that more students score in the middle categories than in the top or bottom categories (see "Normal curve" sidebar for the breakdown).

♦ *Grade equivalents.* These scores, which are shown as decimals, tell you something about how your child compares to *average* children of other ages. For example, if your child gets a grade equivalent of 3.2 on a math test, it means that her score is about what the *average* 3rd-grader in the second month of school (the second month is November—September is 0, October is 1, etc.) would have received if he took the same test that your child took.

Students can score above or below their actual grade level. (But, don't interpret high grade equivalents to mean that your child should skip a grade. High grade equivalent scores do not mean that your child would perform well on a test designed for an older child, just that your child did as well as an older child would have on a test designed for your child's grade.)

♦ *Normal Curve Equivalents.* These scores are rarely shown in children's individual test reports (or are only given in combination with other scores) because they are somewhat harder to interpret than percentile ranks and grade equivalents. They are similar to percentile ranks in that they show you how your child scores relative to other children her age across the country. Like percentile ranks, high scores are better than low scores and scores over 50 indicate that your child scored better than the average child in her grade or age group. But unlike percentile ranks, normal curve equivalents are distributed in equal intervals over the normal curve. (In contrast, percentiles are farther apart at the high and low end and closer together in the center of the curve.) See the graph in the sidebar to compare the two scales.

Scale scores on *criterion-referenced tests* translate into:

♦ *Proficiency scores or performance levels.* These show how well your child has mastered your state's prescribed

curriculum for your child's grade level.
◆ Different tests present these scores in different ways. Some simply list a proficiency level (such as failing, needs improvement, proficient, or advanced). Others use check boxes to show your child's proficiency. Other test reports present a graph of proficiency levels and show a "bar" which represents your child's "probable" range of scores. This probable range takes into account the fact that all tests have error and shows the range of scores your child would likely get if she took the same test over and over again (or different versions of the same test).

◆ Some tests explicitly point out areas in which your child could use improvement.

◆ Some states, such as California, also give you your child's "reading level," which you can use in conjunction with the state reading list to look up free reading books that would be appropriate for her to read.

"Which test scores should I pay attention to?"

On a norm-referenced test, the easiest numbers to interpret are the national percentiles and the grade equivalents. National percentiles can tell you if your child is average, or above or below average. Grade equivalents can tell you if he is scoring "at grade level" (judge his score according to when he took the test—probably in about the eighth

month of his most recent grade—not when you receive the scores). Both of these scores will tell you how your child compares to other children.

On a criterion-referenced test, pay attention to your child's proficiency level. To be "on track" according to your state's curriculum standards, your child should be at least proficient in all areas. Although it's good for your child to be "proficient" or above-proficient on criterion-referenced tests, you should also pay attention to your child's national percentile rank (if it's included on your child's test report). That rank will give you an idea of how your child compares to other students his age nationally, which is useful because it will help you assess the quality of your state's proficiency standards. Some states have very high standards (e.g., expecting children to master fractions in the third grade), while other states have very low standards. Obviously, scores of "proficient" mean more in states with higher standards than in states with low standards. If your child's test report does not include norm-referenced scores, look at your state's curriculum standards to make sure that they seem appropriate.

"My child's scores seem low. When should I get concerned?"

Before you get too concerned about your child's test scores, remember that all tests reflect some "error." Many factors can influence a child's test scores: feeling ill, noise outside the classroom, or test anxiety, to name a few. So, if your child's scores seem low, think back to the days of the test and try to think of any reason why the test scores might not reflect your child's true skill level. Also, if your child is very young or if this is his first time taking a standardized test, remember that standardized tests require some test-taking techniques that your child may not have mastered yet (e.g., students must first figure out answers in a test booklet and then accurately transfer those answers to an answer sheet). However, with those caveats in mind, you should talk with your child's teacher (either current or former) about his test scores if:

◆ *Your child's test scores are very different from his most recent grades.* If your child consistently receives very high or very low grades in a subject and his achievement test scores are the opposite (for instance, he gets straight As in reading but scored at the ninth percentile on his reading test), you should bring this discrepancy to the teacher's attention. The difference may reflect one of several problems—all of which should be dealt with early.

- *Your child may have severe test anxiety* which is preventing him from showing his skills on standardized tests. Since he will have to take many tests in his lifetime, you and the teacher should work to lessen this anxiety as soon as possible (see Chapter 3 for some tips).

- *Your child's teacher (or the school in general) may be holding your child to low standards.* If you child gets straight As but is scoring well below grade level—and those test scores are accurate—then your child's teacher is giving him misinformation about his performance. Ask the teacher to explain your child's grades to you.

- *Your child may be underachieving in school.* If your child gets high test scores but usually gets low grades, he's probably "slacking off" in school. Either he's not turning in work, not studying for tests, or misbehaving. Either way, you should talk with the teacher and see how you can help your child earn grades that reflect his knowledge and abilities. If your child is not underachieving, then perhaps the school is holding him to particularly high standards—again, you should discuss the discrepancy with his teacher.

◆ *Your child's test scores are far below your perception of your child's skills.* This is obviously the most subjective of all criteria. But if you feel that your child reads very well (for instance, he competently reads books at or above his grade level) but he scored below grade level on his reading achievement test, it's worth talking to the teacher, just to make sure that nothing is wrong. Likewise, if you have a sense that your child is one of the brightest among his friends and he scores below his school's average, you should probably talk with his teacher.

Of course, even if your child's test scores don't indicate a discrepancy with his grades or his skill-level, you might be concerned if his scores are very low. If his academic performance, overall, is low, you may want to consider getting a tutor or finding a school that can better cater to his learning style. Most academic difficulties are best tackled sooner rather than later. See Chapters 2, 3, and 6 for more information on what to do if your child is struggling in school.

Test Scores on a Normal Curve

Scores on standardized tests are typically distributed in a "normal curve" (sometimes called a "bell curve"). Most students score in the center of the distribution (creating the hump)—with the average score at the 50th percentile. As you can see, very few (only 4%) students get the very highest and the very lowest scores. Percentiles, normal curve equivalents, and stanines all tell you how your child scored relative to the other children in his age group across the nation. Although they use slightly different metrics, all of these scores give you very similar information about your child's test performance.

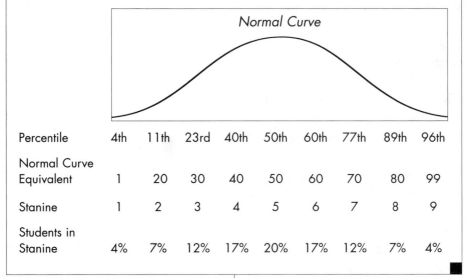

					Normal Curve				
Percentile	4th	11th	23rd	40th	50th	60th	77th	89th	96th
Normal Curve Equivalent	1	20	30	40	50	60	70	80	99
Stanine	1	2	3	4	5	6	7	8	9
Students in Stanine	4%	7%	12%	17%	20%	17%	12%	7%	4%

"Why should I worry about test scores when my child is only in elementary school?"

There's no point, really, in worrying about a young child's test scores. But you should pay attention to them for several reasons:

♦ *Children's test scores can give you a good benchmark for your child.* If your child attends a very challenging school and sometimes struggles for good grades, but gets very high test scores, you can feel comfortable that you are challenging her sufficiently (and that your child is struggling with work that is actually quite difficult). On the other hand, if your child is getting good grades easily but does not score well on an achievement test, your child's school may be too easy. You should discuss this possibility with your child's teacher.

♦ *Low test scores may signal test anxiety or poor test-taking skills, which should be dealt with early.* You don't want to deal with test anxiety or poor test-taking skills when your child's preparing for the SAT—deal with it now. If your child drastically underperforms on her achievement tests talk to her teacher, work on reducing her anxiety, and teach her some test taking strategies (see Chapter 3).

♦ *High test scores may signal that your child needs extra challenges or qualifies for a gifted program.* High test scores can lead to extra opportunities for children, such as entrance into gifted enrichment programs. If your child scores in the top 75th percentile (or above) on a standardized test and is not already enrolled in a gifted program, ask the school what its requirements are for the gifted program (be aware that some districts' cutoffs are as high as the 95th percentile).

Educational Materials You Should Have at Home

THERE ARE MILLIONS OF EDUCATIONAL BOOKS, TOYS, AND "TOOLS" ON THE MARKET FOR parents and children to try out—some are essential and others are completely unnecessary. Below is a list of materials that families should try to keep on hand for research projects, homework assignments, and "educational" fun. I've placed an asterisk (*) by items that families should prioritize—many (like dictionaries) are inexpensive and very handy. Others (like computers and Internet access) are more expensive and, obviously, you need to decide whether or not these large purchases fit within your budget. Many of the "essentials" on this list are readily available for public use—for free—at public libraries (and probably at your child's school as well). So, if you have a library nearby, you may not need reference books or Internet access at home. But, if your budget allows, having these materials at home will make research projects and everyday homework much more convenient both for you and your child (and, if your child relies on you for transportation to the library, having these materials at home will also enable her to work more independently).

Reference books

Almanac—almanacs are great reference books, and there are many designed especially for kids. They include short bits of information on a wide range of topics. Sort of like condensed encyclopedias (with lots of statistics), they are excellent starting places for research projects and great for looking up answers to kids' most random questions.

Atlas—a book of maps (try to find one that is up-to-date—many countries' boundaries have changed in recent years). Although hardcover atlases are expensive, paperbacks are cheaper and easier to replace. (Globes are good substitutes for atlases as long as you don't need detailed maps.)

Dictionary—the most basic dictionaries describe the definitions, pronunciations, and parts of speech of most words. More advanced dictionaries also contain synonyms and antonyms as well as pictures and short encyclopedic entries about famous people and places. Look for a dictionary that has easy-to-understand definitions (it's frustrating for children to look up words and find that they do not understand the definition) but beware of children's dictionaries. Children's dictionaries often lack a wide range of words. (Before you buy a dictionary, try looking up a few challenging words to make sure that the dictionary you're considering is comprehensive enough for your needs.)

Ideally, you should have a children's dictionary (for your children to use) and an adult dictionary for you to use when your children's dictionary falls short.

Encyclopedias—a book (or set of books) that contains factual information about a range of topics. Although some simple encyclopedias (especially those designed for children) come in one or two volumes, most come in sets of approximately 20 alphabetical volumes. Libraries have up to date encyclopedia sets, so it is not necessary to have a set at home. However, having a set of encyclopedias at home will provide a great resource for research reports and will help your child research topics that she finds interesting.

Rhyming Dictionary—a book that lists words by the sound of their final syllables. They are a little hard to get used to (if you want to find a word that rhymes with gobble, you would look up "ble") but they can be really helpful when kids are trying to write poetry.

Thesaurus—a book of synonyms and antonyms. A thesaurus can help your child build his vocabulary and use a diverse range of words in his writing.

Subject-specific science and history books—The *Eyewitness* series has dozens of books on history and science topics that are full of facts, information, and pictures. Children enjoy flipping through them and often use them for research reports.

Reading Materials

At least a couple of your child's favorite books—so she can revisit them.

At least a couple of books your child hasn't read but wants to read—so she always has reading material available. (These can come from regular library trips.)

At least one book your child would like to be able to read someday—so she has something to look forward to and strive for.

Magazines your child enjoys (that, ideally, are close to her reading level). *Sports Illustrated for Kids, People for Kids, Vogue for Kids* and other popular magazines are great (even if they are not particularly academic). Many children also enjoy more serious magazines such as *Time for Kids* (this is great if your child has to do current event reports), *National Geographic Kids, Ask* (a science magazine), or *Cricket* (a fiction magazine). (Check out Cobblestone Publishing at http://www.cobblestonepub.com/ for a wide variety of magazines—from preschool through middle school—on a wide range of topics.)

A public library card.

Math and Science Supplies

A ruler—ideally one with standard and metric measurements (e.g., inches and centimeters).

A compass—the kind that you use to draw circles. They typically have a pencil on one end and a point on the other end that can be opened and closed to make bigger or smaller circles. (Available at most drug stores and discount stores.)

A protractor—these are semi-circle shaped rulers (usually clear plastic) that can be used to measure angles and make pie charts.

A calculator—This will come in especially handy if you want to spot check long problems in your child's math homework. It will also be handy if your child is motivated to use math to solve a real life problem but you don't want him to get too frustrated over the big numbers.

Building toys or blocks—These can be regular blocks, Legos, or sets like K'Nex which allow children to build fairly complex machines and animate them with small motors. Having some toys like this will help your child explore building, planning, and basic engineering.

Technology

Computer with a word processing program with spell check. Make sure you have good, up-to-date virus protection software on your computer (viruses can be picked up through e-mail or the Internet, and they can render your computer useless—protect yourself).

Internet access. The Internet has revolutionized the way that children (and adults) do research. Internet access is a wonderful tool for research reports (it brings child-level reference material right to your computer) and also a great resource for looking up answers to everyday questions. Your child can also use it for educational games, to write e-mails or instant messages, and to visit educational Web sites (everything from Harry Potter pages to sites where you can "dissect a frog" virtually). You will also find the Internet to be a great resource for researching schools, summer programs, and other education related issues as well as for buying books. If your budget will allow, subscribe to a service (such as DSL or cable Internet) that is relatively fast. More and more sites contain many graphics and animations and it can get frustrating waiting for them to load on a dial-up connection.

Software for learning how to type. Many children enjoy the challenge of learning how to type. Software turns it into a game. And, learning to type correctly will save your child a lot of time writing up reports for the rest of her academic career (and probably beyond).

Math computer games. (See Chapter 5 for more information on how to choose the best games for your child.)

Vocabulary computer games. (See Chapter 5 for more information on how to choose the best games for your child.)

CD-Rom Encyclopedia—these digital encyclopedias work just like book encyclopedias. But, in addition to text entries, they often have pictures, sound clips, and video clips. These are great if your Internet goes down, if your Internet connection is slow, or if you want your child to be able to do "computer" research without accidentally pulling up x-rated Web sites.

Games

Word games in which children build words from letters such as: Scrabble or Boggle (either the adult versions or the kid versions—which have bigger letters and allow shorter words).

Thinking games such as Trivial Pursuit (for kids), Cadoo (the kid version of Cranium), Brainquest the Game, or Scattergories.

Strategy games such as: Backgammon, Battleship, Connect4, Checkers, Clue, Clue Jr., Chess, Mastermind, Othello, or Risk (which also teaches geography).

Math/Counting games such as: Smath (a math version of Scrabble), Mancala (an African counting game), Sorry (or any game where children roll dice and count spaces to move around a board), or Monopoly (or any other game that uses money).

Games that build children's memories (such as Memory or Simon).

Playing cards. A regular deck of cards

can be used for all kinds of games with educational components, from War, in which children need to compare the relative size of numbers, to Rummy and Old Maid, in which players have to group similar cards and develop strategies based on simple probability. (Get a book of card games and let your children explore new games too.)

Learning Aids

Flashcards with addition, subtraction, multiplication, and division facts.

Manipulatives (items to count with and practice arithmetic with—even normal building blocks or beans will work). If your child struggles to do math with fractions or money, you might consider investing in manipulatives that represent different fractions (sometimes these are called "fractals" and they come in disks cut into different numbers of "slices") or money (or use real money).

*A clock with hands (or a toy clock with hands—something you can use to teach your child to tell time with a non-digital clock).

*A digital clock (or toy clock) you can use to teach your child to tell time on a digital display.

Madlibs. These little paperback books are great for teaching kids grammar in a fun way. They are full of funny little stories with missing words (each blank is paired with a part of speech—noun, verb, etc.). Kids (working alone or—even better—in pairs) come up with words for each missing part of speech and then fill in the story—which always turns out kooky and sometimes turns out hilarious. Madlibs are cheap and great for traveling.

Books with mindbenders or puzzles. Lots of kids like to work on word searches, logic puzzles, mazes, crossword puzzles, and other pencil and paper games. Keep some around the house for your child to work on if he gets bored. Although kids often just think of these puzzles as "fun," many look strikingly similar to "analytic" problems on the LSAT (used for law school admission). To make sure your child is interested in the puzzles you get for him, let him go to the store with you and pick them out. Also check the Internet for puzzles (for instance, http://www.mysterymaster.com has dozens of logic puzzles of varying levels). You can make your own puzzles at http://www.puzzlemaker.com.

Electronic "Quizzers"—There are dozens of electronic learning devices on the market and they have improved considerably since the days of "Speak 'N Spell." Today, you can buy toys that take a variety of different cartridges so that they can quiz students on different subjects (e.g., spelling, math, history, science) for different grade levels. For instance LeapFrog's TurboTwist toys have cartridges for grades 2-8 and cover all academic subjects. Most of these toys are relatively affordable (usually about $30 for the machine and about $10 per cartridge). Kids usually like the fact that the tests are electronic and they provide a good way for children to quiz themselves.

Electronic "Reading Tools"—LeapFrog's LeapPad and Fisher Price's PowerTouch take books (and corresponding software cartridges) and turn them into interactive "reading" experiences for children. Easy books teach counting and the alphabet. More advanced books tell stories and teach phonics, spelling, and other language arts skills. Children use their fingers (on the PowerTouch) or a "magic pointer" (on the LeapPad) to have the computer read stories to them (as they turn pages), help them sound out and spell words, and prompt the computer to tell them about different characters and animals in the story. Children can even use the toys to play games related to the story (some books even teach children words in Spanish). The books are designed to simulate the experience of reading with an adult—and succeed (at least to some extent). Although these products are pricier than the "quizzers" ($30–$50), they would make a great gift for young pre-readers whose appetites for reading exceed the time that you can spend reading with them. They would also be good for children who aren't fascinated by books but can be lured into reading by electronic bells and whistles.

Art and Music supplies

Crayons, colored pencils, or pens. Keep colored writing tools around the house. Children frequently need to color reports or worksheets for homework. (See Chapter 4 for other materials you should keep around the house to be prepared for reports and projects.) And, if your child is especially talented or interested in art, keep other art supplies handy, as well, so that she can explore and develop her talents. (If she's really interested, art lessons may be in order, too!)

Musical instruments and sheet music. Not every child has an aptitude for music. But many children love music and learning how to read music and play an instrument can be life-enriching. If your child is interested in music, an inexpensive keyboard or a recorder (and lessons either from you or from a music teacher) would be a fun way for her to begin to explore her interests.

How to Make Charts and Graphs

G RAPHS AND CHARTS ARE A GREAT WAY TO DISPLAY DATA OF ALL KINDS. FOR EXAMPLE, your child might want to use a chart to show the data he collected for his science project. Or you might want to use a chart to describe your child's progress (for instance, you might choose to graph his spelling test scores to see how they improve as he studies more). This appendix describes the three most common types of charts and graphs and how to make them.

Pie Charts

Pie charts show how an entire group is broken up into different-sized pieces. So, for example, let's say your child decided to see how many cars in your neighborhood "rolled through" your local stop sign in an hour (see the sample science projects in Chapter 4 for more information). He might make the following chart and gather the following data:

BEHAVIOR	FREQUENCY
Stopped	‖‖‖‖‖‖‖‖‖‖‖‖‖‖‖‖‖‖‖‖=20
Didn't stop	‖‖‖‖‖=5

Now he knows that 20 cars stopped and 5 did not stop. He would probably want to turn those numbers into percentages. By adding his two totals, he knows that he observed 25 cars. 20 out of 25 stopped. 5 out of 25 did not. $20 \div 25 = .80$ $.80 \times 100 = 80$ percent and $5 \div 25 = .20$ $.20 \times 100 = 20$ percent.

So, the table could also read:

BEHAVIOR	PERCENTAGE
Stopped	80%
Didn't stop	20%

Now, because the group that stopped and the group that didn't stop are part of a whole (all of the cars that your child observed—100 percent), a pie chart will display these data well.

Pie charts are circular (like pies).

The entire circle represents the whole or 100 percent. The pie chart gets divided into sections to represent your different groups (in this case, those who stopped and those who didn't stop). One of the easiest ways to make a pie chart is to use a computer program like Microsoft Excel or the spreadsheet portion of Microsoft Works (type Pie Chart into the search line of the "Help" function in either of these programs and it will show you how to enter your data and make one like the one below).

Pie chart:

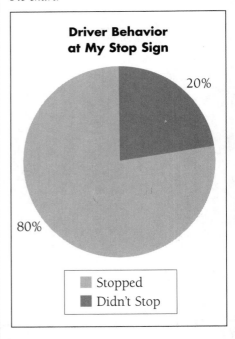

Or, your child can draw his own pie chart. He will need something round to trace (the mouth of a cup or glass will work well), a protractor (see Appendix 6 on materials you should have at home for more information), and some pens, crayons, or colored pencils.

Help your child follow these steps (also see the diagram below):

1. *Draw a circle.* This circle represents 100% (in this case, all of the cars he observed).

2. *Use the percentages in your table to find out how many degrees of your circle you should mark off.* (Every circle has 360 degrees. Your protractor is probably a half circle and probably shows you 180 degrees.) To figure out how many degrees to mark off, multiply your percentage times 360 (so, 20% × 360 = 72 degrees).

3. *Use the protractor to mark* 0 and 72.

4. *Draw straight lines from each mark to the center of the circle.* Those two lines should meet and form a "pizza slice" shaped chunk.

5. *Color the chunk one color and the rest of the circle another color.*

6. *Make a legend* (the little box) to show which group is which color.

When you color in your slices, your pie graph should look like the computer-generated one above. Make sure you add a legend (the little box under the computer-generated pie chart) to tell whomever is looking at the chart which group is which. Add percentage labels to the slices if you like. (Note: You can show more than two groups in a pie chart—although anything more than four or five groups will probably become too confusing. If you have more than four or five groups, consider using a bar graph.)

Bar Graphs or Bar Charts

Bar graphs and bar charts are the same thing. They are used to show differences between several groups. Say, for instance, that your child observed at a stop sign for an hour (like above) but instead of taking note of who stopped and who didn't, took note of the colors of the cars that rolled through the stop

Step 1

A circle is 360 degrees around.

Steps 2 & 3

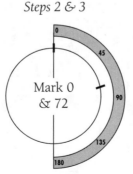

Mark 0 & 72

A protractor is usually a half circle = 180 degrees. Tick marks show each degree.

Step 4

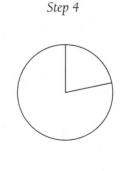

Draw lines from the marks to the center to form a "slice."

sign. He might end up with data that looked like this:

CAR COLOR	FREQUENCY
Blue	|||=3
Red	||||||=6
White	|||=3
Tan	|=1
Silver	||=2

A pie chart showing these data would be hard to interpret—too many slices that are too similar in size. A bar graph gives you a quick, visual way to see the differences between the different colored cars. As you can see from the following graph, more red cars than other cars rolled through the stop sign.

The easiest way to make a bar chart is to use a spreadsheet program on the computer (enter "bar chart" into the search line in the help menu and the program should walk you through the process of making a bar chart). You can also make a bar chart by hand (see figure below to get an idea of what it should look like). Use a piece of graph paper so that the bars will line up evenly.

1. Draw a vertical line and a horizontal line to form an "L." The vertical line is called the y-axis and the horizontal line is called the x-axis.

2. Label the x-axis with your different categories or groups. Space them evenly across the x-axis.

3. Label the y-axis with a scale of numbers that will include all of your frequencies. (If you can, start at zero (0), because that makes the graph eas-

Bar chart:

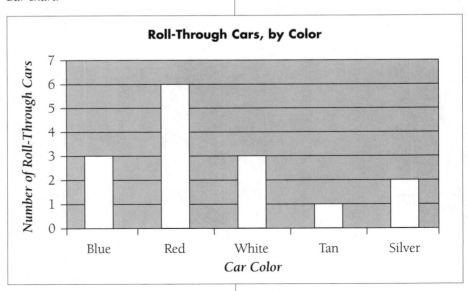

iest to understand.) Label the y-axis with numbers in even intervals (you can go one-by-one, by twos, by fives, or by whatever interval will fit as long as the intervals are equal and evenly spaced).

4. *Above each category, draw a rectangle whose highest point is even with the number on the y-axis that matches the frequency for that category.* Make the rectangles wide enough so that you can see them but narrow enough so that they don't touch each other.

5. *Color the different bars different colors if you like.*

6. *Put a title on the graph and label each axis.*

Frequencies or Percentages?

When you present data, you always have to decide whether to show raw frequencies (how many red cars rolled through) or percentages (the percentage of red cars that rolled through). For simplicity's sake, I've graphed frequencies in the bar chart and line graph. However, these frequencies could be misleading. For instance, if most of the people in your neighborhood drive red cars and all drivers are equally likely to roll through the stop sign, your child would see more red cars rolling through *just because* there are more red cars overall. In that case, it would be more accurate to show percentages. So, your child might record the fact that 20 red cars passed the stop sign and 5 red cars rolled through—thus 25 percent of red cars rolled through (compared, perhaps, to only 5 percent of tan cars). You plot percentages on the y-axis in exactly the same way you plot frequencies.

So, overall, any time your child shows frequencies as data, he should ask himself if the frequencies are misleading. To take another example, more cars might run the stop sign between 6 P.M. and 7 P.M. simply because more cars go down the street at rush hour—not because the drivers are in a bigger hurry to get home. In this case, your child should conclude that the frequencies are misleading. So, he should divide the frequencies (the number of cars that ran the stop sign between 6 P.M. and 7 P.M.) by the total number of cars in that category (the number of cars that arrived at the stop sign between 6 P.M. and 7 P.M.) and create percentages. He should then present and graph those percentages.

Line Graphs

Bar graphs and line graphs are very similar. But, while you use bar graphs to show how frequencies differ across different categories, you use line graphs to show how frequencies change over time. Because time is continuous, you use lines to connect the frequency points rather than bars (thus, the name line graph).

To use the same example, let's say your child watched the stop sign for an entire afternoon/evening to see if people were more likely to run the stop sign during rush hour. These are the data:

TIME	FREQUENCY
3 P.M.	|=1
4 P.M.	|||=3
5 P.M.	||||=4
6 P.M.	||||||||=8
7 P.M.	|||||=5
8 P.M.	||=2

With a line graph, you'll be able to see how rolling-through behavior changes over the course of an afternoon/evening.

Like pie charts and bar charts, line graphs can be made using computer spreadsheet programs (use the help menu to learn how). To make a line graph by hand, start the same way that you would to make your bar graph:

1. *Draw a vertical line and a horizontal line to form an "L."* The vertical line is called the y-axis and the horizontal line is called the x-axis.

2. *Label the x-axis with your different times.* Space them so that the intervals reflect the amount of time that's passed. For example, the interval between 3 and 5 P.M. should be twice as large as the interval between 3 and 4 P.M.

3. *Label the y-axis with a scale of numbers that will include all of your frequencies.* (If you can, start at zero (0) because that makes the graph easiest to understand.) Label the y-axis with numbers in even intervals (you can go one-by-one, by twos, by fives, whatever will fit as long as the intervals are equal and evenly spaced).

4. *Above each time point for which you have data, draw a dot at the point on the y-axis that corresponds with the frequency for that time point.*

5. *Use a ruler to connect each of the dots.*

6. *Put a title on the graph and label each axis.*

You can plot frequencies for several groups on the same line graph (for instance, one line for the cars that ran the stop sign and one line for the bicycles that ran the stop sign). Make the lines different colors and create a legend (like the one below the pie chart) that shows which line represents which group.

Line graph:

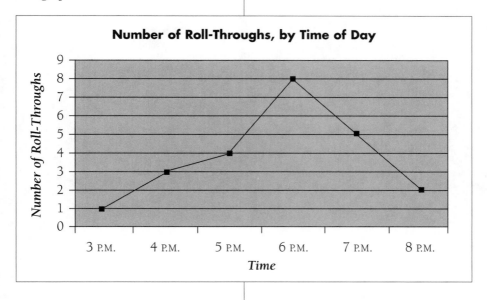

Recommended Resources and References for Parents

V ISIT YOUR LOCAL BOOKSTORE AND YOU'LL SEE DOZENS OF BOOKS ON EDUCATION. Likewise, the Internet abounds with resources for parents. This appendix (which has turned out to be a rather eclectic collection of resources) lists and describes the resources I found most helpful while doing the research for this book. It also includes a relatively small number of books and Web sites that I think provide especially valuable information and activities. Obviously, these references may not hit upon your particular needs and they may not be ideally suited to your child or family. However, I hope that these books and Web sites will serve as a useful starting point in your research—almost all of them refer to still other resources.

Books/Learning Materials

Books:

How to Get Your Child to Love Reading
by Esme Raji Codell (Algonquin Books).

This book is a little quirky (the author likens children's literature to a potato—an ingredient with many creative uses), but the author clearly knows children's books. Her book contains dozens of lists of various types of books (from poetry that children will love to fiction books set in different countries to books of particularly gross science experiments). She also includes scores of ideas about how to expand on your child's interest in reading (from cooking to building a puppet theater).

Great Books for Girls, Great Books for Boys, and *Great Books About Things Kids Love: More than 750 Recommended Books for Children 3-14*
by Kathleen Odean (Ballantine).

You may not always agree with the author's definition of books that are particularly good for boys or girls, but these books are great resources for parents and children who are searching for good books (each book lists over 600 children's books). Using these books, you can browse titles at home and either shop online or go to the bookstore or library with books in mind.

Catalogs/Online Booksellers:

Alibris
(http://www.alibris.com)

Alibris can be a good (although not always the cheapest) source of used books.

Amazon.com
(http://www.amazon.com)

Amazon.com is probably the most famous online bookseller. The site is useful not only for finding books but for reading reviews of books, toys, and software. Although you can't trust every review that you read, many of them will give you (and your child) a sense if you might like a book or if a computer game will be useful in improving your child's math skills.

Barnes and Noble
(http://www.bn.com)

Like Amazon.com, Barnes and Noble's online bookstore offers a wide range of books along with customer reviews and ratings.

Bookfinder
(http://www.bookfinder.com)

Enter a title or author and Bookfinder will find you used copies (often quite cheap) of the book you are searching for. You have to pay shipping and handling but you can still get some bargains, especially if you buy several books from the same vender (and have them shipped together). Beware, first editions and other collectable books may be quite expensive.

High Noon Books
(http://www.academictherapy.com/)

High Noon (a division of Academic Therapy) produces books designed for older students who read at the first- through fifth-grade levels. The books have adolescent and pre-adolescent content but employ relatively simple plots, simple sentence structures and controlled vocabulary. You can order these books online or through the catalog.

E-Bay
(http://www.ebay.com)

If you are looking to buy children's books in bulk, look at E-Bay. Sometimes people sell entire collections for relatively low prices.

Magazines:

Cobblestone Publishing
(http://www.cobblestonepub.com)

The publisher produces a wide range of educational magazines, on topics ranging from fiction to science, for children of all ages. Annual subscriptions (5-12 issues) cost between $24-$36.

Web sites:

BookAdventure.org
(http://www.bookadventure.org)

This Web site, sponsored by Sylvan Learning Centers, is designed to motivate kids to read. It allows children to search for books according to their age, reading level, and interests, create book lists, quiz themselves on books that they have read, and earn prizes for reading (if they get enough points on their quizzes). The quizzes are challenging and a great way to "check" how well your child understands her pleasure reading. Kids have to register (for free) in order to take quizzes and qualify for prizes.

Scholastic Booksellers
(http://www.scholastic.com)

You probably know about Scholastic from the "book orders" that your child brings home from school. Their Web site (click on the "family" section from the home page) has a number of resources for families and children including articles, games, and booklists organized by subject.

Curriculum

What Your Kindergartner Needs to Know through *What Your Sixth-Grader Needs to Know* by E.D. Hirsch, Jr. (Dell Publishing).

Hirsch's Core Knowledge Series has a book for every elementary school grade level. Each book details the skills that children should have, the books they should read, the information they should learn, and the math techniques they should master at the specified grade level. Although you should not require (or even expect) your child's school to stick to the books perfectly, they are great reference for parents who want to brush up on their second-grade math or history knowledge before the school year starts or for parents looking for suggestions for "quality" pleasure reading for their children.

Enrichment Ideas and Activities

Books:

Make Your Kids Smarter: Top Teacher Tips for Grades K to 8
by Erika V. Shearin Karres
(Andrews McMeel Publishing).

This book contains 50 tips to help children think, learn, and practice school skills. Many of the tips are creative and interesting. If your child likes to do little projects and assignments, this book would be a good investment.

Web sites:

EdBoost Education Corporation
(http://www.edboost.org)

From the homepage, click on the "Virtual EdBoost" button to go a page that links to dozen of children's sites. Some of the sites feature on-line flashcards for math practice, science experiment ideas, forums where students can post their own poetry and stories, and online almanacs and encyclopedias designed for children.

The Exploratorium
(http://www.exploratorium.edu/)

This Web site, which is part of the Exploratorium Museum of Science, Art, and Human Perception in San Francisco, is a wonderful resource. Click on the "Explore" tab at the top of the Web site and you and your child can explore online exhibitions (including optical illusions and sports science!) and learn about hands-on activities you can do at home (from making candy to dissecting a cow's eye). This site also has links to other fun, more specific sites (such as http://www.froguts.com where students can virtually dissect frogs and other animals).

The Discovery Channel
(http://school.discovery.com/ and http://kids.discovery.com)

This Web site (which is tied to the television station) has fun online activities (even lessons to learn languages) as well as enrichment toys that can be ordered online. Click on "Brain Boosters" for mindbenders of all kinds and use "Puzzlemaker" to create mazes, wordsearches, crossword puzzles, and many other types of puzzles. There is also a "Science Fair" link with lots of tips for creating good science projects.

Gifted Education

Family Education Network
(http://www.familyeducation.com)

This Web site is designed to bring together the Internet's best education resources. The site contains a number of links to good Web sites, articles (on topics ranging from gifted education and enrichment activities to ADD/ADHD and home schooling), and general education tips. It also has message boards on a variety of topics for parents and educators. One particularly good article for parents of gifted children lists the national and regional programs that offer summer camps for gifted children (http://www.family education.com/article/0,1120,23-12281,00.html).

The National Association for Gifted Children (NAGC)
(http://www.nagc.org)

This nonprofit organization provides a wide range of information for parents of gifted children, from legislative updates and state-specific policy information, to lists of toys to buy for gifted children and summer camps designed for gifted children.

Learning Difficulties/ Special Education

Books:

Parenting a Struggling Reader: A Guide to Diagnosing and Finding Help for Your Child's Reading Difficulties
by Susan L. Hall and Louisa C. Moats (Broadway Books).

This wonderfully accessible book is a must-have for any parent whose child struggles with reading. The book helps parents check their children for learning disabilities, tells parents how to find and assess psychologists, and discusses remediation techniques for students with reading-related learning disabilities. The authors also discuss

how parents can help their struggling readers at home. One of the most useful chapters in this book guides parents through the IEP process. (I would recommend this chapter to any parents going through the IEP process—even if their child does not struggle specifically with reading.)

The Complete IEP Guide (2nd Ed.)
by Lawrence Siegel (NOLO Press).

This book is an excellent reference book to help any parent navigate the legal issues involved in the IEP process. NOLO Press specializes in legal guidebooks, providing case law, sample forms, as well as easy-to-understand legal advice. The book even has templates for the letters you should write to your child's principal to start the IEP process, request services, and request a due process hearing.

Web sites:

U.S. Department of Education Web site
(www.ed.gov)

To access information for parents, click the "Parent" tab at the top. Then, from a menu at the right, you can access a section on special education. The index page for IEP information is: http://www.ed.gov/parents/needs/speced/iepguide/index.html.

IDEA Practices
(http://www.ideapractices.org)

This Web site is funded by the U.S. Department of Education and provides a number of resources for parents, advocates, teachers, and administrators. It also includes the full 1997 IDEA law at: http://www.ideapractices.org/law/index.php.

The National Dissemination Center for Children with Disabilities
(http://www. nichcy.org/)

This government Web site contains accessible information (and links to more in-depth information) on specific learning disabilities, federal special education laws, how to work with your special-needs child at home, and how to communicate with your child's school regarding your child's learning difficulties. If you are requesting tests or negotiating special education services for your child, look at the free online publication: "A Parents' Guide: Communication with Your Child's School Through Letter Writing." (NICHCY, Parent Guide 9, October 2002) (http://www.nichcy.org/pubs/parent/pa9.pdf.) The site also has a booklet for students who are going through the IEP process.

The Council of Educators for Students with Disabilities
(http://www.504idea.org/)

This Texas-based organization is dedicated to providing information about IDEA and Section 504 to educators and parents. The Web site includes several helpful "Question and Answer" pages about special education laws and processes.

SchwabLearning.org
(http://www.schwablearning.org/)

Schwab Learning is a nonprofit Web site that calls itself "A parent's guide to helping children with learning difficulties." The site contains a number of articles, message boards, and links that will be helpful for parents of children with learning disabilities.

Reed Martin, J.D.
(http://www.reedmartin.com)

This attorney, who specializes in special education advocacy, has posted a Web site with a number of helpful articles containing caselaw and information for parents who are dealing with special education, IEPs, due process, or other legal conflicts with schools. Although I can't vouch for the accuracy of all of the legal information, the free articles will give you some idea of the avenues available for you and how a lawyer or advocate might be able to help you.

Learning Styles/Homework Styles

Learning Unlimited: Using Homework to Engage Your Child's Natural Style of Intelligence by Dawna Markova and Anne R. Powell (Conari Press).

This book details the different ways in which children learn. It will be very helpful for parents who fight with their children about how, when, and where they do their homework. The book explains how parents can assess how their child learns best (visually, auditorily, kinesthetically). It helps parents develop techniques to maximize their children's achievement by tapping into their individual learning styles.

Motivation

Motivated Minds: Raising Children to Love Learning by Deborah Stipek and Kathy Seal (Owl Books).

This book provides easy-to-follow, practical advice about how to nurture a love of learning in your child. It discusses ways to motivate children, how and when to use rewards and punishments, and how to encourage children to want to learn.

Parent Involvement Organizations

National PTA
(http://www.pta.org/)

National PTA is a child advocacy group that has local chapters in many U.S. Schools. Its Web site has some good parenting information and information on how to start a local PTA chapter. You can also write the National PTA for information at: 330 N. Wabash Ave-nue, Suite 2100, Chicago, IL, 60611.

PTOToday.com and the National PTO Network
(http://www.ptotoday.com/)

The PTO Web site provides information for parents and parent-teacher organizations that are not affil-iated with the National PTA. The National PTO Network is a network that independent PTOs can join and share resources. You can also write to PTO for information at: 200 Stonewall Blvd, Suite 6A, Wrentham, MA 02093.

Science Projects

Janice VanCleave's Guide to the Best Science Fair Projects
(John Wiley & Sons) and other books by Janice VanCleave.

Janice VanCleave has a wide selection of science fair books, many of which are targeted to particular interests. She has books on (to name a few) weather, the solar system, nutrition, earth science, earthquakes, electricity, plants, microscopes, magnets, and volcano experiments. These books are full of great ideas, but not all of the ideas use the scientific method. So, when you use these books, make sure your child chooses projects that will meet his teacher's requirements.

Index

Books Available from Santa Monica Press

Blues for Bird
by Martin Gray
288 pages $16.95

The Book of Good Habits
Simple and Creative Ways to
Enrich Your Life
by Dirk Mathison
224 pages $9.95

The Butt Hello
and other ways my cats
drive me crazy
by Ted Meyer
96 pages $9.95

Café Nation
Coffee Folklore, Magick,
and Divination
by Sandra Mizumoto Posey
224 pages $9.95

Cats Around the World
by Ted Meyer
96 pages $9.95

Childish Things
by Davis & Davis
96 pages $19.95

Discovering the History
of Your House
and Your Neighborhood
by Betsy J. Green
288 pages $14.95

The Dog Ate My Resumé
by Zack Arnstein and
Larry Arnstein
192 pages $11.95

Dogme Uncut
Lars von Trier, Thomas Vinterberg
and the Gang That Took on
Hollywood
by Jack Stevenson
312 pages $16.95

Exotic Travel Destinations
for Families
by Jennifer M. Nichols and
Bill Nichols
360 pages $16.95

Footsteps in the Fog
Alfred Hitchcock's San Francisco
by Jeff Kraft and
Aaron Leventhal
240 pages $24.95

Free Stuff & Good Deals for
Folks over 50, 2nd Ed.
by Linda Bowman
240 pages $12.95

How to Find Your Family
Roots and Write Your
Family History
by William Latham and
Cindy Higgins
288 pages $14.95

How to Speak Shakespeare
by Cal Pritner and
Louis Colaianni
144 pages $16.95

How to Win Lotteries,
Sweepstakes, and Contests
in the 21st Century
by Steve "America's Sweepstakes
King" Ledoux
224 pages $14.95

Jackson Pollock:
Memories Arrested in Space
by Martin Gray
216 pages $14.95

James Dean Died Here
The Locations of America's Pop
Culture Landmarks
by Chris Epting
312 pages $16.95

The Keystone Kid
Tales of Early Hollywood
by Coy Watson, Jr.
312 pages $24.95

Letter Writing Made Easy!
Featuring Sample Letters for
Hundreds of Common Occasions
by Margaret McCarthy
224 pages $12.95

Letter Writing Made Easy!
Volume 2
Featuring More Sample Letters for
Hundreds of Common Occasions
by Margaret McCarthy
224 pages $12.95

Life is Short. Eat Biscuits!
by Amy Jordan Smith
96 pages $9.95

Marilyn Monroe Dyed Here
More Locations of America's
Pop Culture Landmarks
by Chris Epting
312 pages $16.95

Movie Star Homes
by Judy Artunian and
Mike Oldham
312 pages $16.95

Offbeat Food
Adventures in an
Omnivorous World
by Alan Ridenour
240 pages $19.95

Offbeat Marijuana
The Life and Times of the
World's Grooviest Plant
by Saul Rubin
240 pages $19.95

Offbeat Museums
The Collections and Curators of
America's Most Unusual Museums
by Saul Rubin
240 pages $19.95

A Prayer for Burma
by Kenneth Wong
216 pages $14.95

Quack!
Tales of Medical Fraud from the
Museum of Questionable Medical
Devices
by Bob McCoy
240 pages $19.95

Redneck Haiku
by Mary K. Witte
112 pages $9.95

School Sense: How to Help
Your Child Succeed in
Elementary School
by Tiffani Chin, Ph.D.
408 pages $16.95

Silent Echoes
Discovering Early Hollywood
Through the Films of
Buster Keaton
by John Bengtson
240 pages $24.95

Tiki Road Trip
A Guide to Tiki Culture
in North America
by James Teitelbaum
288 pages $16.95

Order Form 1-800-784-9553

	Quantity	Amount
Blues for Bird (epic poem about Charlie Parker) ($16.95)	_____	_____
The Book of Good Habits ($9.95)	_____	_____
The Butt Hello . . . and Other Ways My Cats Drive Me Crazy ($9.95)	_____	_____
Café Nation: Coffee Folklore, Magick and Divination ($9.95)	_____	_____
Cats Around the World ($9.95)	_____	_____
Childish Things ($19.95)	_____	_____
Discovering the History of Your House. . . ($14.95)	_____	_____
The Dog Ate My Resumé ($11.95)	_____	_____
Dogme Uncut ($16.95)	_____	_____
Exotic Travel Destinations for Families ($16.95)	_____	_____
Footsteps in the Fog: Alfred Hitchcock's San Francisco ($24.95)	_____	_____
Free Stuff & Good Deals for Folks over 50, 2nd Ed. ($12.95)	_____	_____
How to Find Your Family Roots . . . ($14.95)	_____	_____
How to Speak Shakespeare ($16.95)	_____	_____
How to Win Lotteries, Sweepstakes, and Contests . . . ($14.95)	_____	_____
Jackson Pollock: Memories Arrested in Space ($14.95)	_____	_____
James Dean Died Here: America's Pop Culture Landmarks ($16.95)	_____	_____
The Keystone Kid: Tales of Early Hollywood ($24.95)	_____	_____
Letter Writing Made Easy! ($12.95)	_____	_____
Letter Writing Made Easy! Volume 2 ($12.95)	_____	_____
Life is Short. Eat Biscuits! ($9.95)	_____	_____
Marilyn Monroe Dyed Here ($16.95)	_____	_____
Movie Star Homes ($16.95)	_____	_____
Offbeat Food ($19.95)	_____	_____
Offbeat Marijuana ($19.95)	_____	_____
Offbeat Museums ($19.95)	_____	_____
A Prayer for Burma ($14.95)	_____	_____
Quack! Tales of Medical Fraud ($19.95)	_____	_____
Redneck Haiku ($9.95)	_____	_____
School Sense ($16.95)	_____	_____
Silent Echoes: Early Hollywood Through Buster Keaton ($24.95)	_____	_____
Tiki Road Trip ($16.95)	_____	_____

Shipping & Handling:	
1 book	$3.00
Each additional book is	$ .50

Subtotal _____

CA residents add 8.25% sales tax _____

Shipping and Handling (see left) _____

TOTAL _____

Name _____

Address _____

City _____ State _____ Zip _____

☐ Visa ☐ MasterCard Card No.: _____

Exp. Date _____ Signature _____

☐ Enclosed is my check or money order payable to:

Santa Monica Press LLC
P.O. Box 1076
Santa Monica, CA 90406

www.santamonicapress.com 1-800-784-9553